PILGRIMAGE
IN TIBET

A Tibetan pilgrim approaching the giant flagpole at Tarboche on the circuit of Mount Kailas. Photo by A.C. McKay.

PILGRIMAGE IN TIBET

Edited by
Alex McKay

LONDON AND NEW YORK

First published in 1998
by Curzon Press

Published 2013 by Routledge
2 Park Square, Milton Park, Abingdon, Oxfordshire OX14 4RN
711 Third Avenue, New York, NY 10017

First issued in paperback 2014

Routledge is an imprint of the Taylor & Francis Group, an informa business

Editorial matter © 1998 Alex McKay

All rights reserved. No part of this book may be reprinted or reproduced or utilised in any form or by any electronic, mechanical, or other means, now known or hereafter invented, including photocopying and recording, or in any information storage or retrieval system, without permission in writing from the publishers.

British Library Cataloguing in Publication Data
A catalogue record for this book is available from the British Library

Library of Congress in Publication Data
A catalogue record for this book has been requested

ISBN 978-0-700-70992-2 (hbk)
ISBN 978-1-138-86230-2 (pbk)

Contents

Acknowledgements   vii

Foreword   ix
A.W. Macdonald

Map   xii

Introduction   1
A.C. McKay

1 Reflections on Pilgrimages to Sacred Mountains, Lakes and Caves   18
  K. Buffetrille

2 On the Geographical and Material Contextuality of Tibetan Pilgrimage   35
  W. van Spengen

3 Hindu Trading Pilgrims   52
  J. Clarke

4 Khyung-sprul 'Jigs-med nam-mkha'i rdo-rje (1897–1995): An Early Twentieth-century Tibetan Pilgrim in India   71
  P. Kværne

5 On Pilgrimage for Forty Years in the Himalayas: The Female Lama Jetsun Lochen Rinpoche's (1865–1951) Quest for Sacred Sites   85
  H. Havnevik

6 On the Way to Kailash 108
   W. Callewaert

7 The Opening of the sBas Yul 'Bras mo'i gshongs according
   to the Chronicle of the Rulers of Sikkim: pilgrimage as a
   metaphorical model of the submission of foreign
   populations 117
   B. Steinmann

8 On the Sacredness of Mount Kailasa in the Indian and
   Tibetan Sources 143
   A. Loseries-Leick

9 Kailas-Manasarovar in "Classical" (Hindu) and Colonial
   Sources: Asceticism, Power, and Pilgrimage 165
   A. McKay

10 Tibetan Pilgrimage in the Process of Social Change:
   The Case of Jiuzhaigou 184
   Peng Wenbin

   Bibliography 202

   Notes on Contributors 220

   Index 223

Acknowledgements

The early inspiration for this work came from my own Indo-Tibetan travels, after which Dr Humphrey Fisher, of the School of Oriental and African Studies (London University), initially guided me into pilgrimage studies. My thanks are also due to Prof. Timothy Barrett and Dr Werner Menski at S.O.A.S., and in particular to Prof. Peter Robb and Dr Julia Leslie for their advice and support over a number of years.

This work was produced during a Leverhulme Trust (U.K.) fellowship at the International Institute for Asian Studies, in Leiden, the Netherlands, and a further IIAS fellowship. It has benefitted from the financial support of the IIAS and I am also indebted to several other institutions for support during fieldwork in the Himalayas and during its completion: the British Academy and in particular the Spalding Trust (U.K.), along with that of Malcolm Campbell (Curzon Press), for his faith in this project. None of the above are, of course, responsible for the content and opinions expressed herein. Unpublished Crown Copyright documents from the Oriental and Indian Office Collection appear by permission of Her Majesty's Stationery Office.

For their assistance during my fellowship in Leiden, my thanks are due to the following authorities and staff of the IIAS: Professors Wim Stokhof and Frans Hüsken, drs Paul van der Velde and Sabine Kuypers, and to Esther Guitjens, Marianna Langehenkel, Karen van Belle-Foesenek, Jennifer Trel, Kitty Yang-de Witte, Ilse Lasschuijt and Automation Officer Manuel Haneveld for his skills in removing "bugs" from the computer.

The authors of articles herein were participants at the Pilgrimage in Tibet conference, which was held in Leiden in September 1996 with the support of the IIAS. My thanks are due to all of the participants, observers and guests for their contributions to that conference, and in particular to the respondents, Professor A.W.Macdonald (Paris) and Dr Toni Huber (Virginia), for their advice during and since that time. Others whose contributions have been of assistance include John Bray, Mona Schrempf, Peter Richardus and Drs Reinhold Grunendahl (Goettingen), Peter Verhagen (Leiden), Michael Aris (St. Antony's College, Oxford), Professors T.E. Vetter, B.C.A. Walraven and W.J. Boot and, in particular, Emeritus Professor Jan Heesterman for his insight and ideas.

Finally, I wish to thank my wife, Jeri McElroy, for her enthusiastic support and understanding during this project.

A.C. McKay
Leiden 1997

Foreword

Pilgrimage observed

The papers brought together in this volume all resulted from the meeting so ably organised by Alex McKay at the International Institute for Asian Studies in Leiden in September 1996. They bear witness to a current upsurge of interest in Tibetan pilgrimage in the university microcosms of several countries. However they also testify to the emergence in the West of a new type of scholar who is not always a member of a university faculty. From the days of Eugène Burnouf to those of J.W. de Jong we were assured that the proper way to study Buddhism was to read, edit and translate its texturral legacy. Closer in time Gregory Schopen has asked for two cheers for Epigraphy and Archaeology.[1] But by and large until very recently what Buddhists did and do has not been a primary preoccupation among those who haunt or gain their living in the groves of Academe. For long anthropologists were in a minority in the fields of Buddhist Studies and they were not expected to display any great philological talent. Such scholars as Richard Gombrich, who addressed himself to both Buddhist precepts and practices were rare in those days.

Today the scholarly scene has changed: anthropologists too read Buddhist books. Not content with visiting pilgrimate-sites, some even go on pilgrimage, speak the local language and read the pilgrims' *Guides* in the text. Such *Guides* find translators in other continents than those in which they are composed.[2] The genre *dkar chag* has recently been studied by Dan Martin.[3] Katia Buffetrille has participated twice in the pilgrimage around A-myes Rma-chen and has demonstrated, in a definitive manner, that what is in the relevant guide-books is not always an adequate account of the local landscapes and its religious features, nor is it a reliable guide to pilgrims' ritual behaviour.[4]

Textual study is no longer enough: the relevant texts and manuscripts must also be adjusted to the cultural context of their creation. A good over-view of such texts has been given by Toni Huber: '... all traditional Tibetan genres', he writes, 'depend upon and invoke two principal sources of authority to identify sacred sources. The main type is visionary authority, based upon "pure visions" (*dag-snang*) of particular landscapes experiences by Tantric lamas in altered states of consciousness, during meditations, dreams and so forth. The "gap" which exists between a pilgrims' mundane experience of a holy place and the splendored *dag-snang* type visionary accounts of an environment's sublime features and properties is technically explained by authors in terms of traditional theories of graded perceptions and cognitive abilities which are related to an individual's karmic (i.e. moral) status, degrees of embodied psycho-physical defilement (*sgrib-gnyis*) and thus their extent of spiritual progress towards awakening. The second type is prophetic authority in the form of citation and analysis of "prophecies" (*lung-btsan*) reputedly made by Buddhas, deities, recognised saints or highly realized lamas about the identity of particular holy places'.[5]

If the relationship between guide-books and landscape has been clarified, and the ethnographic description of pilgrims' behaviour considerably improved, it is still difficult for the Western researcher to formulate valid generalisations about what pilgrims – whether illiterate or not – actually experience at any given site. Pilgrims even when they move in groups or come from the same village, are a mixed lot, some being more mystically inclined than others, some having read more, meditated more deeply, heard more tales and teachings than others. If believers among them see more and something else than what is in front of their eyes, there seems to be a quasi universal need among human beings to people landscapes with stories.

A.W. Macdonald

Notes

1 *Bones, stones and Buddhist Monks, Collected Papers on the Archeology, Epigraphy and Texts of Monastic Buddhism in India*, Honolulu, University of Hawaii Press, 1997.

2 Mathew Kapstein, 'The Guide to Crystal Peak', in Donald S. Lopez, Jr, (ed.), *Religions of Tibet in Practice*, Princeton, Princeton University Press, 1997, pp. 103-119. Toni Huber, 'Guidebook to Lapchi', in *ibid*, pp. 120-134.
3 Dan Martin, 'Table of Contents (*dkar chag*)' in José Ignacio Cabezon and Roger R. Jackson (eds.), *Tibetan Literature, Studies in Genre*, Ithaca, Snow Lion, 1996, pp. 500-514. See also, in the same volume, John Newman, 'Itineraries to Shambhala', pp. 485-499.
4 Katia Buffetrille, 'The Great Pilgrimage of A-myes Rma-chen: Written Tradition, Living Realities', in A.W. Macdonald (ed.), *Mandala and Landscape*, Emerging Perceptions in Buddhist Studies: No. 6, New Delhi, D.K. Printworld (P) Ltd, 1977, pp. 75-132.
5 Toni Huber, 'Colonial Archeology, International Missionary Buddhism and the First Example of Modern Tibetan Literature', in Petra Kieffer-Pülz and Jens-Uwe Hartmann (eds.), *Bauddhavidyāsudhākarah, Studies in Honour of Heinz Bechert on the occasion of his 65th Birthday*, Swisttal-Odendorf, 1997, pp. 297-318: the quotation is from p. 306.

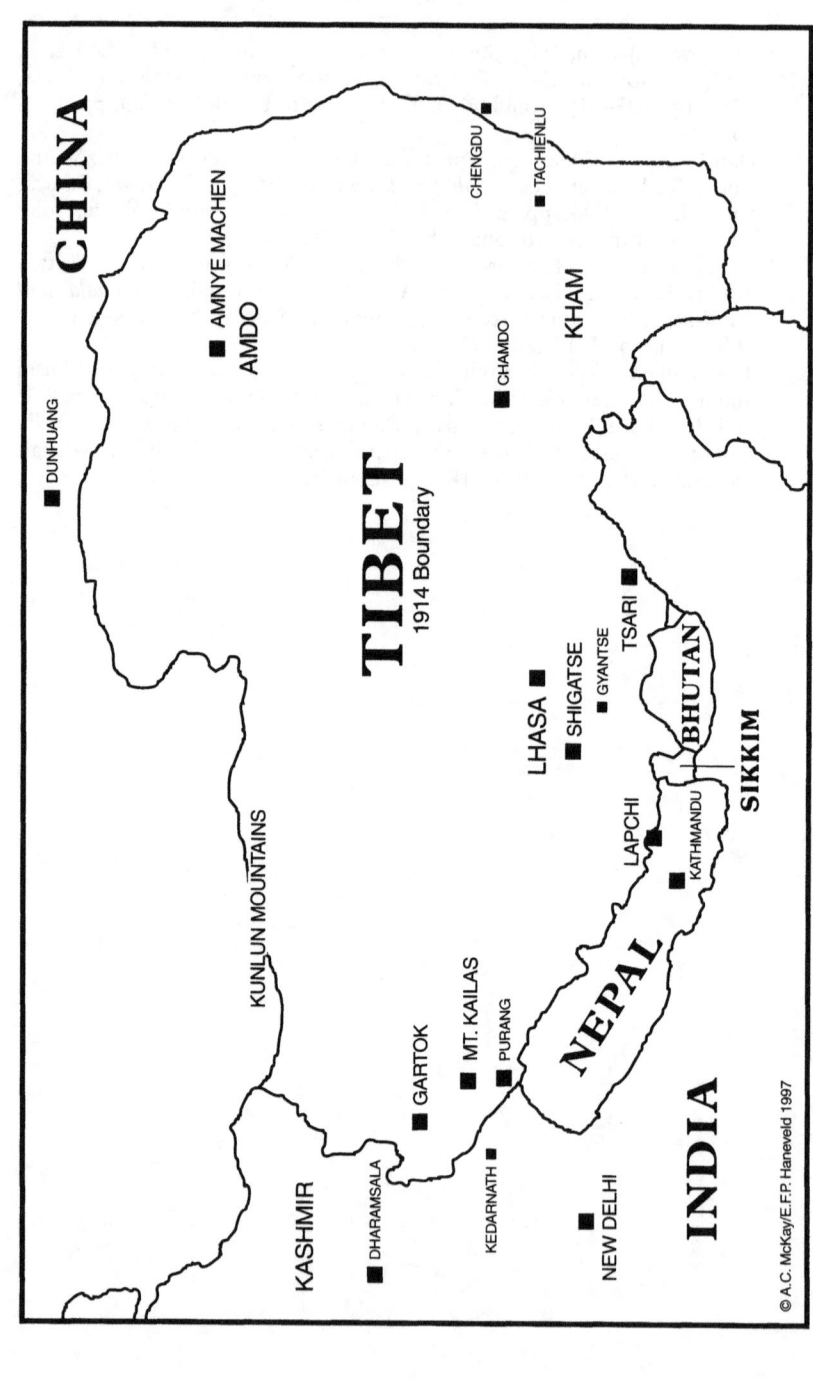

Introduction

Alex McKay

Pilgrimage is a core element of religious practice in the Tibetan cultural world. Indigenous monastic authorities have disputed its spiritual value in the past,[1] and the practice was suppressed by the Chinese political authorities during the 1960s and '70s. But pilgrimage today remains not only an almost universal feature of Tibetan society, but also serves as a prominent indicator of local and national cultural identity. Through an examination of pilgrimage in Tibet we can, therefore, gain great insight into a wide variety of aspects of Tibetan history, culture, and identity, as well as illuminating wider fields and disciplines of study.

It is not my intention in this introduction to attempt any detailed analysis of the state of the field, to suggest methodologies, or to construct any theoretical frameworks from which our work might progress.[2] Indeed, perhaps the widest possible range of approaches free of excessive theorising or the strict imposition of disciplinary boundaries is currently most appropriate to a field of study which is still, if not in its infancy, in a youthful phase of growth. But in order to locate the articles that follow in their wider context, I shall offer a selective account of the historical imperatives of the pilgrimage process generally and a sketch, from the historian's perspective, of the growth of the Tibetan pilgrimage studies field.

As a human phenomena, pilgrimage is generally defined as a journey to a sanctified place, undertaken in the expectation of future spiritual and/or worldly benefit. We may add to that definition an element of time, or a separation from usual place, in order to distinguish it from regular worship.[3] While journeys, types of destination and precise motives are all cultural variables, pilgrims generally travel to a centre which has sacred connotations within their religious tradition because they believe that the journey (and particularly the sacrifices they make and hardships they undergo), will bring a reward. In that sense, pilgrimage is a transaction, an investment in the future.

Because of the element of motion over time, the nature of that transaction is rarely if ever free of economic considerations. The pilgrim must buy, sell or seek charity to survive en route, and at the focal destination, if it is at all developed, the pilgrim makes offerings to religious institutions or practitioners there. The more pilgrims are attracted to a region and to a particular place, the greater the economic stimulus to the community and the centre is involved. Pilgrimages can thus become events of major economic importance.

Because they are of such economic importance, and because they involve the movement of people and their gathering together, often in large numbers and in areas on the periphery of, or beyond the control of, the centre, pilgrimages are also an issue of authority; of concern to both religious and secular powers, who thus seek to influence and control the phenomena.[4] A particular challenge is posed to the various authorities by individuals and groups of individuals who have adopted itinerant pilgrimage as a long-term or permanent lifestyle. Ways must be found to incorporate them within the religio-political system which sustains and unifies the network of sacred places which constitutes the wider sacred geography.

If such issues of authority are successfully negotiated, political and economic interests usually encourage the closer integration of a pilgrimage into the religious tradition[s] of the dominant culture and lead to deliberate strategies designed to stimulate its growth (visits by religious or political elites, improved security of travel and so on). This process is a major factor contributing to the "systemisation" of a pilgrimage site by religious and political authorities.

The process of systemisation, which is ongoing, involves the establishment of institutions to house, feed and instruct pilgrims, and an increase in structures of worship – temples, priests, sacred images, and so on.[5] In addition, there is an associated growth of rituals and of oral or literary traditions concerning the site which serve to locate the pilgrimage within a particular religious tradition. These developments are all indicators of the incorporation (or at least attempts to incorporate) a site within a belief system.

These developments are rarely uncontested. The process of contestation may continue to be expressed in various forms even after the apparent triumph of a particular authority, with the survival of earlier beliefs, often in radically altered forms. Competition may also arise between various sects or sections of authority over control of a site and the economic and social power with which it is associated. In particular, the incorporation into the centre of the religious and/or political power of a site located on or beyond the periphery of existing authority challenges existing power structures, local and regional, with unpredictable results.

As pilgrimage sites become established and systematised, they develop fixed populations under the control of local authority. Neither process is static, and as and when the authority changes, the new powers must include (or suppress), the pilgrimage site and the local population within their own system of government and/or belief. Thus pilgrimages to a particular site, and the sacred centres themselves, may decline as a result of such changes, or become subject to new understandings and meanings within a new belief system, which may radically – even violently – alter the pilgrims' focus.

The individual pilgrims, and their experiences and understandings of their journey, as well as pilgrimage sites themselves, may therefore, be seen against an ever-changing backdrop of politics and economics, sectarian and political competition and co-existence, and issues of power and authority. The pilgrim, even the renunciate, is a part of a religious phenomena, but also of a socio-religious and political system in constant flux.

Yet, despite this worldly setting, the ideal of the individual pilgrim in religious traditions and mythologies is of one who is primarily concerned with the spiritual aspects and experiences of the journey, and unconcerned with those temporal dimensions, upon which, being more easily classifiable and open to analysis, scholarship is apt to focus. Such ideal pilgrims do indeed exist, and the core experience they undergo may be one largely beyond the analytic and descriptive classifications of scholarship. Yet without an understanding of that ideal dimension, an understanding liable to arise more from empirical or participatory experience rather than textual studies, pilgrimage as a human phenomena cannot be fully comprehended. It is a strength of this collection that the contributors have all participated in the cultural milieu which they discuss.

❊ ❊ ❊

The Western academic study of Asian pilgrimage is a relatively new field of enquiry, one initially shaped by work within the monotheist

Christian and Islamic traditions. Much stimulus was provided in the 1970s by the works of the social scientist Victor Turner and by scholars who engaged with Turner's somewhat idealistic theories of *communitas* and *liminal/liminoid* states. After pioneering work in the 1960s and '70s by Indic scholars such as Surinder Bhardwaj and Swami Agehananda Bharati, and by Anne-Marie Blondeau and A.W. "Sandy" Macdonald in Himalayan and Tibetan studies, Asianists in general and Tibetologists in particular have increasingly come to involve and to focus upon this issue.

The greatest stimulus to Tibetan pilgrimage studies came with the gradual opening of that region to tourism in the 1980s, making fieldwork there a possibility. Not since the time of pioneers such as Giuseppe Tucci and Robert Ekvall had Western scholars interested in pilgrimage been able to travel in Tibet. The result of this modern freedom was a new generation of researchers who enjoyed the benefits of direct access to their subject culture.

An attraction of pilgrimage studies is that it touches upon, or offers a point of entry from, a number of different disciplinary backgrounds. In practice however, within recent Tibetan and Himalayan studies it has been a field dominated by anthropologists, perhaps because their focus is immediately closer to cultural actualities than that of the historian or textual specialist. As a result of the modern anthropologist's concern with 'the social construction of space and social being',[6] this has resulted in a significant growth in our understanding of Tibetan concepts of sacred space and the relationship between these "power places" and the peoples of the Tibetan cultural world.

A landmark in this growing understanding was provided in 1994–95 by a series of four editions of the *Tibet Journal* (an academic outlet produced by the Tibetan exile community), devoted to the subject of sacred space.[7] Those editions were under the guest editorship of Toni Huber, whose own works have been instrumental in shaping the development of the field in the 1990s.[8] Further testifying to the growth of the field has been the appearance of several volumes of essays devoted to aspects of pilgrimage and sacred space in recent years [to which this present work will add].[9] Mention should also be made of the new French "school" of pilgrimage scholars, several of whom are represented in this collection, and who owe much to the inspiration of Blondeau and Macdonald.

It was this climate of increasing interest which led to the International Institute for Asian Studies sponsoring the Pilgrimage in Tibet conference which was held in Leiden on 12 & 13 September

1996, a conference of which I was organiser and Macdonald and Huber acted as Respondents. As a small, tightly focused gathering of specialists, it was a valuable opportunity for participants from various disciplines to exchange ideas, approaches and information. Following the conference, ten of the participants were able to provide articles for this collection.

Pilgrimage studies have thus become one of the main sources for an increased understanding of Tibetan culture, history and identity. There remains much to be learned about the origins of Tibetan pilgrimage, of its gender relations, economic imperatives, spiritual motives and much else. Equally we may speculate at length as to whether the present integration of Tibet into the modern capitalist economy will lead to a decline in pilgrimage there, or whether, as a result of Tibetan strategies of resistance to Chinese imperialism, the role of pilgrimage as an agent in the construction and strengthening of Tibetan identity, and the tendency to use pilgrimage as an issue in a political sphere (as for example, with the Sino-Indian agreement allowing a limited number of Hindu pilgrims to Mount Kailas), there will actually be a growth of the phenomena. But if it is the function of the anthropologist to highlight the need for scholarship to take into account local cultural assumptions and conceptualisations concerning universal religious phenomena,[10] equally it is the function of the historian to describe identity and pilgrimage as process, to ask questions concerning the sources, nature and application of power within that process, as well as to chart the movements of those processes through time in relation to neighbouring and universal phenomena.[11] The need to take into account such factors, and to balance the anthropological concern with space and the historians' concern with time, meant a historical theme was suggested for this volume; albeit a loosely applied one. We may hope that this preliminary interplay of the two distinct disciplines of anthropology and history will enrich both each other's interpretation of the subject and the field as a whole.

❀ ❀ ❀

Several of the articles herein also concern the cultural world of Hindu India, although they involve Tibet in the sense of it being the pilgrim subjects' "centre". *Pilgrimage in Tibet*, therefore, may be understood to deal with the many components of the Tibetan cultural world. This socio-political sphere was not static, but in constant flux, and did not exist in isolation, but drew upon, and contributed to, its neighbouring cultures, "major" and "minor", local and regional. Indic, Sino and Tibetan cultures thus each enriched each other, as did sub-cultures at every level. This interplay between traditions was continuous over time, with ideas, like goods, exchanged, adapted, expressed and understood within each cultural context, along trans-Himalayan networks of traders and pilgrims, cultures and states.

No attempt has been made in this volume to standardise the contributor's systems of transcription from Tibetan, Sanskrit and other Asian languages. Thus, for example, we read of [Mount] Kailas/Kailash/Kailasha, according to the author's choice. The wide variety of transcription systems, and their appeal to different disciplines and functions unfortunately remains a major weakness of Tibetology, in particular in its appeal to a wider audience.

Given the inevitable overlap of sources in such a specialised area of study, a general bibliography has been used, which may also act as a separate resource in itself. The contributors' articles have been ordered to provide the following sequence: overviews of pilgrimage, examinations of types of pilgrim, studies of the interplay of mythology and politics, and finally a case study of modern pilgrimage.

❉ ❉ ❉

The volume opens with a schematic outline by Katia Buffetrille discussing the process within the relationship between Buddhism and popular beliefs by which the establishment of Buddhism as the dominant culture in Tibet transformed pre-existing indigenous understandings of sacred geographical sites such as mountains, converting them into Buddhist pilgrimage places. She concludes that mountains attracting pilgrims are those which were (and in most cases still are) traditionally considered to be territorial gods (*yul lha*) before being transformed into sacred mountains for Buddhist pilgrimage.

This process of 'Buddhacisation' involved the construction of new understandings of place through the ritual appropriation of existing sacred space, often by means of transferring concepts of sacred geography from Indian sources.[12] In this process pre-existing indigenous deities were subjugated or converted into Buddhist deities and Buddhist concepts were superimposed onto the cult of the territorial god. This involved an associated "mandalization" of the landscape within the Buddhist understanding (often with the *yul lha* being incorporated into the mandala as a protective deity) and an "opening" of the sacred centre, involving the "discovery" of the circumambulation path by a charismatic Buddhist figure.

This process has produced two, overlapping types of sacred mountain in Tibet. Firstly, those where the primary worship remains that of the *yul lha*, who are associated with the local community and its origins, and who are worshipped by seasonal rituals largely carried out on the side of the mountain. Secondly there are those mountains (*gnas ri*[13]) which are now sacred to the wider Buddhist tradition. There, the original *yul lha* deity has been superceded by a Buddhist deity and the primary form of worship is the essential ritual act of Buddhist pilgrimage – circumambulation, following the Indian *pradaksina* ('moving to the right') model.[14]

This transformation process was of great political significance. *Yul lha* rituals were at the heart of the political organisation of the territory surrounding the mountain, and the transformation of a *yul lha* mountain into a Buddhist *gnas ri* was marked not only by the introduction of circumambulation rituals but also by new religious and political structures which drew the region into a wider system and identity.[15]

We cannot usually date this process with any exactitude, not least because it was not a linear process and is often ritually ongoing, with local variants (as will be seen in the paper of Peng Wenbin). Thus the extent to which it has progressed varies greatly. But Buffetrille has found that although there is architectural evidence from the 7–10th century period for the existence in Tibet of the Buddhist pilgrimage ritual of circumambulation, there are no dated historical sources for Buddhist pilgrimage within Tibet before the 13th century.

Given the importance of this conversion model, more research is needed which compares this with the Sanskritisation process which occurred within India, and with the affect that had upon local deities there.[16] Within India, the Sanskritisation process began much earlier, and may have provided a model, or some aspects of the model, of "Buddhacisation". Certainly both processes have led to a great multiplication of sacred entities and understandings, including the survival of elements of ancient beliefs. Similarly, we need consider the process as it applies to the history of Bon, how that belief system (in its various forms over time) related to, or determined, local deities, and whether there was also a process of "Bonicisation", predating or contemporous to, the processes of Sanskritisation and Buddhacisation.[17]

There are other questions we also need to ask; to what extent did these processes assist what political powers and religious authorities? How might this process compare with that which occurred during the spread of other religious traditions? To what extent and at what levels was this process resisted and to what extent do narratives of conversion with their symbolic violence, represent a retrospective ideological justification, idealising what we might otherwise describe as an equivalent to imperialism; the age-old story of the conquest, subjection, and forced conversion of the weak by the strong?[18]

We next turn to the wider material context of Tibetan pilgrimage, which is examined by Wim van Spengen. There was [and is] an almost invariable overlap between the spiritual and material goals of the pilgrim. Pilgrimage also has its social aspects, with organised groups of pilgrims banding together for safety in the face of the dangers of nature and of man. This chapter discusses the economic environment of pilgrimage, the economic survival strategies adopted, and the extent to which both spiritual and material needs, as well as social intercourse, were catered for by the overlap of pilgrimage centres and trading fairs. Both sites and fairs could, from various perspectives, be placed in hierarchies ultimately encompassing the entire Tibetan cultural sacred map of the world – in a network which stretched as far as the sacred places of the Buddha in India, to Omei Shan in Szechuan and to Urga in Mongolia.

From the perspective of a geographer, van Spengen discusses the different understandings of landscape held by Tibetan pilgrims and Western scholars. He also reminds us that pilgrimage to sacred urban centres of Tibetan cultural power was at least as popular as to those geographically peripheral sites whose Buddhacisation may be seen within a context of political expansion strategies. Pilgrimage to urban sites has received much less emphasis within Tibetan studies (in contrast to Indic studies, where the reverse is true), and clearly that issue requires the development of somewhat different understandings and models.

In stressing the range of pilgrimage sites, this chapter also raises the question of a wider indigenous (both Buddhist and non-Buddhist) understanding of the entire Tibetan landscape as a sacred space; a classification for which there is textual support and Indian parallels, as well as recent political manifestation in the form of promotions such as that of "Tibet: Zone of Peace", formulations which offer possible, if somewhat idealistic, grounds for negotiation of the Sino-Tibetan problem.

Van Spengen points out that pilgrimage contributed to a circulation of goods, particularly small items of value such as precious stones, and the numerous lay travellers whose economic existence revolved around trading at pilgrimage sites raises the wider question of when pilgrimage stops and lifestyle starts – a question more complex still in discussing the trading activities of monastic practitioners and religious renunciates.[19] John Clarke's contribution provides a case study of one particular aspect of the interplay of trade and pilgrimage. He discusses the evidence concerning Hindu renunciates who travelled to Tibet from India. The majority of these "Gosains" were, in contrast to the idealistic popular perception of renunciation, heavily engaged in trading activities and they played an important role in Indo-Tibetan trade during the 18th and early 19th centuries, before they fell from favour with the Chinese authorities in Tibet.

Drawing on the evidence of an 18th century painting now in the Bodleian library, which depicts pilgrims from Oudh, Clarke describes how groups of these Gosains visited various parts of Tibet on an annual cycle of trade and pilgrimage. This cycle included attendance at various religious festivals throughout the subcontinent and visits to the southern tip of India to purchase pearls. These were favoured items to trade into Tibet with, because their high value and low weight made them suitable for individuals to carry over long distances.

There was a high level of organisational structure behind these trading patterns, and the Gosains became an economically successful community. They also acted as political intermediaries between the East India Company and the Panchen Lama, in particular the well-known Gosain, Purangir, who travelled on behalf of both the British to Tibet and the Tibetans to Peking.

The three following papers provide us with personal insights into Tibetan pilgrimage from three comparatively recent, but very different, perspectives; those of a Bon-po monk, an itinerant female practitioner most closely associated with the Nyingma tradition, and a contemporary Western academic.

Per Kvaerne describes the colourful biography of the monk Khyung Sprul, who made three journeys from Tibet to India during the period 1922–1948. Khyung Sprul was both a pilgrim and a Bon "missionary", spreading that doctrine – although not always explicitly – and visiting the various Bon sacred sites. His travels demonstrate the wide range of Tibetan pilgrims as well as of Bon sacred sites, but his pilgrimages also encompassed many Buddhist centres such as Sarnath and Bodh Gaya, and even the Sikh centre of Amritsar. To Khyung Sprul, both Bon and Buddhist perceptions were equally valid. He travelled widely in Kinnaur, where, in an echo of earlier reformers he acted to suppress animal sacrifices to local *yul lha*.

Khyung Sprul, who eventually founded a monastery in the traditional Bon heartland of Western Tibet, was also forward-thinking enough to use the modern technology available in India to publish religious texts for mass circulation in Tibet. Such endeavours clearly contributed to the modern character and survival of Bon, and remind us of the affect of technology on understandings of existence. Can he be seen as part of a Bon "revival" in this period, as evidence of a continuing process of contestation between Bon and Buddhism, or as a demonstration of the close links between two branches of the same family?

Hanna Havnevik similarly examines the biography of a Tibetan pilgrim, but in this case the female practitioner Lama Jetsun Lochen, whose travelled extensively during the period 1865–1904. As a wandering lay practitioner, she was subject to a "process of sanctification', as recognition of her sacred qualities, by both herself and outsiders, accumulated over time.

Jetsun Lochen was born to a mother who was herself an itinerant pilgrim, and from her earliest years was accustomed to travelling extensively throughout the Tibetan cultural world. Accepted in her youth as a gifted reciter of *manis*, she sees herself only as a "poor beggar". After acquiring a "root guru" within the Nyingma tradition, and strongly influenced by the "Ris med" movement, she becomes part of a band of "cotton clad" pilgrims, visiting sites made sacred by such figures as Milarepa, Padmasambhava and Shabkar. Eventually ordained as a nun in the 1890s, she continues with renunciate and *siddha* practises and becomes a highly regarded figure.

This article raises issues of gender in Tibetan pilgrimage and in the wider Tibetan cultural world, a field of enquiry still in its infancy.[20] It appears that while in some spheres femininity is considered advantageous – as for instance in goddess worship rituals – and that among the Nyingma there is more scope for the female practitioner, they often faced considerable prejudice. Jetsun Lochen was frequently discriminated against by patriarchal authorities, including being excluded from particular sites on the grounds that her presence would render them inauspicious. That she accepts these restrictions apparently without complaint suggests that this situation was inherent in the Tibetan system, with women denied full participation in most spheres of religious authority. Even charismatic female authority was limited largely to the popular sphere, with only a handful of female religious figures included in the structure of incarnate authority. We need more research into the nature and structure of the gender aspect of these power relationships and of their development, and to ascertain how these varied with place and within particular spiritual traditions and organisations.

A totally different perspective is provided by the account of Winand Callewaert, describing in prose and poetry his 1996 journey to Mount Kailash. There are numerous difficulties in blending the personal experience of a multiplicity of spiritual traditions and the academic perspectives, and such attempts are unusual in this type of forum: not the least remarkable aspect of this chapter is its absence of footnotes! In the past we have had the learned travel accounts of scholars such as Tucci and Snellgrove, and Don Lopez has more recently provided a stimulating examination of the practical and theoretical problems that he faced in converting Tibetan Buddhist teachings and understandings into Western academic forms.[21] But Callewaert's blending of Western and Asian perspectives in a travel account is perhaps closer in spirit to that of Anagorika Govinda in his *Way of the White Clouds,* albeit closer to Mark Twain in style![22]

Using as a backdrop his understanding of Asian cultures and belief systems, and familiarity with their textual traditions, Callewaerts brings out the reality of pilgrimage as it is experienced by a western traveller – dominated by the physical hardships, rough wayside shelters, bitter cold, endless dust and the physical irritations it brings, extreme reactions from extended emotions, and with periods of exhausted emptiness. Anyone who has travelled in a truck to Mount Kailas will appreciate the significance of the heartfelt words 'Dust, dust, dust.' Yet there are also spectacular camps with open horizons, stimulating philosophical discussions, even altered states of consciousness, and certainly suspension of everyday Western belief structures, and a closeness to the earth, along with a sense of history and of joining a tradition.

In comparing his account with those of Tibetan pilgrims, perhaps the most notable difference is that descriptions of the hardships of the journey are largely absent from Tibetan accounts – as Havnevik has noted in her article. As van Spengen demonstrates, hardships are a consistent feature of Western narratives. Are these literary conventions, or physical differences, and do they affect our view that pilgrims regard the overcoming of hardship as beneficial to their journey? Clearly adaptation to the environment is a major factor, but such are the range of perceptions represented in Western (and other non-Tibetan) accounts, that their almost uniform response to the Tibetan environment suggests specific cultural rather than physical factors at play here.[23]

Whether the other notable factor, that of spiritual disappointment, or at least the gaining of understandings very different to those sought or expected, is a cross-cultural phenomena, is a question for further research, not necessarily within Tibetan studies.[24]

Brigitte Steinman's paper uses literary evidence to provide a specific example of the process of Buddhacisation outlined earlier by Buffetrille. She describes how the chronicle of Sikkimese history, written in 1908 by the Maharaja of Sikkim himself, may be read as a history of the conquest and take-over of the land of the Lepcha and Limbu peoples by Buddhist invaders from eastern Tibet. While this is presented in the literature as being a religiously pre-ordained progression within the grand Buddhist schema, we may recover and articulate the "voices" suppressed by "official" history through an analysis of this text.

We may read of the transformation of Sikkim beginning with a gradual expansion towards that region in the life-time of the Buddha. A progression is presented from Sikkim as a "Hidden Land" described in *terma* texts, towards the predestined "opening" of the land to Buddhist influence, and then of the genealogies associating the new Sikkim ruling clan with the Minyak clan whose origins were in eastern Tibet. The landscape is subject to the gradual process of mandalization, with Lepcha pilgrimage places being co-opted into the new religious geography. As with the Tibetan Buddhist account of Milarepa vanquishing the Bonpo magician at Kailas, we have the subjection myth of the Limbu shaman, with the inevitable triumph of the Buddhist and the voluntary submission of the autochotonous powers. Yet we can read indications of Lepcha resistance here, and of the violent imposition of the new faith, as shown by the account of the lynching of the Lepcha wizards. But in the religious literature of this type, this process is presented as preordained, immanent; a religious order is grounded in the text. Buddhism easily triumphs, the whole process serving to legitimate the ruling dynasty and serve the religious model of pacification and Buddhacisation.

In this reading the importance of pilgrimage sites derives from their function of deliminating the sacred kingdom. There are overlapping mythologies of place, from Lepcha, and Bhotia mythology, but the hegemonic account is of course by the dominant culture, the Buddhist state. One element of authority which is clearly apparent is the close association between religious topography and taxable areas. Once a region was "opened" by the religious elite, they began the process of establishing a taxation base within the borders of this *'mandala* state-system'.

There is another model of pilgrimage sites; one with far greater popularity in terms of numbers of supporters than that understood by academics. That is the understanding held in the popular imagination of lay pilgrims and passed on largely by means of oral recitation, although based on both textual literature from within the tradition holding it sacred and upon local traditions. Andrea Loseries-Leick focuses on that mythological understanding of the major pilgrimage site of Mount Kailasa, previously referred to in Callewaert's paper.

Kailasha is held sacred in the various Buddhist, Bon, Hindu, Jain and Tantric traditions, and through their understandings as expressed in oral and textual traditions we can understand the value and meaning of pilgrimage and the religious exercises associated with it from the perspective of the actual pilgrims. In addition, these mythologies provide evidence that pilgrimage to Kailasha pre-dates by a considerable period the introduction of Tibetan Buddhist pilgrimage as indicated in Tibetan Buddhist sources, and perhaps lead us to conjecture what discoveries could be made if we able to obtain archaeological evidence from the region.

My own paper (McKay) contrasts the understandings of Mount Kailas presented in the "classical" Hindu textual accounts with the evidence concerning the pilgrimage contained in British imperial sources, in order to suggest that the modern Hindu understanding of Kailas was strongly influenced by British frontier officers at the turn of this century. They constructed an image of Kailas which presented it as a desirable pilgrimage centre for all types of Hindu; a construction designed to stimulate the pilgrimage in order to bring revenue to frontier districts. In the preceding centuries, however, it was apparently a site visited only by a small group of renunciates of a particular sect. A reading of the classical texts in this light suggests this has been the case for a considerable period, and also that the accounts of visits to Kailas given in texts such as the *Mahabharata* more probably refer to journeys to a different mountain, one within present-day India's borders.

Kailas, it is argued, was largely an 'ideal' pilgrimage place, and not seen as a destination for ordinary caste Hindu pilgrims. In the early Indian perspective it was located beyond the periphery of the ordered world, in the "wilderness" – which might be drawn into the "known" by the presence and power of Hindu renunciates travelling and practising there. But this transformation process never progressed to the point where the region developed the structures associated with a Hindu pilgrimage site, although under British patronage that process had begun by the 1930s and '40s, only to be prevented by the Chinese takeover. Kailas thus remained outside of the political boundaries of India.

In conclusion we are brought into the present day world of conflict and accommodation between tradition and modernity. Peng Wenbin provides a case study based on fieldwork in the region of Jiuzhaigou, where Tibetan and Chinese cultures meet. It provides an illustration of the complexity of Tibetan pilgrimage in the political context of China today, as well as examining the impact of social, political and economic change upon a local pilgrimage site.

The local people, who identify themselves as Tibetan Bonpo, have recently begun making pilgrimages to the local sacred site, Mt. Rdzadkar, after a period in which it was forbidden by the communist Chinese authorities. The revival of religious activity in the area in 1982 was followed by an immediate, and perhaps largely spontaneous revival of customs such as pilgrimage. But the popularity of this act of worship has subsequently been affected by the rapid growth of the region as a tourist area. The pilgrimage and tourist seasons overlap, with the result that the numbers making this pilgrimage have declined greatly since the initial revival, with most local people preferring to take advantage of the economic possibilities offered by the tourist trade, rather than undertaking pilgrimages.

Wenbin describes the actual pilgrimage undertaking. Although the presiding deity of the mountain is apparently a local *yul lha*, pilgrims circumambulate the mountain, besides performing other rituals more immediately associatable with *yul lha* worship. The gaps between ideal "monastic/textual" practise of pilgrimage and actual lay pilgrimage are also shown by the ignoring of prescriptions on food such as onions.

There is thus a tension between modern economic needs and traditional practises, between spiritual merit and material gain, between generations, and between the need to reaffirm identity and the need to make money. Yet despite the influx of tourists and the Chinese promotion of the region as a tourist site, there has been a strengthening, or a reaffirmation, of Tibetan identity there. Much of this follows the personal narrative of the abbot of the local monastery, but an "authentic" Tibetan identity is in the process of being keenly constructed by the village leaders, thus connecting this region to the Tibetan core culture.

❋ ❋ ❋

We have observed that there are numerous questions concerning pilgrimage in Tibet which remain to be investigated. But that there are particular characteristics to Tibetan pilgrimage practice which provide a multi-disciplinary basis from which to proceed is apparent, with a number of these having been discussed in the foregoing chapters. Although we cannot be entirely assured that understandings and meanings of these features have remained consistent despite local variations and political and cultural change, certain broad tendencies and features do appear to persist across time. The expansion and growth of a pilgrimage place beyond the merely local, for example, depends upon it being drawn into a dominant model of sacred landscape imposed by a universal religion, a model which doubles as a landscape of control – a sphere of authority, ordered, taxed, and made subject. Similarly we can see the continuing interplay of trade and pilgrimage, the material processes which enable pilgrims to survive, and even to prosper economically. We can observe codes of meaning in textual traditions which indicate patterns of contestation at sacred sites, the suppression of existing beliefs and cultures, and even of individual lives. And we can, in focusing on the individual, see the power of belief and of culture which lies behind the undertaking of a pilgrimage and which sends the pilgrim across what is, to the outsider at least, an exceedingly harsh landscape.

❊ ❊ ❊

In dealing with a living tradition such as pilgrimage, we may perhaps, in conclusion, offer without comment the following popular proverb from eastern Tibet:

'ADVICE TO TRAVELLERS ON THEIR WAY TO LHASA',[25]

The scales of Chamdo do not weigh;
The Draya folk resent horse play,
And when at Kiangka no one may
Upon the threshold steps delay;
Remember too that Batang wives
Are much inclined to changeful lives;
And if in need you must not try
Good tsampa at Litang to buy;
And Oh! beware, no one repeats
The gossip heard on Hokou streets. *

* 1: Cheating is a fine art in Chamdo
  2: The Dray folk are bold and warlike
  3: The Kiangka winds are very boisterous
  4: The Batang women are reputed to be very immoral
  5: Litang is nearly 14,000 feet high
  6: Hokou village is highly endogamous.

Notes

1 See Huber 1990: 121–165
2 See for examples of such models in the Indian context, Morinis 1984; Dubey 1995: VI.
3 Morinis 1984: 2., favours separating pilgrimage from regular worship by defining a pilgrim as one who 'consciously sees himself to be so'[!?], although he also classifies pilgrims into those with spiritual and those with worldly aims (*ibid*: 60), and states that the 'journey from home to shrine is a[n]. . . defining aspect of all pilgrimages' (*ibid*: 218–19). In regard to Tibetan pilgrimage, however, there are specific characteristics, often overlooked, which mean that it is, as Huber states, 'difficult to define, with many aspects, and a meditational dimension as well'; Huber 1994c: 37.
4 As Epstein and Peng Wenbin state, pilgrimages often 'disrupt and subvert the states totalizing project by reasserting local spatial identity'; Epstein & Peng Wenbin 1994: 22.
5 This is not to deny a spontaneous element in this movement.
6 Epstein & Peng Wenbin 1994: 21.
7 See *The Tibet Journal* 1994–95 volume XIX, numbers 2, 3, & 4, and volume XX, number 1. In that the journal is produced from within the Library of Tibetan Works and Archives in Dharamsala, these developments can be seen as having been at the initiative of the Tibetan exile community.
8 See the various works of Huber in the bibliography.
9 See bibliography, Macdonald 1997; Karmay & Sagant 1997; Blondeau & Steinkellner 1996; Huber 1998b (forthcoming); also see the variety of papers in Ramble & Brauen 1993; Kvaerne 1993, *et al*.
10 See the review by Lionel Caplan of William Sax's *Mountain goddess: gender and politics in a Himalayan pilgrimage* [Oxford: OUP, 1991] in the *Bulletin of the School of Oriental and African Studies*, vol. 58 (2) 1995: 393–94.
11 As stated by Bowman 'An historical investigation of the evolution of pilgrimage networks would show that popular pilgrimages now closely integrated with the social practices of their cultural environments were not spontaneously generated out of those milieus but were imposed upon local populations through the agency of "universal religions!"'; Huber 1990: 156, quoting Bowman, G., 'Anthropology of Pilgrimage' in Jha, M., (ed.), *Dimensions of Pilgrimage. An Anthropological Perspective*, New Delhi: Inter-India Publications, 1985.
12 Re this transference from India, see Huber 1990.
13 *Gnas* is generally translated as meaning "place" in the sense of "sacred" or "power" place, hence *gnas-skor*: "pilgrimage", or literally "going around a

place". For a wider discussion of this concept, see Huber 1994c, who points out that '*gnas* in the term *gnas-skor* always carries the double meaning of the actual physical place, and of the residence or existence of deities, entities or beings believed to be powerful or significant in some way by the pilgrims who go there.' (Huber 1994c: 31).

14 A model which, however, as Huber points out, has become subject to indigenous Tibetan understandings distinct from those of "classical" Indic Buddhist formulations as understood in most Western scholarship: Huber 1994c: 34–37.
15 Regarding the political role of *yul lha* mountains, also see Karmay 1994.
16 Re Sanskritisation in the Himalayan context, see for example Seeland 1993, esp.: 356. As Macdonald (1990: 207–08) has pointed out however, the process of Sanskritisation, as currently formulated, involves an element of social mimesis (or "social climbing"!) absent in (Madhyamaka) accounts of Buddhacisation.
17 See, in that regard, the description of gShen-rab's descent from 'Ol-mo-lung-ring to Shang Shung (Zhang zhung) in Ramble 1995: 92.
18 Regarding the role of Tibetan literature in presenting a particular perspective, see, for example, Macdonald 1990; Huber 1997: 234–41.
19 Buffetrille (Buffetrille 1997: 87), has pointed out the similarity between the normal lifestyle of the nomadic population, who compromise the majority of pilgrims, and their lifestyle on pilgrimage. There is, of course an added dimension in that, as Anagorika Govinda put it 'the pilgrimage in the outer space is actually a mirrored reflection of an inner movement or development'; Govinda 1966: XIV.
20 See, for recent articles exploring that issue, Huber 1994b; Havnevik 1990, forthcoming/ongoing.
21 See Tucci 1956, 1989; Snellgrove 1989; Lopez, D., 'Foreigner at the Lama's Feet', in Lopez, D. (ed.), *Curators of the Buddha: the Study of Buddhism Under Colonialism*, Chicago/London: University of Chicago Press, 1995.
22 Govinda, 1962/1966.
23 Compare, for example the wide range of perceptions presented by the "Nietzschian superman" Sven Hedin, the American Buddhist Theos Bernard, the Jesuit monk Ippoliti Desideri, the British imperial officer Charles Bell, the Japanese monk Kawaguchi Ekai and the Indian *pandit* Swami Pranavananda: all react to the hardships of the Tibetan environment.
24 Other recent travellers to Kailas (of both European and Indian origin) with whom I have been in contact have had similar experiences, an issue I hope to consider in the future.
25 'Advice to Travellers on the Way to Lhasa', proverb translated by J.H. Edgar, in the *Journal of the West China Border Research Society*, vol. IV, 1930–31: 4. [The original uses 'Ch'mdo' rather than 'Chamdo'.]

Chapter 1

Reflections on Pilgrimages to Sacred Mountains, Lakes and Caves[1]

Katia Buffetrille

In Tibet, pilgrimages are one of the most important religious demonstrations of the lay people. In fact, at the beginning of the nineteen-eighties, when religious liberalisation was instituted by the Chinese authorities, one could see pilgrims thronging to the temples and monasteries, and also starting again their traditional peregrinations to sacred mountains, lakes and caves. Thirty years of repression did not seem to have reduced their religious fervour.

I recently completed a Ph.D. on pilgrimages to sacred mountains, lakes and caves in Tibet proper and in the Sherpa area of East Nepal. The choice of these components of the landscape was motivated by the fact that they form a unity in the Tibetan conception of space: a mountain is generally associated with a lake, and in that case, the first is regarded as the father, and the second as the mother. With regard to caves, their location inside mountains, and also the part they play as retreat and meditation places for practitioners, makes them an important component of this whole.

One of the interests the subject holds is the mixture of several traditions. One finds traditional practices that may be described as "popular" in the sense that they do not belong to any learned tradition; and also Buddhist beliefs and influences coming from the periphery of Tibetan culture, all of them difficult to identify even today. The aim of this study is not to separate Buddhist actions and beliefs from ones that can be called non-Buddhist but rather to understand how this synthesis has taken place and is still evolving, and why and how some elements have been retained in the form they have been.

Because of their representativeness, I chose to focus my studies mainly on three mountains, the pilgrimage routes of which I followed:

Kailash (western Tibet), A myes rMa chen (eastern Tibet) and rTsib ri (southern Tibet). With regard to lakes, I studied the pilgrimage to 'O ma mtsho, in East Nepal, and with regard to the caves, those to Halase-Maratika, also in East Nepal. It is necessary to point out that a Tibetan expression exists to express what one translates generally as "sacred mountains": *gnas ri*; *gnas* means "place" but, in this context, the term is understood as "sacred Buddhist place". On the other hand, there is not, as far as I know, a specific term to distinguish a "sacred lake" from an ordinary one. For example, the expression *gnas mtsho* (made up by me) was unknown to all my informants.

In this article, I intend only to present the main results of my research, and to point out still open questions in order to stimulate further understanding of a phenomenom full of strong and surprising vitality.

Preliminary remarks

Before taking up the subject itself of pilgrimages to sacred mountains,[2] I would like to underline that there are no dated historical sources which testify to the practice of Buddhist pilgrimages in Tibet during the first diffusion of Buddhism (7th–9th centuries). Sources mention them from the 13th century onwards, but one should not forget that, from the beginning of the second diffusion (end of 10th–11th centuries), the number of the Tibetan religious practitioners who went to India, Kashmir or Nepal in quest of Buddhist teachings was great. During these travels did they visit the sacred places? Are they not the precursors who introduced the idea of pilgrimages to Tibet itself? Whatever the answer, the two oldest pilgrimage accounts appeared later: one was composed by Chag lo tsa va, a Tibetan man of religion who went to India at the beginning of the 13th century;[3] the other by O rgyan pa (1230–1309),[4] a disciple of rGod tshang pa mGon po rdo rje (1189–1258)[5] who went to Swat in the second part of the 13th century and wrote an "account" about his journey. These first documented Buddhist pilgrimages were made by religious people whose destination was the Indian world. I will not, however, discuss Buddhist pilgrimages to India because of limited space.

Pilgrimages involve the practice of circumambulation. Indeed, a pilgrim is defined as a *gnas skor ba* – "one who goes around a sacred place" – by the rite he must perform at the end of his travels,. This ritual act seems testified to during the Royal period by the building of ambulatories around the *cella* of temples, the initial construction of which goes back to the 7th–10th centuries.

One may wonder when the tradition of pilgrimages to sacred mountains (and also to lakes), and their circumambulation first appeared. After the new blossoming of Buddhism in the 11th century, the 'Bri gung pa masters Gling ras pa (1128–1188)[6] and 'Jig rten mgon po (1143–1217)[7] sent numerous practitioners to the famous bKa' brgyud pa sacred places of Kailash,[8] Tsa ri (south-east of Lhasa, near the Indian border) and La phyi (southern Tibet, near the Nepalese border). These practitioners attracted others. Whether the tradition of pilgrimages to sacred mountains started at that time is something only a systematic study of the biographical and autobiographical literature may reveal, (without being sure that this survey would bring conclusive answers). As far as Kailash is concerned, rGod tshang pa is credited with the opening of this sacred place (*gnas sgo phyed ba*). When O rgyan pa, his disciple, went to Kailash, he meditated there, as he writes, among a crowd of five hundred ascetics, but he did not undertake a circumambulation of the mountain; at least he does not mention it in his guide.[9]

The territorial god (*yul lha*)

During this research, a first conclusion imposed itself quite quickly: the mountains to which pilgrims went and still go were mountains traditionally considered to be territorial gods (*yul lha*) before becoming mountain holy places (*gnas ri*),[10] a typical Buddhist concept with which all the literature spoken about above is associated. Territorial gods are mentioned as early as the Dunhuang manuscripts (7th–10th centuries). Most scholars agree that the concept of territorial god, and thus its cult, preceded the arrival of Buddhism.[11] This cult, which appealed mainly to laymen, thrived until the Chinese occupation, and has recently begun again, as witnessed at least in some regions of Tibet.[12]

Without pretending to describe in these few lines the nature and the role of the *yul lha*, one may simply state that the various studies which have been done agree on the anthropomorphism of their representations, and more particularly, on the relations they maintain between each other, similar to those of human society. I shall give just a few examples:

Kinship ties
- descent: the father of gNyan chen thang lha mountain is 'O de gung rgyal; his mother is a goddess called g.Yu bya gshog cig, "Turquoise Bird with One Wing"[13].

- marital unions: A myes rMa chen has as wife (*yum*) dGong sman lha ri, "The Excellent Goddess dGong ma". (It happens sometimes that mountains marry human beings, as is the case with gNyan chen thang lha[14]).
- adulterous liaisons: it is said that the mountain rGya gangs bKra shis lha mo of Shangtsa district, protectress of the Nachuang tribe, and the wife of Yabang mountain, fell in love with A myes rMa chen and had an illegitimate son, which occasioned the anger and revenge on the part of her husband[15].
- *antagonist relationships*: the one which matched A myes rMa chen against A myes gNyan chen, mountains located south of the city of Linxia (Chinese province of Gansu).[16]

To come back to the contemporary situation, one notes that if there exist *yul lha* mountains (Brag dkar mountain, Shar khog country, A mdo)[17] and *gnas ri* mountains (Kailash) separately, there are also mountains on which these two concepts are superimposed (A myes rMa chen, for example), and it so happens that territorial gods may reside on a mountain that is considered a mountain holy place (*gnas ri*), one example being rTsib ri.

The process of Buddhicisation

Thus my interest was directed towards what I call "the process of Buddhicisation",[18] which leads to the transformation of a mountain territorial god whom laymen worship once or twice a year *on the slope of the mountain*, into a Buddhist mountain holy place around which pilgrims *perform a circumambulation*.

This process is carried out through the subjection of space, human beings and time:

At first, it consists of a ritual appropriation of space, in which written sources serve an important function. Pilgrimage guides describe in a more or less detailed manner the subjection of the indigenous deities and the installation of the *maṇḍala* of a Buddhist deity (generally that of Cakrasaṃvara), within the landscape. In fact, Buddhist authorities did not try to supplant the *yul lha* but rather to incorporate them and to transform them into protectors of the Law, while allowing them to retain numerous characteristics of territorial gods. The objective of a pilgrimage guide is to lead the ordinary pilgrim from the simple perception of a physical landscape to the conception of the place as a sacred landscape. These texts are literary stereotyped projections of an internal vision of spiritual reality destined to convey the pilgrim towards a supernatural level. Texts of this kind are in fact nothing other than a tantric *sādhana*.[19] The pilgrim knows the content of these texts through the transmission of knowledge by religious people met along the pilgrimage routes. Thus it is in the written sources, passed on orally by religious people, that the sacred landscape becomes superimposed on the real landscape for one who does not perceive it.

Moreover, the appropriation of space also takes place in a concrete manner, on the physical plane, and leads to the subjection of living beings. One day a great religious man "opens the pilgrimage" (*gnas sgo phyed ba*) and so allows access to the site. The coming of practitioners and the construction of religious buildings takes place; supernatural imprints of divinities and saints line the circumambulation paths. Thus there is an objective marking of the landscape by religious people leading the pilgrim to act according to what he sees and what religious people say.

Buddhicisation affects also wildlife, which is, in the system of the *yul lha*, the latter's own property. A hunter who ventures to kill it risks being struck by the *yul lha*'s thunderbolts, if he does not have a preliminary agreement. Wildlife on a Buddhist mountain is often taken to be an emanation of the spiritual world; hunting is prohibited in the territory of a mountain in an even stricter way than in daily life, where Buddhist precepts are not always respected.

Time also falls under this calculus and the time of pilgrimage is determined, in a more or less precise manner, according to Buddhist criteria: within a period of twelve years, one year is particularly auspicious for certain pilgrimage places, and the merits acquired at that time are said to be much more numerous. The choice of the year can be determined by the year when the pilgrimage was opened by a great religious figure, or by the birthday of a saint or of a Buddhist event. Sometimes the month and the day are also defined, and correspond to an important date in the Buddhist calendar.

One can understand why spiritual and temporal Buddhist authorities showed such an interest in diverting sacred mountains and *yul lha* ritual to their own uses. This ritual, which involved various competitions, such as horse-racing, archery and gun-shooting, was at the heart of political organisation. For example, E.H. Walsh describes the election of new chiefs in the Chumbi valley (southern Tibet) at the beginning of the century.[20] The ceremony took place on the 15th day of the 4th month (a very important date in the Buddhist calendar),[21] in front of a stone altar located under a tree and dedicated to the *yul lha*. The two chiefs at the end of their mandate threw the dice; the two candidates who obtained the highest throw were the newly elected ones. The chiefs asserted to E.H. Walsh that they held their power not from the Tibetan government but from the territorial god who expressed itself through the throwing of the dice. An appointed chief became master of the soil, if over a delimited territory.

The ritual to the territorial god was a life-giving ritual if one conceives life "as the energy which allows a battle to be won, a good harvest to be obtained, sickness to be overcome or health of the mind to be preserved".[22] It allowed the revival of the environment and that of the society which depended on this environment.

For A. Hocart, it is the ritual more than the economy which founds the state.[23] One may say simply that he who has ascendency over life-giving rituals has power. Rituals thus exercise crucial political clout, which explains the interest temporal and spiritual Buddhist authorities showed for the cult of the territorial god and its implications. Just as a centralised state is slow to tolerate the independence of local powers, so too its authorities could only reluctantly admit the designation of local chiefs in the name of a territorial god. They could neither accept the territorial gods, nor could they, for fear of violent opposition, suppress them completely. The solution arrived at was one of Buddhicisation: the *yul lha* were deliberately transformed into "mountain holy places" (*gnas ri*); new cults and the practice of circumambulation materialised and consolidated this take-over.

The transformation of a *yul lha* mountain into a *gnas ri* mountain had important consequences. First, it led to the depersonalisation of the first of the two, and this is confirmed by the iconography: the anthropomorphic god which is the territorial deity, gives way to a mountain sacred place which, when represented, appears in the shape of a mountain, or sometimes of a *stupa*. This changed drastically the conception Tibetans had of their environment and of their relationship with the mountains and with nature. Out of a mountain of local symbolical import, Buddhism makes a mountain of universal symbolical scope. Whereas only the inhabitants of a particular territory can worship the *yul lha*, and expect prosperity, honour, power, etc., as a result, every living being can worship a *gnas ri* mountain and expect from the pilgrimage done around it, according to the individual's merits, a positive answer to their requests. There is also a transformation from a deity associated with a limited territory, and with the people who reside on it, into a deity to whom everyone can have recourse. A mundane deity (*'jig rten pa'i srung ma*, "a protector who belong to the phenomenal world") is turned into a transcendental one (*'jig rten las das pa'i srung ma*, "a protector who has passed beyond the phenomenal world"). The requests the pilgrim addresses to the *yul lha* are direct and establish a contractual relationship between him and the god. This law of exchange demonstrates the non-transcendental nature of the supernatural entities who dwell at the site. The more a mountain becomes a mountain holy place (*gnas ri*), the more this logic based on an exchange between pilgrim and divinity tends to disappear. The old equivalence between the two partners vanishes, giving way to an attitude of veneration in which the pilgrim implores the deity to grant him what he desires. Once the mountain has become completely "Buddhicized", the pilgrim acts as if he were in a temple.

In short we can say that Buddhism intervenes in territorial, social and political organisation, breaking down the local structure.

But the result of Buddhicisation occurred unequally over the Tibetan area, with various outcomes which, according with my studies, reflect different factors: the interest manifested by political and religious authorities towards a particular sacred place, the social, religious and geo-political context as well as any encountered resistance.

A myes rMa chen and Kailash, two mountains, two states of Buddhicisation

To put this process of Buddhicisation into perspective, we may compare A myes rMa chen, a mountain on which the two concepts *yul lha* and *gnas ri* are superimposed, and another mountain I would qualify as *gnas ri*, Mount Kailash. The aim of this comparison is not to show two different stages in the process of Buddhicisation, one minimal and the other maximal, but to show different states, Buddhicisation being neither a linear process nor a monolithic one.

A myes rMa chen: I know of only two pilgrimage guides dedicated to A myes rMa chen Mountain: one bears the title *Yul rma chen gangs ri'i gnas kyi rten bshad gdul bya'i 'gro blo'i dad brgya'i padmo 'byed pa'i nyin byed snang ba*, "Explanation of the Supports of the Holy Site, the Snow Mountain of the Land of rMa, [an Explanation] called Sun Which Opens the Hundred-petalled Lotus of Devotion amongst

Living Beings Who Are to Be Converted".[24] Everything suggests that its author belonged to the Jo nang pa school;[25] the second is a Bon po text, *rMa rgyal (s)pom ra'i dkar chag mdo(r) bsdus*, "A Short Guide to rMa rgyal (s)pom ra",[26] credited to Vairocana.[27]

The Jo nang pa guide installs the *mandala* of Cakrasaṃvara within the landscape, but the *yul lha* rMa chen spom ra is still present, as he is in the Bon po guide. While Zhabs dkar Tshogs drug rang grol (1781–1851)[28] is mentioned, the texts do not speak about the lineages of practicants. The physical subjection of the territory is still going on: sacred sites exist along the circumambulation path, but they are few, and their names do not have Buddhist connotations. In 1990, there were only a rNying ma pa monastery and a *stupa*; in 1992, a temple was in the process of being completed.

This pilgrimage attracts mainly nomads from the surrounding areas. The pilgrims know only one circumambulation path, whereas all my informants in Kailash knew perfectly that there were three, corresponding to the spiritual capacities of living beings. The behaviour of the pilgrims comports with a mountain not totally subdued to Buddhism: most of them perform the circumambulation on horseback in disregard of Buddhist principles. Many of them carry a gun and engage in playful activity at the halting-places. They perform various ritual acts I would qualify as popular, in that they are not prescribed by pilgrimage guides: they lift stones, carry them, weigh their sins by hanging from a projection of the cliff; they cross the *smyal lam*, the "path to hell";[29] they try to "delight" the god, to "please" him. They hunt not far from the mountain and apologise to the Buddhist deities, engraving prayers on stones arranged along the circumambulation path; but it is to rMa chen spom ra, represented as a warrior-god, that they address their requests, and it is from him that they expect their fulfilment.

The horse-year is said to be the most auspicious for the pilgrimage, but I have not heard about a particular month or date.

Kailash: With regard to Mount Kailash, the Buddhist written sources are numerous. To quote as examples:

- *gNas chen gangs ri mtsho gsum chu bo bzhi dang bcas pa gtan la dbab pa lung don snang bar byed pa'i me long*, "The Mirror Which Reveals the Meaning of the Scriptures, a Definitive account of the Great Holy Place [formed by] the Snowy Mountain, the Lakes [Three in All] and the Four Rivers".[30] The author is Ngag dbang 'phrin las.

- *Gangs ri chen po ti se dang mtsho chen ma dros pa bcas kyi sngon byung gi lo rgyus mdor bsdus su brjod pa'i rab byed shel dkar me long,* "The Crystal Mirror, an Analysis Which Briefly Explains the story of the Events Which Occurred at Ti se, the Lofty Snowy Mountain, and at Ma dros pa Lake" by dKon mchog bsTan 'dzin chos kyi blo gros (1869-1906),[31] 34th abbot of 'Bri gung.
- *'Dzam gling gangs rgyal ti se'i dkar chag tshangs dbyangs yid 'phrog,* "A Guide to Ti se, King of the Snowy Mountains of the World, Called Beautiful Melody Which Delights the Mind," a Bon po guide by dKar ru Grub dbang bsTan 'dzin rin chen (1801–?).[32]
- *Gangs ri mtsho gsum gyi (d)kar chag,* "A Guide to the Snowy Mountains and the Lake, three (in all)," a Bon po guide by Ye shes rgyal mtshan (13th century, according to C. Ramble 1995: 102).
- *Gangs mtsho'i ngo mtshar gyi che ba ji ltar gnas tshul,* "A Description of the Great Wonders of the Snowy Mountain [Kailash] and the Lake [Månasarovar]," by Chos dbyings rdo rje.[33]

We learn that the Buddha spoke about this mountain in his prophecies. The existence of a "protector of the field" (*zhing skyong*) called Gangs ri lHa btsan, or Ti se lHa btsan, is sometimes taken note of, but the guides provide him a function only within a Buddhist framework. Attention is also drawn to the uninterrupted presence of famous practicants in fairly impressive numbers, from rGod tshang pa's time to 1965. Buddhicisation is inscribed in the landscape in a concrete figuration. The "mandalisation" (to borrow Grappard's expression from Japan[34]) is total: in the center rises Mount Kailash, and four temples were built in the four cardinal points; four prostration sites (*phyag tshal sgang*) indicate the four directions. All the mountains and all the larger rocks bear the name of Buddhist divinities or divinities subjugated to Buddhism. Supernatural imprints are numerous. Three circumambulation paths are well known, and each of them is intended to be used by the particular kinds of living beings as becomes their spiritual elevation: one outer (*phyi skor*), the longest, for ordinary human beings; the second, the intermediate one (*bar skor*) for the ḍāka and the ḍākinī, and the third, the inner one (*nang skor*), for the five hundred *arhat*. It seems to me that the existence of three such paths, in most of the sacred places, is indicative of the process of Buddhicisation in that they institutionalise the progress of the pilgrim as he participates in the sacred landscape.

Pilgrims come to Mount Kailash from every part of Tibet, undoubtedly attracted by its fame; but also they know that the

Buddhist deities who reside there are able to fulfil their wishes. Thus, Buddhicisation changes their mentality and their ritual behaviour: their gestures are pacified; reserve gives way to demonstration. They come on foot to the sacred place, slowly and modestly, wearing simple clothes, and without weapons, in an attitude of respect, with bowed head. Their main ritual acts are prostrations, offerings and the recitation of *mantra*, during which they follow the instructions the pilgrimage guides prescribe. Kailash is represented not by an anthropomorphic god but in the form of a *stupa* or in its own form, that of a mountain. The time factor is also very important, not to say paramount: one is advised to make the pilgrimage to Mount Kailash in a horse-year, and on the 15th day of the 4th month, which is, as we saw, a very important day in the Buddhist calendar.

Kailash shows a very advanced state of Buddhicisation, some of whose stages are unknown: for example, how were all traces of the *yul lha*, including his name, eliminated, assuming there was a *yul lha* in the first place?

In A myes rMa chen the stage has been set. One may wonder if rMa chen spom ra will cede his place to Cakrasaṃvara, and if so how and when. Of course, from a Buddhist point of view the *yul lha* has been subjugated, but he still serves a preeminent function: pilgrims evoke only him; it is he to whom the pilgrimage is dedicated. Will he of his own free will, if one may so say, withdraw in the face of his successor? Whereas elsewhere one can merely imagine the ambiguity of the relation or the past conflict between the *yul lha* and the Buddhist deity, without being able to define it with anything other than the soothing and self-prompted descriptions of the Buddhist masters, in A myes rMa chen one is still a witness to the events: the ambiguities are still perceptible. The process is continuing, and there is still resistance to it. The adoption of principles of the Buddhist Law brings about a conflict of values. There is a difference between the (not always integrated) written norm which is Buddhism, and the unwritten practices which belong to a popular tradition. One sees nomads hunting close by the mountain and begging pardon, at the pilgrimage site, to the Buddhist divinities, to Vajrasattva or the Buddha, but not to Cakrasaṃvara, which underlines the latter's lack of significance for the lay pilgrims, or the ignorance they have of his presence.

There is nothing to insure that A myes rMa chen will become a second Kailash: on the one hand, the social and geographic contexts are different and may lead to different outcomes; on the other hand, strategies for the implantation of Buddhism differ (not to forget the importance, at the present time, of political changes). Thus, in the case of rTsib ri, a mountain holy place (*gnas ri*) in southern Tibet on which resides one (or several) *yul lha*, the main pilgrimage was compulsory in the past. The inhabitants of each of the villages around rTsib ri had to participate in turn in an organisation called *sKor chen las pa* "Workers of the Great Pilgrimage," an expression used to designate the members as well as the organisation itself. This participation which, according to my informants, was also compulsory, was shared in terms, year by year, among the households of a village. The organisation differed slightly from one place to another, but its aim was the same: to allow the greatest number of villagers to do the pilgrimage by giving them barley flour (*rtsam pa*) and beer (*chang*). Each village had a field, given to it by the administrative authorities, the produce of which was totally allotted to the pilgrimage. Each year some families were appointed to work this field. I have tried to show that the organisation of the pilgrimage was cast in the mould of a ritual dedicated to the *yul lha*, the aim of which was to obtain good harvests and to prevent calamities (mainly hail).

What was the purpose of this transposition? The story of rTsib ri, which appears in its origins as a mountain territorial god (the persistence of a *yul lha* bears witness to this), identifies it as a flying mountain which came from Bodhgayā[35] to cover a lake, the waters of which emitted harmful vapours that killed a host of men and animals; but it is also a condensed version of the three great bKa' brgyud pa sacred places – two reasons not to see rTsib ri any longer as a *yul lha* mountain but as a *gnas ri* mountain.

Nevertheless, a cult to the territorial god was kept alive until the Chinese occupation. In overlaying the organisation of a traditional festival on a purely Buddhist phenomenom, the spiritual and temporal authorities signalled the interest they attached to the Buddhicisation of this mountain territorial god and also, perhaps, the difficulties they encountered during the process. Does not the denial of the previous existence of rTsib ri (the tradition says that in the past, before the mountain came from India, there was just a lake), indicate a desire to eradicate totally the status of rTsib ri as territorial god?

One should beware of an oversimplified explanation which would classify this mountain as being at an intermediary stage of Buddhicisation between Kailash and A myes rMa chen. One should consider it in its own context, as conditioned by the environment, local populations, and probably also by the political system or, perhaps more exactly, the political powers in the area.

At the end of this brief presentation of the process of transformation of a mountain territorial god into a Buddhist holy mountain, it seems worthwhile to underline some of the characteristics pilgrimages to sacred mountains possess in their own right. One of them is that they have certain features traditionally associated with the cults to territorial gods. Pilgrimages to sacred mountains (but also ones to lakes and caves) are very important for the community and its survival. A pilgrimage allows someone to restore his position in society who has infringed a prohibition or committed very serious offences (perhaps even crimes) which lead to a disordered state affecting the whole community. One striking example is the pilgrimage to mChod rten nyi ma, a sacred place at the Tibeto-Sikkimese border, where it is possible to go in order to "wash away" the defilement generated by incest.[36] These pilgrimages impinge on many aspects of the daily life of the people, such as sickness, death, or the desire to obtain material wealth.

According to what I have observed, the lay pilgrim moves within a system that is not defined exclusively either by notions traditional prior to Buddhism, or by Buddhist notions proper. It is a composite system harbouring a unique vision of the world, and endowed with its own coherence. Sometimes there is a confrontation between two ideologies, sometimes a peaceful cohabitation, sometimes the transformation of one by the other.

Halase Maratika caves

The contemporary study of sacred mountains in a way gives "snapshots" of various stages in the process of Buddhicisation, but it does not allow one to really follow this process. So it is specially interesting to see it at work in the caves of Halase-Maratika, in East Nepal.

The name Maratika is known in the literature as early as the 12th century from the *bKa' thang Zangs gling ma*, a treasure-text, *gter ma*, discovered by Nyang ral nyi ma 'od zer (1124 or 1136 – 1192 or 1204); but at that time the place refered to by that name was located south of Mount Potala, the palace of Avalokiteśvara, in India. The transfer of this name to the site of Halase, in Nepal, occurred at an unknown date. The holy place of Halase-Maratika seems, in the past, to have been little frequented by Tibetan pilgrims. It was chiefly a sacred place for Hindus, though at present, they are being supplanted little by little by Sherpa and Tibetan Buddhists.[37] One can observe as it occurs the process of Buddhicisation: the ritual appropriation of the space is well under way, and the physical subjection is far advanced. Religious events are on the increase: Tibetan hierarchs come regularly to practise rituals or for retreats (this is the case for 'Khrul zhig Rinpoche, a rNying ma pa hierarch); and it is here that the young mKhyen brtse Rinpoche (the reincarnation of the great rNying ma pa master) received a new name in December 1995 and, in April of 1996 sacred dances (*'cham*), took place for the first time,.

The example of Halase-Maratika shows that there is a firm intention on the part of Buddhist authorities in exile to map out a new sacred geography based on sites outside of Tibet, known through the texts. It is a way to keep the Tibetan past alive, and thus to participate in the collective memory of Tibetans. To assert in this way a continuation with or renewal of the past is to go far beyond simple religious purposes. The diaspora and the Tibetan community in Tibet proper share the same past, which materialises in the sacred places. By instilling the consciousness of a national identity, the Chinese occupation reduces the sense of belonging to a religious community. The Tibetan nation, although cut in two, still exists as long as the national cohesion of the population in exile is asserted and the latter's link with the population in Tibet retained. Tibetans do not try to create new sacred places but only to revive the ones collective memory knows.

During our times of disorder, the revitalisation of pilgrimages, both in Tibet and in India and Nepal, is one of the manifestations of the political and cultural identity of Tibetans. By going on pilgrimages, Tibetans seem to assert their identity; wandering along the pilgrimage routes, they map out their territory anew and reappropriate their space in the face of the Chinese occupant.

Conclusion

It is now time to give a definition of pilgrimages to sacred mountains as far as the facts and their analysis allow.

In Tibet, pilgrimages to sacred mountains are a collective undertaking (very seldom an individual one), based on family relationships or on locality, around a mountain holy place, the sacralization of which is recognized by greater or fewer numbers of Tibetans depending upon its degree of Buddhicisation. Pilgrims perform a circumambulation and ritual actions, which vary in accordance with the degree of Buddhicisation. These acts allow them to obtain the realisation of their wishes. Their aim is, in the first place, to obtain material benefits to which spiritual benefits attach, and this in a rather stereotyped way. The requests pilgrims make involve an exchange with the supernatural entities who dwell at the site.

The popular nature of the pilgrimages to sacred mountains and lakes must be underlined. All the information is in agreement: men of religion are devoted to meditation, and it is the lay people who are pressed to go on pilgrimages, as was clearly expressed by the doctor in theology (*dge bshes*) of Brag shing thog (Takshindo), in the Sherpa area, when he said, speaking about 'O ma mtsho Lake (Solu):

> Only those who are interested in this present life go to 'O ma mtsho Lake. But those who are thinking of the future life do not go there because the *yul lha* and the *shi btsan*[38] do not have the power to give merits for the future life. What do we get from going to 'O ma mtsho? Money, children, cattle. Monks need neither money nor children nor cattle.[39]

At the end of this study, the confrontation between written sources and observation allows the broad outlines of a typology to be drawn. However, numerous questions have not received an answer; most of them run up against our ignorance about the history of pilgrimages in Tibet as a phenomenom.

First of all, as already stated, there is the question of the origin of pilgrimages to sacred mountains (and lakes), and also that of circumambulations.

One does not know either when and under what circumstances the term *gnas* appeared for the first time with the meaning of holy place. Sa skya Paṇḍita (1182–1251) uses it in his critical treatment of the traditions of sacred geography and pilgrimages[40]. The same question arises for the expression *gnas ri*. The most ancient mention I have found is in a pilgrimage guide to mChod rten nyi ma, attributed to rGod ldem (1337–1408). In this case also, a systematic survey of the Tibetan literature would be necessary in order to arrive at an answer.

Moreover, one problem I did not approach in my study is that of rights to the soil. We saw that the *yul lha* was associated with a fixed territory and its population. When a mountain territorial god becomes a mountain holy place, what happens in terms of rights to the soil?

Lastly, in contradiction of the typology I draw, one may point out some "aberrants". Observation has showed that the Sherpas go around lakes but do not go around mountains; this I explain by the fact that the latter are seen as *yul lha* rather than *gnas ri*. We saw above that the mountain is, generally speaking, associated with a lake. Thus can we understand a pilgrimage around a lake as a substitute for one around a mountain?

Only some of the questions which arose during my research are set forth here. The studies of other researchers will add to our knowledge about pilgrimages to sacred mountains, lakes and caves. A study of the latter constitutes a privileged subject for anthropological work, profiting from present observation in order to help to understand the past. But it also offers a real "laboratory" where it is possible to observe the contradictory forces at work in contemporary Tibetan society: Buddhism against popular beliefs, traditional culture against modernity.

Notes

1 It is impossible to thank in this article all the people who gave me their support and advice while I was writing my Ph.D. I am particularly grateful to A.M. Blondeau and R. Hamayon who, by their corrections and suggestions, helped me to improve this article; also to the participants of the IIAS "Pilgrimage in Tibet" conference, the questions and remarks of whom enriched my research, last but not least, to P. Pierce (Nepal Research Centre, Kathmandu), to whom I owe the correction of the English translation and a careful draft reading. My sojourn in Kathmandu in 1996 was possible due to the Lavoisier scholarship granted by the French Foreign Ministery.
2 One might think that the title of my article is misleading. In fact, because of lack of space, I deal very little with the subject of lakes. Nevertheless, because they form a part of my study and are associated with mountains in the Tibetan conception of landscape, I chose to mention them.
3 Roerich 1967: 459–570.
4 Tucci 1940 and Roerich, 1949, 1976: 696–702.
5 Roerich 1949, 1976: 680–686 & 700.
6 Disciple of the great bKa' brgyud pa master Phag mo gru pa (1110–1170). For more information about him, see Roerich 1949, 1976: 552–559.
7 Also called 'Bri gung Chos rje, he founded the 'Bri gung pa school, one of the four main branches of the bKa' brgyud pa school. He was a disciple of Phag mo gru pa.
8 Petech 1988: 355–369.
9 Tucci 1940: 41.
10 This is the case as far as the mountains on which I worked are concerned. The possibility is not excluded that some mountains were, from the very beginning, considered as *gnas ri*, "mountain holy places."
11 Nebesky-Wojkowitz 1956, 1975: 4; Stein 1962, 1981: 182; Tucci 1973: 194; Karmay 1994: 412.
12 See, for example, the description Karmay 1994: 112–120, gives of the cult of the territorial god in Sharwa country (A mdo), a ritual he attended in 1985.

13 Nebesky-Wojkowitz 1956, 1975: 206.
14 Yuthok 1990: 145.
15 Ma Lihua 1993: 193–198. I was not able to restore the Tibetan spelling of Shangtsa, Nachuang and Yabang.
16 For these legends, see Li An Che 1949: 39–40; Rock 1956: 27; & Stein 1959: 454.
17 Interview with S.G. Karmay, held in February 1990.
18 I use the term "Buddhicisation" in a broad sense: it includes the same process set in motion by the Bon po clergy. This choice explains itself if one follows the idea of Snellgrove (1968, 1987), taken up by P. Kvaerne (1976, 1995), according to which 'the Bon religion was a peculiar but authentic form of Buddhism,' (Kvaerne 1995: 136) as far as 'rituals and other religious practices, as well as meditational and metaphysical traditions' are concerned (Kvaerne 1995: 13) I do not use the term "Lamaisation" because it overplays the role of religious authorities to the exclusion of political ones in this process.
19 I use the term *sādhana* in a broad sense.
20 Walsh 1906: 303–308.
21 On this occasion Tibetans celebrate the birthday, the illumination and the *parinirvāṇa* of the Buddha, whence the name of this festival: "Three Festivals in One" (*dus chen gsum 'dzom*).
22 Hocart 1936, 1978: 479. My translation from the French.
23 Hocart 1936, 1978.
24 A monk I met in rMa chen prefecture gave me this guide in 1990. For a presentation and translation of it, see K. Buffetrille (1997).
25 The Jo nang pa, from the name of their main monastery, Jo mo nang, constitute one of the main schools of Tibetan Buddhism. They were founded by Kun mykhen Shes rab rgyal mtshan (1292–1361). Its followers were condemned by the Fifth Dalai Lama (17th century) because they maintained what the dGe lugs pa school thought were heterodox points of view. Some of their followers escaped to the eastern part of Tibet, and the Jo nang pa monasteries fell under dGe lugs pa control.
26 Tashi Tsering (LTWA), Dharamsala, provided me a copy of this guide.
27 Vairocana is a great 7th century translator acclaimed by both Buddhists and Bon pos. For a translation of this guide, see Buffetrille 1994: 20–23.
28 See Ricard (1994) for an English translation of his biography.
29 These "paths to hell" are one of the constant features of places of pilgrimage. They are often narrow cavities burrowed in the rock or narrow paths between two rocks. To succeed in passing through them purifies the devotee from his sins and ensures them an easy crossing during the intermediary period between death and rebirth (*bar do*).
30 This guide was published in Dharamsala along with others under the title *Tibetan Guides to Places of Pilgrimage*. It is in the form of a Tibetan book (*dpe cha*), and comprises thirty-two folios written in cursive (*dbu med*).
31 Concerning dKon mchog bsTan 'dzin chos kyi blo gros 'phrin las rnam rgyal, see Huber & Rigdzin 1995: 12. A translation of chapters 6 and 7 is now out; Huber and Rigdzin 1995: 10–47.
32 Norbu and Prats (1989) are the editors, having worked on two versions of the text. They give a transliteration along with the translation of some

parts. Recently, Ramble 1995: 102–105 provided a short analysis of this guide.
33 This guide was published in the first issue of the review *Bod ljongs nang bstan*: "*gangs dkar ti se'i gnas kyi dus chen rta lo 'khor chen la rten 'brel*", 32–62. It is a recent work written especially for the horse-year, during which it is particularly auspicious to do the pilgrimage. A full translation is given in my Ph.D. (1996).
34 Grappard 1982.
35 On rTsib ri and flying mountains, see Buffetrille 1996a.
36 See Buffetrille (forthcoming).
37 See Buffetrille 1994a: 1–70 & 1994b: 81–94.
38 A Sherpa monk from Junbesi explained to me that after their death, some men are born again as *btsan*. It is necessary to propitiate them because, if they feel displeased, their acts are malevolent. If on the contrary, they are pleased, they succumb to the requests of the people.
39 Interview held in August 1991.
40 Huber 1990: 121–165.

Chapter 2

On the Geographical and Material Contextuality of Tibetan Pilgrimage

Wim van Spengen

Far from being a fading habit in a secularizing world, pilgrimage remains one of the more outstanding and persisting characteristics of the world's major religions. Within a religious context, the act of pilgrimage is usually regarded as devotional and penitential; that is, primarily a cultural exercise. However, pilgrimage is also conditioned by a full set of material parameters. This paper sets out to explore the geographical and material contextuality of Tibetan pilgrimage. As such, it asks questions as to how, where and when, and to a lesser extent why, pilgrims set out on the road.

The most striking feature of pilgrimage as a physical act is its movement in earthly space. But here already generalization must give way to differentiation. Movements of pilgrimage may be short-term and short-distance, but may equally well develop into something of a lifestyle spanning the width and breadth of the Tibetan culture area. Pilgrims may fend for themselves, or be catered for in certain places. They may combine a little trade with a large dose of religion, or feature as traders who take their chance to enrich their *karma* in passing. Pilgrims fill the fairs and courtyards of monasteries, the highroads and byroads of Tibet. They circumambulate lakes and mountains, climb high mountain passes, and suffer from a variety of diseases. They differ from each other in background, wealth and objectives. No two pilgrims are the same.

Going on pilgrimage, in a geographical sense, is first and foremost going on an extended journey. As such, the act of pilgrimage falls within the general category of travel, not merely of travel for pleasure, but also for profit. In fact, the pleasure can turn into profit where outdoor life heightens the senses and prepares the pilgrim for a geo-transcendental experience of the 'power places' he visits. Chan speaks in this connection of 'sin-destroying localities'[1] and the *Skanda Purana* long ago summed it all up by stating:

> In a hundred ages of the gods, I could not tell thee of the glories of Himachal. As the dew is dried up by the morning sun, so are the sins of mankind by the sight of Himachal.[2]

But in the journey itself too, the chances of pilgrim's progress are greatly enhanced by the transcendental experience of place and landscape. The Dutch philosopher and phenomenologist, Ton Lemaire, once phrased it as follows:

> A journey projects us into the landscape of others; by going away from home we give up, for the time being at least, our attachment to a known environment and expose ourselves to the experience of other places (. . .) Both the vitality and vulnerability of the traveller give the journey the character of an initiation, a 'rite de passage': the self-inflicted pain to gain entrance into a new physical and metaphysical world.[3]

Behind these [pilgrim] journeys lies hidden the quest for adventure and psychological healing, not to speak of spiritual purification.

The geography of pilgrimage in Tibet

What is often, but cannot be, ignored in any discussion on pilgrimage in Tibet, is the geographical setting *in* which and *through* which the phenomenon of pilgrimage takes shape. Looking at the geographic environment *tout court*, the modern scientific mind sees nothing more in a place than a specific location expressed in degrees longitude and latitude, as well as endowed with particular physical qualities. But for the Tibetan pilgrim the locational and physical qualities of a place possess an inherent meaning anchored in its specific geomantic characteristics. According to Chan, there can be no doubt that 'geomancy, or the art of divination by geographical features, plays a vital role in determining [a place of pilgrimage in Tibet]'.[4]

Dowman too, sees places of pilgrimage as 'focal points of energy'. In the words of the latter, 'the pilgrim's destination is always a special point of the earth's surface endowed with a powerful mystique'.[5] Even the routes towards these 'power places' are littered with geographical features that, through a 'Tibetan cultural reading of the landscape'[6], are able to ward off the dangers of the road and at the same time bring a little merit to the pilgrim. But can we fully agree with Chan's view that 'the sanctity of a site is largely derived from its special natural and physical attributes, rather than from the shrine erected there'[7]? After all, it is possible that the 'Tibetan cultural reading of landscape', in its 'unorganized' form, came under pressure with the rise of Tibet's now dominant order, the Gelukpa, who favoured more 'organized' forms of pilgrimage to shrines, and particularly to Incarnations attached to their newly founded or converted monasteries. In this connection we may even speculate on a decline of pilgrimage to 'natural' places of power. But the reverse may also be true in the sense that, as a reaction to the rise of Gelukpa power in outlying areas, there was an *increased* pilgrimage to local and regional sites, invoking the full geomantic power of place to emphasize a specific regional or doctrinal identity.[8]

The metaphysical quality of a power place is activated by the human agency of the pilgrim. In order to extract the inherent merit from a place it is necessary to reenact the age-old praxis of circumambulation. As Blondeau has rightly observed, the essential element of Tibetan pilgrimage appears to lie in the movement around a sacred object, after the ancient Indian *pradaksina* model.[9] Be it mountain or lake, town or temple, the Tibetan pilgrim makes the tour(s) as thousands of his co-religionists have done before him.

Mountains seem to be particularly important, because in early myths of state they served as liminal places of contact where heavenly beings were transformed into earthly rulers.[10] This fact betrays a pre-Buddhist element in the creation of sacred place, a sign of geomantic perfection on the basis of which the Buddha-isation 'drama' of Tibet could unfold. The establishment of Songtsen Gampo's demon-suppressing temples,[11] together with Padmasambhava's efforts at introducing the Indian Buddhist pilgrimage cult of Tantric *pitha* sites, may be seen as the basis for a nascent Buddhist pilgrim network in the Tibetan realm. Together with a later phase of Lama-isation, in which spiritual masters like Milarepa 'opened up' specific places for pilgrimage, these 'events' became the subject of rival conversion myths concerning Tibetan holy places, the analysis of which has recently been attempted by Toni Huber under the label of a 'sacred geography controversy'.[12]

Pilgrimage became such an institutionalized feature of Tibetan regionality that several pilgrim guides to mountains and shrines came to be written. Pilgrim itineraries around sacred mountains and lakes were spelled out step-by-step, whole pilgrim rounds to a variety of sacred places annotated, while later versions even catered for the need of pilgrims going to Bodh Gaya and related places in India.[13] For Lhasa, we have a seventeenth century guide in a translation by Grünwedel (1919), written by the 'Great Fifth' Dalai Lama, in an attempt to emphasize Gelukpa authority.[14] Nowadays Lhasa is well described, not least because of the two modern pilgrim guides by Dowman (1988) and Chan (1994). It should be noted that the latter two appear to lack the doctrinal bias of earlier Tibetan guides, as is for example the case with *Mk'yen Brtse's guide to the holy places of Central Tibet* in a Nyingma and Sakya direction.[15]

In addition to these, transliterations, translations and annotations of traditional Tibetan pilgrim guides for the main sacred mountain sites of Tibet have become available over the past ten years. For Ti-se or Kailash, we have DeRossi Filibeck (1988), Norbu and Prats (1989) and Huber and Rigzin (1995), and for La-phyi and Tsa-ri, DeRossi Filibeck (1988, 1990). Further we now have the *thèse de doctorat* of Katia Buffetrille (1996), combining fieldwork and textual analysis with regard to several places of pilgrimage in Tibet and the Himalaya.

Generally these guides have a much deeper meaning than to show the exact geographical location of sites and routes alone. In the interplay of written guide and oral traditions which may be heard on the spot from local lamas and site-keepers, a conscious effort is made to show the beneficial effects of a victorious Buddhist tradition over older demons and deities whose historically enacted drama of conversion makes now possible the safe visit of pilgrims to the site.[16]

Lhasa as the supreme focus of pilgrimage in the Tibetan Buddhist world, harbouring its highest incarnation, the Dalai Lama, attracted pilgrims from all over Tibet and even beyond. Particularly at the time of a major festival, such as the great Monlam Prayer following the Losar or New Year celebrations, the population of Lhasa, which at the beginning of this century was perhaps between fifteen and twenty thousand, swelled to four or five times this number.[17] Tashilunpo too, the seat of the Panchen Lama near Shigatse, drew tens of thousands of pilgrims; single audiences at major celebrations bringing together six thousand pilgrims and lookers-on before the great Living Buddha.[18]

The range of the great power places of Central Tibet was considerable. Pilgrims flocking to Lhasa and surrounding places came from Ladakh, Ngari, the Himalayan border districts of India, the kingdoms of Nepal, Sikkim and Bhutan, faraway districts in Southeast Tibet like Pome and Zayul, petty semi-independent states like Mili and Chala, nomad countries all over Tibet, the provinces of

Kham and Amdo, further from Mongolia, and even Southern Siberia, the homeland of the Buddhist Kalmuks and Buriats. In its range, the above pilgrim network resembles the Lhasa-centred network of towns and routes, though more routes from all over Tibet could and should be drawn in to obtain a picture nearer to reality.[19]

It is possible, and even probable, that the importance of regional centres of pilgrimage has always been underestimated, in particular those outside the confines of Central Tibet. Besides the multi-faith Tise/Kailash, which is relatively well-known,[20] as well as the big Gelukpa monasteries of Kumbum and Labrang in Amdo,[21] there were many places of pilgrimage never or seldom visited by outsiders, and consequently we are only erratically informed about them. We know little, for example, about the holy mountain-side of La-phyi on the Nepal-Tibet border and one-time abode of Milarepa,[22] which was, according to the Cambridge botanist Wollaston,[23] visited annually by thousands of pilgrims, or about the cave sanctuaries at Halase.[24] What about the faraway Targo-gangri with its associated lake,[25] tradition-rich Kongpo Bon-ri,[26] or the relatively unknown Takpa Siri in the district of Tsari, where various villages are said to have subsisted on the money they could earn by providing transport for the numerous pilgrims?[27] Or again, the holy mountains of Shar Dung ri, Northeast of Sungpan,[28] Amnye Niangchen, East of Labrang,[29] Amnye Machen,[30] the twin-peaks of Dorjetroleh, Northeast of Gartok in Kham,[31] Kawakarpo, the 'mountain of silver snow' on the Salween-Mekong divide,[32] and Gangarling, 'holy mountain of the outlaws', to the west of the kingdom of Mili,[33] as well as mighty Minya Gongkar,[34] the pilgrim function of which is as yet not quite understood. Last but not least, Murdo, the local identity-guardian in the Gyalmorong area that is supposed to have drawn in the proper season anywhere between three and ten thousand pilgrims.[35] Thus, all these mountain sites generated considerable flows of pilgrims, especially at the time of a twelve-year 'High Pilgrimage', contributing to a culturally defined *espace-mouvement*, and perhaps, but not necessarily so, to political integration.

From a geographer's point of view, mountains, lakes, rivers, caves, and passes – all geographical features revered by Tibetans – together with the flows of pilgrims they generate, constitute the geographicity of the Tibetan pilgrim world. The written-in-the-earth quality of these sacred places is made manifest by the pilgrim journey which obtains meaning through the generation of merit. But temples and monasteries too, as the repositories of sacred objects or the seats of Incarnations, became the physical expression of the constructive imagination of human beings in their creation of Buddhist sacred landscape. It is this 'meaningful' man-environment interaction which lies at the root of the phenomenon of pilgrimage. But there is more to say about the generation of pilgrim flows than in cultural geographic terms alone. Indeed, pilgrimage was the trade opportunity of a lifetime, ranging from the pedlar's hawking to the prince's caravan trade.

The economic environment of pilgrimage[36]

Human beings, being human after all, and therefore standing in need of catering for their daily needs, were swift to recognize the economic possibilities of the pilgrim journey. Though it is impossible to tell whether pilgrimage created trade or vice versa, it seems undeniable that the large flows of pilgrims generated by Lhasa and a few other centres of national importance contributed to the growth of a trade network spanning the length and breadth of Tibet and even beyond.[37] But regional centres of pilgrimage too, drew numerous worshippers.

The high mobility of people in the context of pilgrimage, the scale at which it took place, as well as the vast distances covered by the pilgrims, all contributed to the likelihood of trade. Pilgrims were sometimes away for over two years and had to barter their way to Lhasa and other places.[38] The pilgrimage of farmers and herders was often combined with petty trade,[39] their cattle being used as walking merchandise. In addition, they might have saved some of their agricultural surpluses while still at home, which were now carried in the form of bundles of tea, parcels of gold dust, and silver talents.[40] Devotees generally managed to combine religion with a little business, and the shops of Lhasa and the fairs of Kailash definitely felt their presence.[41]

At times of great religious festivals, supra-regional fairs under the protection of the monasteries saw the gathering of numerous trading pilgrims. The demand generated by the seasonal clustering of large numbers of pilgrims also brought together regular traders from all over Inner Asia and adjoining countries. In addition, *fakirs*, mendicants, and charlatans tried their luck, performing their tricks and selling their magical medicines. Perhaps we can do no better than to cite at some length the eye-witness report by Susie Rijnhart, who assisted in the celebration of the yearly 'Butter God Festival' at the monastery of Kumbum in 1897:

For some days previous to it the roads leading to the lamasery are literally covered with travellers arriving from China, Mongolia, and all Tibetan territories. Some are mounted on horses, driving before them their heavily-burdened yaks; others, of higher rank, are borne on stately camels, with long retinues of pedestrian pilgrims following behind. There are priests with closely shaven heads and wooden knapsacks thrown over their shoulders, and laymen with long, tattered sheepskin gowns and short wild-looking hair. As the pilgrims arrive, the rooms of the lamasery are first occupied, then the black tents of the Tibetans begin to rise until the entire valley and hillside become as one vast encampment resounding with the shouts and laughter of men, women and children, the whining of camels, the neighing of horses and mules, the barking of dogs, the clattering of gongs and cymbals, the blowing of horns and the ringing of bells. On the main road to the temple are scores of white tents of Mongol and Chinese merchants who come not only to pay their respects to the Buddha, but to dispose of their wares, consisting chiefly of cutlery, needles, cloth boots, tea, charm-boxes, idols and other articles.[42]

Of course, not all of these fairs were of the same importance. In fact, there was a whole hierarchy of greater and lesser sacred places with their corresponding fairs, structurally perhaps, not unlike the geographer's Central Place system. Sacred places of different levels had corresponding pilgrim fields, creating a kind of nested hierarchy ultimately encompassing the entire population of Tibet and its culturally related border worlds.[43] In practice, such a set-up meant that some fairs were held less often than others, were of longer duration, and offered a greater variety of goods, in addition to a high or even temporarily increased degree of sacredness of the locality involved. The twelve-year 'High Pilgrimage' and corresponding Khumb mela near Kailash is a good example of the latter.[44]

Let us briefly cast a glance now at two very specific Tibetan items of luxury trade, that were often to be seen at places of pilgrimage: medicinal herbs and precious stones.

Temporary and chronic illness has always been part and parcel of the *condition humaine*, and pilgrims too, did not escape that predicament. Weakened perhaps by insufficient food on their long journey across high passes, quite a few of them were afflicted by strange ailments that needed to be cured. As the mountainous areas of the Himalayas and eastern Tibet yield many a medicinal herb of proven effect, herb collectors and medicine sellers plied their trade successfully at the crowded fairs. Monasteries too, were sometimes centres of herbal medicine preparation.[45] At the fairs, herbs also changed hands from collectors to wholesalers, who transported greater quantities to the lowland markets of India and China.[46] But pilgrims themselves too, collected the medicinal herbs of their choice on the slopes of holy mountains and in unfamiliar habitats.

The step from herbal medicines to precious stones such as traded at the fairs of Tibet, is less than one might think at first sight. In a world as full of symbolism as traditional Tibet undoubtedly was, gem-stones had their own meaning attuned to the need of the hour. One of them was the healing power that stones were thought to possess, and consequently their appreciation as medicine ranked next to their valuation as ornaments. Turquoise, for example, the widely appreciated gem-stone of Tibet, was in high demand in both qualities.[47] In addition, coral, pearls, amber, rubies and jade found their way into Tibet, their low weight for value quality making them a preferred item for the itinerant traders and pilgrims plying the fairs. Precious stones came from Afghanistan, India, Burma, and Turkestan,[48] but less so from the Himalayas.[49] If they could afford it, Tibetans spent fortunes on ornamentation. The Tibet explorer William Gill, in his *River of Golden Sand*, left us the following significant passage:

> The Tibetans, both men and women, are possessed of a taste also amounting to frenzy for coral and turquoises; and the immense quantity of these that are used is surprising. The scabbards of their swords, the covers of their charm-boxes, their earrings or bracelets, all are ornamented with coral and turquoises.[50]

Consequently, precious stones commanded a profitable sale, and not only in pilgrim centres.

Tibetan pilgrimage came to extend beyond its immediate cultural domain from the beginning of the nineteenth century onwards. The one exception to this general statement was the Kathmandu valley in Nepal, which had already been visited for centuries by Tibetans, particularly in wintertime.[51] Since the era of the seventeenth-century Malla kings, when free circulation across the Himalaya was still the rule, Tibetans increasingly had come to create their own niche in valley society, a position best visible near the stupas of Bodnath and Swayambunath.[52] The German scholar Kurt Boeck, in his well-illustrated book on his journey to India and Nepal in 1898, gives an interesting impression of what he calls the Tibetan village of Bodnath.[53] According to him, Tibetans visited the Kathmandu valley in wintertime to exchange salt, yak tails, and woollen blankets for grain, and in addition were dealing in gold dust, turquoise, agate, rubies, and other precious stones, together with medicinal herbs.[54]

Apart from these pilgrimages and trading ventures into the Kathmandu valley, journeys to places well outside the Tibetan cultural sphere of influence, in particular India, did become fashionable in the course of the nineteenth century.[55] The holiest place to visit for the Tibetans was Bodh Gaya, where Buddha attained enlightenment under a *pipal* tree. As the Indian plains are scorching hot in summertime, these journeys of pilgrimage took place during the winter season, and over time were accelerated in pace and volume by the beginnings of railway transport in the Ganga Plain, and by the increasing orientation of Central Tibet towards a rising British-Indian *économie-monde*. These journeys of pilgrimage, especially in its extended form throughout the northern plains and the Indian Himalayas, were instigated by the rich, who gained merit by paying poor people to go on pilgrimage for them.

From the beginning of the twentieth century onwards, they came to regard Kalimpong in the Sikkim Himalaya as their main point of departure. However, Kalimpong also became the refuge of stranded pilgrims, who, venturing into the plains, had lost all their money and now tried to make ends meet by selling off their personal belongings.[56] The more successful traders and pilgrims on their way to Bodh Gaya, often passed through Calcutta, satisfying both their natural curiosity for things beyond the Tibetan ken and their passion for trade.[57]

To avoid a one-sided picture, it should be mentioned here that similar developments took place in eastern Tibet, though on a smaller scale. With the rise of Tachienlu on the Sino-Tibetan border, quite a few Tibetans, ventured into China, especially to the great pilgrim mountain of Omei Shan in southern Szechuan.[58] Urga in Mongolia too, as the seat of a primary "Living Buddha", became the object of pilgrimage and trade for Tibetans from Amdo, as well as for monastic trade missions from all over Tibet.[59] The two-year stay of the Dalai Lama in Urga (1904–1906) may temporarily have emphasized its renown as a centre of pilgrimage.

Thus, pilgrimage to sacred places, whether by private pilgrims or monastic missions, had a definite economic effect apparent in the commercial activities accompanying major religious festivals. In fact, these fairs, as they were commonly called, have been defined as 'annual gatherings of buyers and sellers at a particular place and time for the purpose of trade, often following a religious function, and accompanied by forms of amusement and entertainment',[60] a description which well fits the Tibetan situation. However, when the scale of the trade increased, fairs often assumed a more secular character, in which the exchange of goods came to dominate the religious celebrations. Markets shifted and became less dependent on the pilgrim public.

The material environment of pilgrimage

Let us now turn to the daily chores of pilgrims. We should note here the observation of General Bower on his journey across the Changtang in 1891, that 'if the truth was known, I expect the mortality [of pilgrims] on the road to be something enormous.'[61] Of course his impressions were coloured by the desolate stretches in Northern Tibet which he had to cross, but a journey of pilgrimage was never without its dangers. Many a mishap lay on the threshold of daily travel and consequently many a pilgrim succumbed to the 'fatigue and tribulation' of the road,[62] not to speak of the danger of being robbed and murdered.

Firstly, we must realise that the geography of Tibet poses its own problems to the traveller and pilgrim. Anyone who would like to know more about the physical geography, climatic conditions and natural regions of Tibet can do no better than to turn to chapter one of Vaurie's *Tibet and its birds*,[63] where a full synthetic description is to be found. From this chapter we learn that physical Tibet is a country of extremes: of distance, relief, winds, temperatures and storms, but that it is not without its niches of agreeable landscape and fine weather. Much depends on the season travelled and the weather encountered, but the threat of sudden change for the worse is always present. In addition, there is the lay of the land, its high average altitude, its breath-taking passes, its steep slopes and cliffs. All these conditions of landscape and climate take on a special meaning in relation to *whom* is attempting to make a journey of pilgrimage and under *what form*.

As to the latter, it is important to ask questions about the *scale* of a particular pilgrim enterprise. Some pilgrimages were very localised, did not take more than a few days, and generally did not make pilgrims venture into unknown territory. These pilgrimages were of a recurring nature and could easily be attempted individually or by a family. A simple example is to be found in the few-day trip to the twin-peak of Dorjetroleh, the setting of a 'red cap shrine' and an object of pilgrimages for the inhabitants of the town of Batang.[64]

Then there are the more extended pilgrimages to regional mountains and Incarnations of some renown. We may think here of Amnye Machen and Yurce which are supposed to be primarily worshipped by the Tibetan Golok tribes living at the foot of the mountains.[65] Slightly upward in scale is Kawakarpo, primarily visited by Tibetans of the Southeast, but not beyond the ken and interest of the inhabitants of Lhasa.[66] Finally we come to a category of nationwide pilgrimages centering on the major power places of Tibet such as the mountain-sites of La-phyi and Tsari, as well as the monasteries of Tashilunpo and Kumbum. Pilgrimages to the latter already fall within the 'once in a lifetime' category. The same applies *a fortifiori* to Ti-se and Lhasa. But it all depends on the relative location of the would-be pilgrim to the main centres of pilgrimage.

With regard to the former, the question as to *whom* went on pilgrimage is important, because wealth, age and gender definitely influenced the outcome of a journey of pilgrimage. Materially speaking, pilgrimage was open to men, women and children alike. Women sometimes acted as porters of heavy loads when trails became unsuitable for pack animals.[67] They had to look after the children as well, and we have an eyewitness report of women carrying their children between their legs while crossing a rope bridge.[68] Children, on the whole, were vulnerable, a fact already noticed by Bower.[69] In cases where relatives were too old or too ill to go on pilgrimage, a ribbon-decorated incumbent in the form of a sheep replaced the beloved ones left at home.[70] Wealthy pilgrims stood a better chance of survival, in particular when that survival depended on the ability to buy the necessary shelter, food and fuel. And then of course there were the fully equipped trade caravans of the wealthy merchants sheltering the richer parties of pilgrims.[71]

For ordinary Tibetans from outlying areas, the pilgrimage to Lhasa was the dream of a lifetime. Tafel relates the story of a number of Zangskar women from Somoland who succeeded in completing a two-year pilgrim trip to Lhasa of which they were rightly proud:

> Before leaving home they had sold off everything, except for their most important household belongings which were stored

away in the local monastery. After that, twenty families had set on the road lock, stock, and barrel, together with some yak-oxen and cows: 'We were very lucky' said one of the elder housewives. 'Only once we were seriously attacked by robbers but lost no more than a man and some yak.[72]

The road must have been hard on these groups of pilgrims, in particular when greater distances had to be covered. Teichman noticed a party of pilgrims returning on foot from Lhasa to their home in Nyarong, looking very footsore and weary.[73] Tichy met a bunch of emaciated Singhalese who were on their way to Kailash, and had already been travelling for over three years.[74]

Next to these lay pilgrims, were the many monks and lamas. It is difficult to make an estimate of the proportion of the clergy going on pilgrimage relative to the total number of pilgrims on the road. Yet, their number must have been considerable as many travel accounts mention them in one way or another.[75] A distinction should be made here between the true pilgrim-lama with a fixed destination and the large group of 'professional' pilgrims who wandered from one sacred site to another as a way of life. Chan speaks of the true *sanyasi* as 'one who has taken the vows of abandonment and who formally renounces all ties, embracing the pilgrimage discipline full-time in order to seek enlightenment'.[76] Yet, as Aris rightly observes, there were inveterate wanderers in the category of lamas too, 'the lives of many of them [giving] the impression that their retreats were secondary to their travels'.[77] A fine example of such a Tibetan yogin existence is to be found in *The Life of Shabkar*, an early nineteenth century autobiography which yields rich insights in the custom of 'yogin pilgrimage', as well as traditional Tibetan culture at large.[78]

There was definitely a dangerous aspect to pilgrimage. References to mishaps, as well as to bad weather and roads, abound in the older travel literature on Tibet. Although we cannot know whether the Tibetan pilgrim felt the same way about these hardships as the European traveller did, the catalogue of travel conditions combed from these travelogues shows a surprisingly broad spectrum of bad circumstance and event. 'Unusual cold'[79], 'tremendous snow-storms'[80], 'devastating landslips'[81], 'avalanches'[82], 'flooding'[83], 'high waters'[84], 'low temperatures'[85], 'torrential rain'[86], have all been noticed. Or again, 'overloaded ferries'[87], 'swept away bridges'[88], 'dilapidated rope bridges'[89], 'forest-fires'[90], and occasional 'attacks by wolves'[91] all figure in the literature. Then there were the illnesses of various sorts, including the dreaded malaria when venturing into India, and the ever-present danger of altitude sickness.[92]

This is not to say that pilgrimage could not be a pleasant experience. It is equally well possible to make a catalogue of fine weather and road conditions from the same travel literature. The point however is that a successful journey overall could be spoiled by one mishap, even to the point of an untimely death. Many pilgrims, especially those of poorer background, were prone to failure for the simple reason that they were not well enough equipped. Better-off travellers too, sometimes died needlessly, because 'they did not take seriously the severity of Tibet's weather and altitude.'[93]

When travelling in larger caravans, the dangers of the road would seem less menacing. Individual pilgrims and small groups of devotees often came together at certain places,[94] joining larger trade caravans when possible.[95] Being part of a larger caravan had the advantage of greater food security and personal safety. But water and fuel could be scarcer and the overall pace might be relatively slow as the countless pack animals had to be watered and grazed along the road. Because of that, there was a tendency for smaller groups of pilgrims to take the shortest routes across high passes along age-old pilgrim tracks of proven merit.[96] Even relatively better-off pilgrims preferred to travel in this way, putting their trust in a single beast of burden, while going on foot themselves.[97]

Perhaps the greatest danger to pilgrims on the road was the threat of brigandage and robbery. Going over the travel literature of Tibet, the threat of being robbed figures on many a page. But with Alexandra David-Neel we might say that 'the threat of being robbed should not be exaggerated. Many aeroplanes crash, but many more don't.'[98] This observation by an experienced Tibet traveller is in all probability not far from the truth, and perhaps reflects the everyday pilgrim experience better than many an excited European expedition report. After all, substantial pilgrim circulation has been reported by travellers over the years, and it is unlikely that this would have been the case under the omnipresent threat of robbery and brigandage. This is not to say that accidents did not happen. Pilgrims were seen carrying arms at times, especially in regions and near places of known disaster.[99] As Ekvall has pointed out, brigandage is the product of the 'weak' state in border areas,[100] but, as should be added, also of opportunity. Structural problems of brigandage were first and foremost concentrated along the main through-going caravan roads,[101] and near places where pilgrims and traders gathered. Such a place, for example, was Nagchu, where pilgrims were screened by the Central Tibetan authorities before crossing Tang-la,[102] but also the very Manasarovar area where the presence of innumerable pilgrims attracted robbers from far and near.[103] The Gangarling region in Kham too, developed over the years into a banditry-infested area, due to Chinese meddling in local frontier affairs, leading to an overall decline in pilgrimage.[104]

Pilgrims tried to overcome these threats by strategies of group and night travel,[105] but could not always avoid encounters with brigands. Another frontier area where pilgrims were under threat of attack was the eastern Himalayan district of Tsari. The daily chores of the pilgrims on the Tsari circuit have been well described by Bailey,[106] including the threat of being attacked by the Lopa [Loba] tribes from across the border. This was not an empty threat as the extremely interesting report by Dunbar shows. It is well worth citing the latter at some length:

> To carry out the Tsari pilgrimage, the devout traveller must go round the mountain, a four days' progress, involving a two days' journey through Loba country. The sacred way runs high up the mountain side and does not dip into the valley below. Rindze [an informant] stated that he went with about 200 other pilgrims and that they were attacked on the south side of Tsari by a band of Loba robbers, armed with bows and arrows and long swords. They had no guns and did not apparently use spears, but they discharged volleys of stones on to the pilgrims, who lost 7 killed during the encounter, others dying afterwards of their wounds and injuries.[107]

To appease these Loba the Tibetan government send a delegation of officials to them each monkey-year when the high '*ronkor*' pilgrimage took place.[108] As this pilgrimage could attract well over ten thousand pilgrims, the safety of roads and pilgrim routes loomed large in the mind of the officials, but perhaps there was a hidden agenda of guarding territorial integrity against a powerful colonial neighbour too. Be that as it may, it secured the many pilgrims a safer journey than would have been possible without government support.

Conclusion

Pilgrimage is the geographically, economically and materially conditioned actualization of the wish to acquire merit and to destroy sin. It takes shape through a more or less extended journey to powerful places which make possible psychological healing, if not spiritual enlightenment. The confrontation with other places lifts up the spirit and brings a knowledge of people and places beyond the local ken. However, the vital experience of pilgrimage, which in the words of Lemaire brings a new *vitality*, is matched by the experience of *vulnerability*, the very human fact of being subject to geographical and material conditions going against the pilgrim. But this vulnerability can also work a positive effect. It has been argued that the harder the road the greater the gain.[109] And indeed, for a Tibetan, it is the hardship of the road that *does* enhance the accumulation of merit, in particular if induced in an artificial way. Pilgrims have been seen carrying stones on their back, prostrating themselves and measuring the road to Lhasa full-length with their bodies. In essence then, the pilgrim experience can be summed up in the transcendence of the tyranny of distance and the hardships of the road. For true pilgrim's progress is measured by toil and not by pleasure.

Notes

1 Chan 1994: 36.
2 After, Hornbein 1965: 90.
3 Lemaire 1970: 99.
4 Chan 1994: 36.
5 Dowman 1988: 3.
6 Meyer 1987.
7 Chan 1994: 36.
8 Huber 1990: 121, cf. Epstein and Peng Wenbin 1994: 39–40.
9 Blondeau 1960: 205.
10 Kirkland 1982: 257.
11 Aris 1979: 17.
12 Huber 1990.
13 Blondeau 1960: 216–217, cf. Aris, 1995.
14 cf. Grünwedel 1919: 9.
15 Ferrari 1958: XXI–XXII.
16 Huber (1994a: 13).
17 Bell 1924a: 95; compare this figure to the eighteenth-century Capuchin missionary figure of 80,000 inhabitants as quoted by Snellgrove and Richardson 1980: 224.
18 Hedin 1910 I: 304, 347–360, see also plates 111 and 112.
19 cf. Hedin 1910 II: 203, 1917 III: 126.
20 Rangachar 1931; Hamsa 1934; Pranavananda 1950; Stoll 1966; Snelling 1983; Tucci 1989: 97–172; Johnson and Moran 1989.
21 Filchner 1906, 1933; Li An-che 1982.
22 cf. Aufschnaiter 1976; Macdonald 1990; Huber 1994a.
23 Wollaston 1922: 10.

24 Prindle 1983: 114–118, see also plate facing page 18; Macdonald 1985; Buffetrill 1994a, 1994b.
25 Photos between pages 280 and 281, 284, 290 and 291 of Hedin 1917 III; Berglie 1981; Brauen (ed.) 1983: 54, map.
26 Kingdon Ward 1926: 101; Karmay 1992.
27 Dunbar 1915: 2–6; Kingdon Ward 1936: 390; Ludlow 1938: 9; Fletcher 1975: photo facing page 84, 94; also Huber 1994b.
28 Tafel 1914 II: 277–278.
29 Li An-che 1948.
30 Rock 1930a, 1956; see also Nebesky-Wojkowitz 1956: 209–210.
31 Duncan 1929: 116–117, 1952: 132.
32 Bacot 1908, 1909: 93–142; Kingdon Ward 1913: plates XXI and XXIX facing pages 98 and 150; Gregory and Gregory 1923: plates XI and XII, facing pages 216 and 232; Handel-Mazzetti 1927: 186–190; Duncan 1929: 51.
33 Kingdon Ward 1924: 228–229; Rock 1931, 1947: 241, 385n, also plates 55–59.
34 Rock 1930b; Heim 1933: 59–133; Imhof 1974.
35 Tafel 1914 II: 229; Epstein and Peng Wenbin 1994: 30, 38–40; for Murdo [Siguniang] see Senft 1983, photo facing page 160, for a further impression of the area see Senft 1984: 62ff.
36 This section has been taken from my thesis and is presented here in a partially revised form; cf. van Spengen 1992: 91ff.
37 Blondeau 1960: 212.
38 cf.Tafel 1914 II: 253.
39 Carrasco 1959: 213.
40 Markham 1876: 83.
41 Sherring 1906: 159, 283–284.
42 Rijnhart 1901: 115.
43 cf. Bhardwaj 1973: 6–7, for an example from the Indian Himalayas.
44 Sherring 1906: 28; Hedin 1910 I: 191.
45 cf. Harrer 1952: 162.
46 Heim 1933: 65, and Figure 45 facing page 56.
47 Walker-Watson 1983: 17; cf. Filchner 1933: 413.
48 Ryall 1879: 450; Kawaguchi 1909: 453–454; Calhoun 1929: 708 ff.; Deasy 1901: 156; for amber, see Jest 1987: 228–230.
49 Heron 1930: 21.
50 Gill 1880 II: 107.
51 Hamilton 1819: 212–213; Oldfield 1880 I: 11; Snellgrove and Richardson 1980: 202; Jha 1995a, 1995b.
52 Wright 1877: 27; Lévi 1905–1908 II: 319, 332, 336.
53 Boeck 1903: 293–301; see also the frontispiece of the same book.
54 *Ibid.*: 294.
55 Blondeau 1960: 218–219, cf. Aris 1995.
56 *Ibid.*: 219.
57 Richardus 1989: 41.
58 Cooper 1871: 76; Baber 1882: 42; Hosie 1905: 9; Hackmann 1907: 9.
59 Tsybikoff 1904: 96; Ossendowski 1922: 235, cf. Tsybikoff 1992.
60 Longman Dictionary (1984).

61 Bower 1894: 163.
62 Huc and Gabet 1987 II: 223.
63 Vaurie 1972: 3–37.
64 Duncan 1929: 109ff.
65 Nebesky-Wojkowitz 1956: 210; Stein 1959: 191.
66 Bacot 1909: 102.
67 Bacot 1909: 137.
68 *Ibid.*: 102.
69 Bower 1894: 163.
70 Bacot 1909: 137.
71 de Lesdain 1908: 257ff.
72 Tafel 1914 II: 253.
73 Teichman 1922: 81.
74 Tichy 1937: 103.
75 cf. Bacot 1909: 108; Lha-mo, R. 1926: 165.
76 Chan 1994: 39.
77 Aris 1988: 9.
78 Ricard 1994.
79 Roerich (1931), 1967: 86.
80 Prejevalsky 1876 II: 185–186; Wilson 1885: 264.
81 Hooker 1855 II: 41.
82 Waddell 1899: 57.
83 Cutting 1940: 207.
84 Tsybikov (1919), 1992: 74.
85 Tsybikov (1919), 1992: 286; Roerich (1931), 1967: 86.
86 Karmay 1992: 532.
87 Tucci 1956: 133.
88 Tafel 1914 II: 186.
89 Johnston 1908: 193.
90 Tafel 1914 II: 173.
91 Tafel 1914 I: 306; Rock 1930a: 154; Roerich (1931), 1967: 57.
92 Tsybikov (1919), 1992: 66–67.
93 Chan 1994: 17.
94 Tsybikov (1919), 1992: 52.
95 de Lesdain 1908: 257ff.
96 Kingdon Ward 1936: 394.
97 Futterer 1900: 301.
98 David-Neel (1953: 405).
99 Bower 1894: 163; Tsybikov (1919), 1992: 51, Duncan 1929: 18.
100 Ekvall 1939: 18.
101 Rock 1956: 127.
102 Bower 1894: 109; Burrard 1915 I: 133, 139; Tsybikov (1919), 1992: 77.
103 Burrard 1915 I: 165, 223.
104 Rock 1931: 13–17.
105 Hosie 1905: 37; also Hedin 1922–23, I.
106 Bailey 1957: 200ff., referring to his 1913 journey.
107 Dunbar 1915: 5.
108 Bailey's Report, as cited by Nebesky-Wojkowitz 1956: 406–407.
109 Macdonald 1982: 25; Huber, personal communication.

Chapter 3
Hindu Trading Pilgrims
John Clarke

The discovery of a company painting (figure 1) in the collection of the Bodleian Library in Oxford has revealed new facets to the activities of that intriguing group of Indian ascetics, the trading pilgrims, or Gosains.[1] The Bodleian painting, originally in the collection of Sir Gore Ousley,[2] shows three pilgrims carrying shoulder poles with wickerwork baskets suspended from them. The inscription on the reverse of the picture describes them as Sinashes (Sanyasis) or trading pilgrims and says that they came chiefly from the province of "Caussia" to the northward of Bengal. The inscription further says that they travelled to the latitude of 10 degrees N on the south-eastern coast of India to buy coral and pearls on an annual basis and that they traded these into the foothills of Nepal. They are mentioned as being under the vow of celibacy. The importance of the Ousley picture lies in its inscription, the only one which I am aware of to date, which not only clearly identifies a group of trading pilgrims but mentions both their goods and the source of those goods. The inscription corroborates what is already known about the Gosains as traders but also tells us for the first time that they bought pearls at source in southern India.

Before discussing this picture in relation to the Gosains trading patterns I would like to give an overview of the meaning of the term itself. One of its earliest recorded uses is in the memoirs of the Emperor Jahangir (1605–1628), where it is used to describe an ascetic with whom he had religious conversations.[3] The word, however, represents the Indian vernacular modification of the earlier Sanskrit term Goswamin, the literal meaning of which is "master of cows" or "one who controls his passions". While these meanings refer to

52

Figure 1: Three trading pilgrims or Gosains, Gorakhpur, c.1770, gouache on paper. From an album of castes and occupations, Bodleian Library, Ousley Add, 167 f. 41 r. Courtesy of the Bodleian Library.

Krishna,[4] Goswamin also came to denote the followers of Chaitanya (1485–1534). The first six disciples of Chaitanya were called the Six Goswamis and later followers became Gosayis.[5] It seems that in Bengal the true meaning of the term had been retained and heads of Vaishnava monasteries or priests there were called Gosains.[6] The term also properly applied to followers of Sri Vallabcharya (1479–1531), who were called Gokulasta Gosains both in Bengal and elsewhere in the north.[7] In both cases such Gosains were Vaishnavites. British commentators, from the late 18th century onwards, following local usage, used the term much more loosely, often synonymously for Sannyasis or Fakirs and to include mendicants from both Vaishnavite and Shaivite orders.[8] There was considerable regional variation in the meaning of the term and in many areas other than Bengal it often referred to members of the Shaivite orders.[9] It can be seen from this discussion that trading pilgrims could have had either Vaishnavite or Shaivite affiliations.

Turning to their economic activities, I would like to focus on the role the Gosains played in trading precious and semi-precious stones from India to Tibet during the 18th and early 19th centuries. Such a role is attested to both by contemporary accounts and the inscription on the Ousley painting. At the end of the 18th and well into the 19th century, coral and pearls formed two of the principal exports of

Bengal to Tibet, together with silks, brocades, broadcloth, tobacco, indigo and conch shells. Returns were made in musk, gold dust and yaktails.[10]

James Forbes, an East India Company officer in India between 1766–1783, encountered many Gosains in his capacity of customs officer at Bharuch in Gujerat. He gives us further details about how they traded, observing that it was usual for them to carry back from pilgrimages to the sea coast, pearls, corals, spices, and other valuable articles. These were then exchanged in the interior for gold dust, musk and other products. Though he does not expand on what 'the interior' means, the mention of two of the most important trade products of Tibet makes the Himalayan connection certain.

The Gosains' trade goods were concealed in their hair or in cloths around their waist.[11] In a minute of 1773, Warren Hastings described them as trading in diamonds in addition to corals and other small articles.[12] George Bogle, who had been appointed to head the first diplomatic mission to Tibet in 1774, found Gosains at Tashilunpho, noting that they traded 'in articles of small bulk and great value'. He noted that 'though clad in the garb of poverty there are many possessed of considerable wealth'.[13] In a report of 1779 he also said that small quantities of European goods imported by the trading pilgrims were highly valued in Tibet,[14] while in 1783, Captain Turner commented that the Tibetan trade was in the hands of a few rich Gosains.[15] In the same year Turner was asked by a Gosain called Sukh Dev if he could accompany his party back to India through Bhutan, as he was afraid that he would be stripped of the considerable wealth that he had accumulated over forty years of trading if he passed through Nepal.[16] At this point the significance of the inscription on the Ousley picture must again be mentioned. For the first time the source of two of the Gosains most important trade goods: corals and pearls, are located.

Strictly speaking, however, sources of coral lay not within India itself, but in the Persian Gulf, the Red Sea and the western Mediteranean.[17] In the 17th century, coral was imported by the Portugese, the Dutch and the English East India Company in large quantities to the west coast,[18] and, after 1650 by the English to Fort St George on the Coromandel coast.[19] The Gosains were, therefore, almost certainly purchasing coral from this latter source.

Though there was a market for both coral and pearls in India,[20] both were consumed in vast quantities within Tibet for jewellery and for the ornamentation of images. Marco Polo mentions the Tibetan addiction to coral as early as the 13th century.[21] Coral and pearls were also forwarded to Chinese central Asia and China itself.[22] The headquarters of the Indian pearl fisheries themselves, from the 1st century AD to the mid 17th century, were based on the island of Ramesvaram.[23] There were good reasons, discussed later in the paper, for devotees to visit the famous temple on this site. To the north smaller fisheries existed in the Palk strait[24] itself, while to the south the fisheries off the shores of Tinnevelly with their headquarters at Tuticorin were preminent from the later 17th century onwards.[25] The latitude 10 degrees north given in the inscription is a line passing a little to the north of Madurai and bisecting the northern half of the Palk straight. Henry Le Beck, visiting a pearl fishery in Sri Lanka during the spring of 1797, paints a vivid picture of a crowd of thousands on the shore engaged in sorting, drilling and selling pearls. Among them were priests, Hindu monks and Fakirs who he described as vagabonds and as 'impertinently troublesome'.[26] One must envision similar scenes at the pearl fisheries on the Indian sub-continent.

Unfortunately there is no information at present on likely routes or timings of Gosain pilgrimages either in India or Nepal. One of the most popular pilgrimage cycles for Gosains in India started with attendance at the Kumbh Mela at Hardwar, Allahabad, Ujain or Nasik in January. In March they would attend a mela at Janakpur in Nepal, the birthplace of Sita, then move down to Bengal. After crossing to the Brahmaputra river for bathing festivals they moved on to the mouth of the Ganges in May, then by the end of June travelled north-west into Bihar or down to Puri and the temple of Jagganatha.[27] It is possible that the trading pilgrims in the Ousley painting took in part of this circuit, but it is perhaps even more likely that theirs was a completely different cycle, especially considering their need to be at the tip of India in March/April for the pearl fishing season.[28]

The Gosains in the Ousley picture are described as from Kasia, a subdistrict within Gorakhpur, at that time part of the Kingdom of Oudh, and very close to the border with Nepal. In the 1770s, Warren Hastings noted that the Gosains were most numerous in just this area of the north Indian hills.[29] The gazeteer for the province of Oudh in 1877 gives a census return of upwards of 40,000 Gosains at that time,[30] while an 1872 census of Gharwhal lists a figure of 2,620 for that district.[31] Such a geographical base would have allowed easy access to the Nepalese Terai, which the inscription on the Ousley painting tells us they were trading into.

The routes that were taken into Tibet varied significantly through the 18th and 19th centuries depending on the political situation as it affected the border areas. Until the unsettled conditions caused by the Gurkha conquest of Nepal in 1768–69 and their subsequent attack on Sikkim in 1774, Nepal had formed a principal trade route between Bengal and Tibet. Trade passed through the Terai, over easy passes, and by routes up the Kosi and Arun rivers before finally entering southern Tibet.[32] As a result of the conquest however, the main routes through the Terai were closed and the Gosains were forced to take less easy routes through Sikkim. When that country was also invaded by the Gurkhas in 1774, the Gosains turned to the use of more difficult paths through the kingdom of sLo (Mustang).[33] The fact that the Gosains in the Ousley picture traded only into the Terai may reflect the new political difficulties of trading through Nepal; suggesting that the painting was executed after 1769.

The Gosains, according to Bogle, had possessed rich and 'very extensive establishments' in Nepal, but they had lost these and been expelled by the Gurkha leader Prithvi Naryan Shah because, like the Kashmiris who were also expelled at the same time, they were seen as supporters of the Malla kings.[34] In 1774, some old Tibetan merchants in Tashilunpho told George Bogle that whereas great quantities of broadcloth and coral had previously been brought there, what then came was 'smuggled in by the fakirs'.[35]

Apart from these routes into southern Tibet, there were a number of other trade routes that the Gosains might have taken. Two main routes converged from the west on Gartok, one from Ladakh, the other following the course of the Sutlej river from Simla. The routes from Almora through Kumaon were the most direct from India to the sacred region and were the most popular pilgrim routes, through of minor importance for trade. If pilgrims did wish to make trade in the region a priority, diversions were necessary to tap the markets at Gartok and Leh, or Lhasa and Tashilunpho, 800 miles away in central Tibet. Even at the sacred region, however, some trade was carried out, mostly at the two main centres of Taklakot, just over the border, and at rGya-ni-ma, some 50 miles to the south-west and about 25 miles from the border.[36] The trade season coincided with the pilgrimage season from July to the early autumn. Taklokot was the largest market and in 1908 Sri Hamsa noted the presence of merchants there from the border Indian areas who had brought Indian cloth, corals, pearls, grain and groceries.[37] At the beginning of the 20th century the District Commissioner of Almora, Charles Sherring, found that both places were full of pilgrims who, as he put it, 'generally manage to combine religion with a little business'; testifying to the continuation of the phenomena. The other great western Tibetan trading centre at Gartok hosted an annual fair in September[38] while another was held in August at rGya-ni-ma; both would have provided extra trading opportunities for pilgrims.

The phenomenon of Hindu trading pilgrims was paralleled on a much larger scale by those Buddhist pilgrims coming to holy centres such as Lhasa, who would also engage in trade. Conversely, traders travelling from distant areas for commercial purposes would naturally have also visited any available local holy sites.[39] These traders, of course, were secular pilgrims, not restricted by any vows regulating ownership or the amassing of wealth. Though it is a well known fact that lamas were frequent traders, in the majority of cases such trading was done primarily on behalf of their own monasteries.[40] The question of the personal as opposed to the institutional wealth of monks and incarnates and associated trading is a complex issue only now being addressed by scholars.[41] Although the large trade of monasteries is well known, the concept of trade conducted on behalf of the monastery as a whole is probably misleading. It seems that there was remarkably little pooling of resources by monasteries as entities in themselves, rather individuals were granted specific resources and these had well defined uses. gNyer-pas or bursars were, for example, given funds to finance monastic events such as a particular ritual and might trade to increase these funds. If profits exceeded the required sum the extra amounts would go to the gNyer-pa and this also meant their natal families.[42] Long trading trips for these purposes would also be combined with pilgrimage.

There was, therefore, a spill-over effect from monastic trading which enriched monks, especially high incarnate lamas. An exact comparison with Hindu trading pilgrims cannot be made at present as we do not know how their trips were organised financially or how their profits were allotted. Did they, for example, undertake trading trips where the total profit was divided according to a set formula, as occurred in Tibet, or were their personal moneymaking activities carried out on separate trips?

Pilgrimage and trade in the Himalayas were in fact relatively minor aspects of the overall activity of the Gosains in South Asia. As a group they were of great economic importance in India in the 18th and for much of the 19th century. In order to understand this wider significance a sketch must be given of the organisational structure of the northern Gosains, who most concern us, and their broader trading activities.

There is agreement that Gosains could be either celibate, *nishprahis*, or married, that is *gharbaris*, though both could also be traders and merchants.[43] Though the porters in the Ousley picture are described as celibate and no other references describe the pilgrim traders in Tibet as married, we cannot be sure that a number of them did not fall into this category. Married Gosains were usually householders who might trade or pursue agriculture while retaining their functions as religious teachers or priests.[44] They often owned their own temples.

There is no doubt, however, that the celibates were numerous and that they commonly engaged in trading, banking and money lending. By the 1780s they were the dominant moneylending and property owning group in Allahabad, Benares, Mirzapur, Ujain and Nagpur.[45] Their vast commercial success rested on the several-fold advantages of belonging to a widespread organisation, or series of organisations, which in many areas had begun to take on the character of corporations.

Firstly, a network of *maths,* or monasteries, stretching from Nepal to the south of India provided a ready-made trading network, giving, in effect, staging posts, support and capital for travelling bands of Gosains.[46] Secondly, travelling in armed groups for protection, the Gosains undertook pilgrimage cycles that allowed them to link productive zones providing good trading opportunities. For example, a particularly important route ran from the Punjab along the Ganges to Bengal.[47] What Warren Hastings described as raiding by 'a set of lawless Bandette', was often in reality an annual cycle of pilgrimage.[48] Thirdly, their religious status gave them a number of benefits, such as reductions in customs rates. The Gosains were often in a position to wield considerable political power at a local level.[49] The use of cycles of pilgrimage and armed protection for their long distance trips meant that they were ideally placed to pass the products of Bengal both to the north-west and into Nepal. The trade in silks, piece goods, copper and spices from Bengal into the Deccan was, however, of even greater importance.[50] In 1848 the Gosains are described as having a major share of the trade of the Ganges in their hands,[51] and they were also major bankers and money lenders in Rajputana and the Deccan, at centres such as Hyderabad and Poona.[52] In many areas they were also landlords and tax farmers.[53]

Their economic success also related to the internal organisation of the *maths*. The *math* owned its own buildings and in some cases (mainly in country areas), its own lands, the profits from which supported the *math*. Additionally *gurus* and *mahant*s had their own property and wealth which were separate from that of the *math*. The *mahant* was responsible for the administration of the *math*s property and also gave out the *math*s money to individual *chela*s for commercial activities. Though the *chela*s had no property of their own, at the death of the *mahant* they each received a share of his personal accumulated wealth.[54] As Bernard Cohn notes in his article on the Gosains, it was the way in which the personal wealth of a *mahant* was passed on at his death that gave Gosains an economic advantage over sons inheriting in Hindu society generally.[55] This was due to the *mahant*'s capital being divided unequally amongst the *chela*s according to their standing in relation to him, giving one or more *chela*s a greater share than the others. This contrasted with outside society where sons received an equal share of their father's wealth which tended to lead to a dissipation of resources. Also, although there were some requirements of the *math* involving expense, such as the feeding of mendicants, the *math*s were not expected like the landed or merchant class to outlay capital for lavish entertainment and other display purposes.[56] It is clear that much of the profit from their personal commercial dealings went into the acquisition of property, with the *mahant*s at Varanasi and in Bihar particularly owning large houses and gardens.

Though this paper is focussed primarily on trading pilgrims, it must be pointed out that a wide spectrum of other secular activities were also pursued by Gosains, sometimes in combination with commerce. Some, for example, hired out their services as mercenaries in the disturbed political conditions of late 18th century northern India.[57] In this they followed the lifestyle of the fighting Naga Gosains, an order particularly important in Rajasthan.[58] In 1793 Captain Kirkpatrick called the Gosains 'at once devotees, pilgrims, beggars, soldiers and merchants'.[59] There therefore existed a degree of interchangeability of lay occupation, with others turning from soldiering to trading. Numbers of Gosains who had been fighting in Bihar in the 1770s, for example, settled in Bengal where they started money-lending and trading along the Brahmaputra river.[60] While some Gosains were Sanyasi traders, others were Sanyasi soldiers, nor as can be seen, were these distinctions rigid.

The pictorial representations of trading pilgrims found in Company paintings encompass many variations in dress and appearance. The dress of the Gosains depicted in the Ousley painting (figure 1), with its small cap, represents the general costume of the north Indian hills and should not be thought of as having a wider generic significance. Though there are no obvious sectarian marks the wearing of *rudraksha* berry necklaces probably indicates that they are Shaivite. In contrast, a painting from Tanjore in the Victoria and Albert Museum (figure 2) shows a group of south Indian religious figures dating to around 1830 with, second from the left, a figure labelled "Gosawyee" in English.[61] He wears a turban, *lhungi* and bears the tripundra Shaivite marks on his forehead. The term Gosain is used differently from region to region and here in the south there is a clear distinction being made between the Shaivite Gosain with his turban and the Bhairagi or Vaishnavite mendicant to his left.

To the Gosain's right in this picture, is a Paundauram or non-Brahmin priest from Karnataka and a Fakir. The Gosain here fits the description of Purangir, agent and favourite of the 3rd Panchen Lama. Purangir was said to have dressed like this on public occasions, but ordinarily wore a Sanyasin's *kaupina*, or loin cloth,

Figure 2: Four male ascetics, Tanjore, c.1830, gouache on paper. From an album depicting castes and occupations. From left: Vairagi or Vaishnavite devotee carrying lota and rosary (inscribed: Bhairagi Loka in Devanagari, Byraugy in English), Pundauram, a non-Brahmin Karnataka priest carrying tongs and rosary, (inscribed in English: Canary pundauram), a Fakir carrying a fan and a bird in a cage (inscribed in English: Phakeer). Victoria and Albert Museum, IM 39.9-1987. Courtesy of the Board of Trustees of the Victoria and Albert Museum.

with a red ochre-dyed cloth around his waist and a tiger skin thrown over his shoulder. The majority of painted representations of Gosains are clothed, many have turbans or caps and most have shoes. Though the variety of dress found in depictions is humble we also know that some Gosains dressed ostentiously. A Bengali book of 1800 describes Dasnami Sanyasi merchants and moneylenders as wearing gold ear ornaments and chains set with diamonds and corals while others wore gold or silver bangles.[62] A miniature from Nurpur, dating to around 1750, which is now in the British Library, shows two lavishly adorned Vaishnavite Gosains, one the head of the *math* at Pindori, wearing conical pearl decorated hats.[63]

Perhaps the commonest representation of pilgrims, however, is that where they carry holy water. The Ousley picture is important again here because, although there are many representations of pilgrims carrying holy water from poles, this appears to be the only painting to date that clearly identifies a group of such pilgrims as traders. Not every pilgrim carrying Ganges water would have been a Gosain and conversely it cannot be said that every Gosain would have carried Ganges water. Nevertheless it becomes obvious that Gosains might easily now go unrecognised in company albums described only as "pilgrims carrying holy water". The carrying of Ganges water is a meritorious act for a Hindu pilgrim, as indeed is the carrying of shoulder poles without any useful load attached.[64] It should also be remembered that Ganges water was itself a saleable commodity and was sometimes carried long distances by Brahmin pilgrims for commercial purposes, as Tavernier found in the mid 17th century.[65] Water may therefore have formed a trade item in its own right.

The most common method of carrying water was within baskets decorated with either flags, as seen in figure 1, or peacock feathers. It is remarkable that close photographic parallels to the Ousley album picture exist from the first decade of the 20th century. Pilgrims were photographed carrying holy water from the rivers Ganges and Narmada and are dressed almost identically with caps and *rudraksha mallas*, carrying poles with tiny flags and wickerwork baskets suspended from them. They also bear the Shaivite sectarian markings.[66] In all respects they are remarkably similar to those in the Ousley picture, though living over 100 years later.

Another painting from Tanjore dating to around 1805 (figure 3), shows a pilgrim from Benares accompanied by his wife. He is described in a Tamil inscription as a shoulder-carrying pole-bearer

Figure 3: A holy-water carrier and his wife, Tanjore, 1805, gouache on paper. From an album of trades, occupations and costume. Inscribed in English: Hausicavady Carren or a brahmin that carries Holy Water from Benares. Victoria and Albert Museum, Al 9254(36). Courtesy of the Board of Trustees of the Victoria and Albert Museum.

from Kashi (Varanasi) and in an English gloss as "a pilgrim carrying Ganges water from Benares". His *urdhvapundara* or Vaishnavite marking, is closest to either the Vishnusvami or Vallabhacharya Sampradaya.[67] Though we do not know that he was a Gosain, he was certainly making a journey of similar length and between comparable points with the Ousley painting Gosains, being painted in Tanjore and having come from Benares.[68]

Though holy water was and is carried as a meritorious act, it is also commonly brought back to the place of residence for ritual use or is sometimes consumed as part of concluding ceremonies at the end of a pilgrimage.[69] We have no descriptions of Gosains carrying Ganges water in Tibet and perhaps as Hindus it would have made more sense for them to have been carrying away water from the holy lake of Manasarovar, as we know some pilgrims did. There were, however, other compelling religious reasons for carrying Ganges water to the coast of Tamilnadu and in particular to the temple of Shiva at Rameswaram. The *lingam* installed in the temple of Shiva by Rama as a pennance for killing Ravana came to be considered as one of the great *lingas* of light, with the power to destroy the worst sins merely through *darshan*.[70] There is a further belief that if water drawn from the Manikarnika Ghat in Benares is poured over the *lingam* in the temple of Shiva there it will grow in size.[71]

The Gosains' activities in Tibet itself can be viewed within the context of the more general pattern of Hindu pilgrimage there. The Tibetan population, particularly in western Tibet, was used to seeing Hindu pilgrims en route to the complex of sacred sites around Mount Kailash. But there are indications in George Bogle's account of his visit to Tashilunpho in 1774 that the Hindu pilgrims were far from accepted there and that their presence depended almost completely on the 3rd Panchen Lama himself. Bogle was sent by Warren Hastings to form a contact with the Panchen that would allow the opening up of trade into southern Tibet through Bhutan to compensate for the routes through Nepal which were then closed.

In his account, Bogle talks of about 150 Hindu pilgrims and about 30 Muslim Fakirs being at Tashilunpho in 1774.[72] Captain Turner, who in 1783 was sent to Tashilunpho as an embassy to the new incarnation of the Panchen, that is to say the 4th Panchen Lama, found that '300 Gosains and Sanyasis were fed by the lama there'.[73] We do not know whether Gosains travelled in bands within Tibet, although Bogle's description seems to suggest that they were unobtrusive, at least precluding an obvious show of armed force. Returning to Bogle's description of the Gosains, he called them

> a worthless set of people, devoid of principle . . . they have no object but their own interest, and, covered with the cloak of religion, are regardless of their caste, of their character, and of everything else which is held sacred among the Hindus.

Bogle goes on to state that

> Their victuals are dressed by Tibet servants; there is no kind of meat, beef excepted, which they do not eat. They drink plentifully of spiritous liquors, and although directly contrary to their vows and to the rules of their order, above one half of them keep women. In their deportment they mix, by a strange combination, the most fawning and flattering servility with the most clamorous insolence. They intrude into every company, give their opinion in every conversation, and convey what they have to say in a voice like thunder. They are universally disliked by the Tibetans, have no protector but the lama, and if he were to die tommorrow they would next day be driven from the palace.[74]

Though Bogle's opinion appears clear and strongly held it seems at odds with his comments on them elsewhere. Namely that

> their humble deportment and holy character, heightened by the merit of distant pilgrimages, their accounts of unknown countries and remote regions, and, above all, their professions of high veneration for the lama, procure them not only ready admittance, but great favour.[75]

It may be significant that the positive comments relate more to their relationship to the Panchen Lama. At another place in his narrative he says that many Gosains come on commercial schemes, but although in reality rich, dress poorly and live off the charity of the Panchen. They received a monthly allowance of tea, butter and flour and a little money and were often given 'something considerable' on their departure.[76]

We have almost no record of Gosains at Lhasa. There is one exception, however, a road bill issued on the authority of the 8th Dalai Lama in 1793 to ensure the supply of provisions and ponies to Daljitgir returning from Calcutta with letters from the British authorities to him.[77] This apparent lack of patronage by the Dalai Lamas may be linked to the greater power and influence of the Panchen Lamas from the mid 18th to the 3rd quarter of the 19th centuries when a sucession of Dalai Lamas died young. It may also be that our picture is distorted due to lack of relevant records.

It appears that the patronage of Gosains by the 3rd Panchen Lama, Blo-bzang dPal-ldan Ye-shes,[78] was based as much on his own intellectual and political interests as on any charitable motive. Bogle says that he knew the Hindustani language reasonably well and would talk to the Gosains every day from his window.[79] By this means he was able to glean information both about the distant countries that they had visited and about the government of India. Although Bogle so roundly condemns the character of the trading pilgrims, it is obvious there existed among them men of intelligence and integrity. These were well placed, with their knowledge of foreign countries, languages and trade routes, to act as diplomats, interpreters and of course guides. Bogle states that during his visit he relied on a Gosain called Purangir for his knowledge of the road, climate and people. Purangir acted as both a private secretary to the 3rd Panchen Lama and his diplomatic agent, visiting Bengal on his behalf on several occasions. Bogle informs us that his first name was Purna, and his second shows that he was a Dasanami of the Giri suborder and therefore a follower of Sankaracharya. Bogle mentions that he had the full confidence of the Tibetan authorities and that he was highly intelligent, knowing a number of languages including Mongolian and Tibetan, also that he had a good knowledge of the commerce of India and Asia.[80] The latter was a practical and not merely a theoretical knowledge as he was also a trade agent. Purangir assisted pilgrims and regular traders in selling their musk and gold dust in Bengal and while there in purchasing a range of Bengali products to return with.[81]

Purangir was also said to have had a reputation for piety and integrity and he was chosen by the Panchen to be the head of a Tibetan Buddhist monastery established by him on the banks of the Ganges in Howrah, Calcutta.[82] Through this project the Panchen hoped to provide a base from which Tibetans could once again visit the Buddhist sites in India, re-opening symbolically the former links with the Indian Buddhist homeland. He was encouraged by Hastings with the grant of lands in 1778 and 1782. Purangir lived there on retirement from active service between 1786 and 1795, when he met an untimely death at the hands of robbers.[83]

Both Purangir and his sucessor Daljitgir were used as political agents by the Panchen Lama and did far more than merely carry messages; on occasion they engaged in diplomacy. In 1774, Purangir had been sent by the Panchen Lama to Warren Hastings in Calcutta in order to negotiate favourable conditions for Bhutan, then concluding a treaty with the British.[84] There are several instances of his serving both the Panchen Lama and the British without compromising his own position, though, as both the Panchen Lama and the East India Company desired the opening of trade between Bengal and Tibet, the situation presented no real conflict of interests.[85]

In 1779, Purangir travelled with the Panchen to Peking to visit the Chinese Emperor and, according to Purangir's account, he was presented to the Emperor in order to directly answer his questions on Warren Hastings. Bogle, following Hastings' orders, had also asked Purangir to press the British case for the opening of direct trade with Tibet and to record the conversations which took place.[86] While still at court, the 3rd Panchen died of smallpox, speaking his last words in Hindi to Purangir.

Purangir acted as an interpreter and guide for Turner in 1783 on the recognition of the new incarnation and two years later independently led a mission again to Tashilunpho.[87] In 1790 he made a private visit to Lhasa and in 1792 again visited Tibet, probably combining pilgrimage with the delivery of letters from the Panchen Lama to Cornwallis.[88]

Glimpses of the religious activities of the Gosains are unfortunately rare, but not surprisingly they fit in with the general pattern of Hindu pilgrimage in Tibet. Almost certainly large numbers of trading pilgrims must have visited Kailash and Manasarovar, the main destinations for Hindu pilgrims, but they attracted little attention from western commentators. We only know something about their activities because of Bogle's stay at Tashilunpho and from the comments of a few other Britishers in India, as there was no one in western Tibet to single them out from the mass of pilgrims.

We do know that Purangir went on pilgrimage to Kailash in 1788, after being given a *lam-yig* by the Panchen Rinpoche entitling him to *'u-lag* (provision of ponies, fuel, and servant cooks at each staging point). He travelled with three attendants and made the usual *parikrama*, along with the bath in Manasarovar.[89]

Other Hindu pilgrims went on very long journeys while undergoing *tapasya* or pennance, some visiting Tibet while so doing. The accounts of two pilgrims who did this were recorded in 1792 and published in *Asiatic Researches* in 1801.[90] Though they are called Gosains we do not know whether they also traded. One of these, Purana Puri, a Rajput *sanyasin*, chose the *urdhbahu,* or arms raised attitude, in which to do pennance. His vow was to maintain this posture for twelve years and additionally not to settle at any one place during this period. This partly accounts for his worldwide travels, which included visits to Afganistan, Arabia, Russia, Iran, Turkey and Malaya. On one journey he entered Tibet from Nepal and went via Tingri to Lhasa. After visiting the Panchen Lama he took 80 days to reach Manasarovar and six to circumbulate it, the usual time being three. He visited Kailash before returning to Lhasa, where he was given letters to take to Warren Hastings in Calcutta.[91]

Paucity of evidence makes it almost impossible to assess numbers of pilgrims, trading or otherwise, visiting Kailash and Manasarovar up to the present century. It is hard, for example, to know whether the treaty negotiated by the British at Lhasa in 1904 which gave Hindu pilgrims free entry into Tibet had any real affect on numbers entering. In 1907, Sherring was told that about 150 *sanyasis* visited annually but that every twelve years a Kumb Mela was held at which up to 400 attended.[92] Bharati gives a figure of 600 pilgrims visiting in 1951.[93]

To conclude, much of my account has rested on the testimonies of British East India Company officials from the late 18th century and it would seem that at this time they had reached the apogee of their economic power. They may have been equally powerful in the preceeding century but the lack of accounts from that period mean that we can form no clear picture at present. The Gosains suffered a severe eclipse in Tibet at the end of the 18th century, the Chinese authorities becoming suspicious of their political activities, probably in the wake of the Nepalese incursion of 1792. Captain Turner wrote that

> a most violent prejudice prevails even against the Hindu Gosains who are charged with treachery against their generous patrons by becoming guides and spies to the enemy and have in consequence, it is said, been prescribed in their customary abode at Tashilunpho.[94]

No doubt Gosains did start visiting Tibet again when the situation cooled, but the sort of official patronage given by the 3rd Panchen Lama may well have been more difficult or even impossible from then on. Looking at the broader picture, Bernard Cohn makes the point that the economic power of Gosains in India decreased as river transport declined in importance with the introduction of rail links from the mid 19th century, especially in relation to the link between the Punjab and eastern India.[95] In the 1970s Gosains were described as no longer engaged in banking or commerce but as still owning large *math*s and houses.[96] Today, according to Cohn, they retain commercial importance only as landlords.

Notes

1 Drawn to my attention in 1985 by Robert Skelton, the then Keeper of the Indian Department at the Victoria and Albert Museum.
2 It forms part of an album depicting castes and occupations dating from c.1760–1800, originally in the collection of Sir Gore Ousley, who was in India in the service of the Nawab of Oudh between 1788–1805.
3 Rogers/Beveridge 1914: 104, 108.
4 Monier-Williams 1974: 367; Yule 1996: 389.
5 Balfour 1871: 378; Russell 1916, vol. 3: 150; Walker 1968: 437.
6 Balfour 1871: 373; Risley 1892: 343, 344; Aiyar 1928–36: 254; Sarcar 1955: 110; Giri 1976: 57.
7 Beveridge 1857: 71; Balfour 1871: 373; Aiyar 1928–36: 254;.
8 The *Tuzuk i Jahangiri* (Rogers/Beveridge 1914: 104, 108) has Gosā'in. The similarly pronounced Gosaeen, a Hindi/Marathi modification of the Sanskrit Goswami is a frequent variation (Yule 1996: 389; Balfour 1871: 378–379; Ghosh 1930: 16). Also commonly found are Gosayi or Gosawyee, Thurston 1909: 298–300); and Ghossain or Goshain (Benett 1877: 24; Ghosh 1930: 16; Bayley 1988: 241). Yule 1996: 389, notes that Gosine was common in the late 19th century.
9 Balfour 1871: 378–379; Benett 1877: 24; Rose 1911: 303–305; Aiyar 1928–36: 254–259; Ghurye 1953: 79, 113; Cohn 1963: 175.
10 Turner 1800: 370; Markham 1876: 128; Cammann 1951: 63; Lamb 1960: 341.
11 Forbes 1813: 226.
12 Ghosh 1930: 18.
13 Markham 1876: 125–126.
14 Sarcar 1931: 124.
15 Turner 1800: 370.
16 Sarcar 1931: 123.
17 Cammann 1951: 63; Yogev 1978: 102–109; Gokhale 1979: 112.
18 Gokhale 1978: 112.
19 Yogev 1978: 106.
20 Gokhale 1979: 112.
21 Yule 1903: 49.
22 For corals see Gerard 1841: 297–298; Aitchison 1874: 164; Warikoo 1988: 72; for pearls see Gerard 1841: 183; Aitchison 1874: 297, 300. For the trade in both products to China see Markham 1876: 125; Lamb 1960: 337, 341.
23 Balfour 1871: 473–474.
24 Schoff 1912: 59 discusses the development of fisheries in the Palk Strait during the 1st century AD.
25 Eliot 1880: 225–226; Balfour 1871: 473–477.
26 Le Beck 1801: 397–399. The fishery was opposite the outlets of the Modaragam Aru and Pomparippu rivers at a bay called "Condatchey".
27 Cohn 1963: 176.
28 Eliot 1880: 226; Balfour 1871: 473–474.
29 Kolff 1971: 214.

30 Benett 1877: 24.
31 Giri 1976: 57.
32 Sarcar 1931: 121; Regmi 1961: 95.
33 Markham 1879: 128.
34 See Markham 1879: 127 on the expulsion of the Gosains from Nepal, and 124–127 on the Kashmiris.
35 Markham 1879: 164.
36 Hamsa 1908: 181; Snelling 1983: 177 quoting Pranavananda who lists the largest markets as rGya-ni-ma, Darchen, Taklakot and Thugolho on Manasarovar.
37 Hamsa 1908: 182.
38 Sherring 1906: 148.
39 Markham 1879: 125; Clarke 1995: 39, 40, see footnote 20, and quoting Bell 1924: 226; Roerich 1931: 256.
40 Clarke 1995: 39, 40 quoting Roerich 1931: 453; Das 1902: 208.
41 Martin Ellis (Edinburgh University) Phd thesis in progress (1996) "Religious Authority and Monastic Structures in Tibetan Buddhism; The Ritual Hierarchies of Lingshet monastery, Ladakh".
42 Information from Martin Ellis (see note 41).
43 Balfour 1871: 378; Risley 1892: 300, who says the married Vaishnavite Gosains in Bengal were termed Grihi or Grihastha; Rose 1911: 304, 305; Sarcar 1955: 113; Giri 1976: 57.
44 Beveridge 1857: 71; Balfour 1871: 378; Benett 1877: 24; Risley 1892: 300; Rose 1911: 304, 305; Sarcar 1955: 112, 113; Giri 1976: 57, 58.
45 Cohn 1963: 176, 177; Kolff 1971: 215; Bayley 1988: 183, 126 footnote 50.
46 Cohn 1963: 181; Bayley 1988: 143.
47 Cohn 1963: 176; Kolff 1971: 217; Bayley 1988: 143.
48 Cohn 1963: 176.
49 Bayley 1988: 143, 184, 185, talks of their exercise of power at the Hardwar Kumb Mela, at major commercial towns and on the fringes of other dominions. A Gosain commander, Himmat Bahadur, carved out a small kingdom in the area of Bundelkhand.
50 Cohn 1963: 177; Bayley 1988: 143, 241.
51 Cohn 1963: 180.
52 Ghosh 1930: 138–156; Sarcar 1955: 180, 274, 276–280; Kolff 1971: 214.
53 Cohn 1963: 176.
54 Cohn 1963: 179.
55 Cohn 1963: 179, 180.
56 Cohn 1963: 180.
57 Cohn 1963: 175 & footnote 2; Bayley 1988: 142, 184.
58 Russell 1916: 155–157.
59 Sarcar 1931: 125.
60 Russell 1916: 156, 157; Sarkar 1955: 82–275; Kolff 1971: 214.
61 For a nearly identical example see Archer 1972: 33: Add or 1644; Tanjore 1822. Also Archer 1972: 247 Add or 1616 from Belgaum on the borders of Karnataka dated 1856. Both BL.
62 Ghosh 1930: 19.
63 Archer 1973, vol. 1: 397, vol. 2: 312.

64 Information from personal correspondence with Dr John Marr (S.O.A.S.), 21 October 1986.
65 Tavernier 1977: 179–180.
66 Russell 1916: vol. 1, fp 184, vol. 2, fp 100.
67 Entwistle 1981/82: 37 nos 27–31.
68 Compare with V&A paintings in Archer 1992: 107, AL 8042: 37 Ganges water carrier, Varanasi c.1815–20 and Archer 1992: 56, AL 8940J, holy water carrier and his wife from Tanjore c.1800. Also BL paintings in Archer 1972: 143, Add or.771, pilgrim from Varanasi carrying Ganges water in baskets, 1830–32 and Archer 1972: 162, Add or.1310, pilgrims carrying wicker baskets, Lucknow 1825–30.
69 Stevenson 1920: 142, 298, 360; Ball 1977, vol. 2: 179–180; Bayley 1988: 128; Fuller 1992: 220.
70 Eck 1983: 289.
71 Bharati 1963: 165.
72 Markham 1876: 87.
73 Turner 1800: 339–340.
74 Markham 1876: 88.
75 Markham 1876: 125–126.
76 Markham 1876: 87.
77 Giri 1976: 104.
78 Cammann 1951: 18 footnote 61 on the alternative numbering of Panchen Lamas, making him the 6th; Richardson 1962: 55 explains the lower numbering as Tibetan, the higher as Chinese.
79 Markham 1876: 87.
80 Bysack 1890: 86–87.
81 Bysack 1890: 87.
82 Bysack 1890: 68–92.
83 Bysack 1890: 90–91.
84 Bysack 1890: 64–65.
85 Cammann 1951: 70–74.
86 Bysack 1890: 66; Cammann 1951: 70–74 discusses the possibility that Purangir invented the audience episode in order to please Hastings.
87 Cammann 1951: 82–101, 106.
88 Sarcar 1932: 87; Camman 1951: 127.
89 Bysack 1890: 87, 99.
90 Duncan 1801: 37–52.
91 Duncan 1801: 43–45; Welch 1978: 80, 81, illus.32, a & b.
92 Sherring 1906: 144.
93 Bharati 1965: 96.
94 Cammann 1951: 142.
95 Cohn 1963: 181.
96 Giri 1976: 58.

Chapter 4

Khyung-sprul 'Jigs-med nam-mkha'i rdo-rje (1897–1955)

An Early Twentieth-century Tibetan Pilgrim in India

Per Kværne

Khyung-sprul 'Jigs-med nam-mkha'i rdo-rje (1897–1955) belonged to a generation of Tibetans who were well aware of, and sometimes even familiar with, the greater world surrounding Tibet, but who were at the same time deeply imbued with traditional Tibetan culture and learning. Like a small number of other Tibetan monks in the first half of this century, Khyung-sprul travelled as a pilgrim in India, and has left fairly detailed records of his travels.

The most famous of these Tibetan monks is of course dGe-'dun chos-'phel (1905–51), who stayed in India from 1935 to 1946. His considerable literary output includes not only various translations as well as original doctrinal and historical works, but also a small guidebook to the Buddhist holy places of pilgrimage in India, first published in 1939 and frequently reprinted thereafter.[1] Another such pilgrim is rKyang-btsun Shes-rab rnam-rgyal, who travelled in India in the mid-1940s, and whose account is remarkable chiefly for its interpretation of the various places he visited in a mental context which is entirely that of traditional Bonpo mythology and ritual.[2]

Khyung-sprul was not, it seems – in contrast to dGe-'dun chos-'phel –, eager to assimilate the knowledge and ways of thought of the outside world. Spiritually and intellectually he remained inside the traditional Tibetan world. He was, however, a man with a practical bent of mind, well aware of the advantages of modern facilities in India. It is also worth noting that his first visit to India was a good deal earlier than that of Gendun Chomphel, as he arrived in Kalimpong in 1922, returning to Tibet in 1925. This visit was followed by two further visits: a prolonged stay, chiefly in Kinnaur, the region along the upper course of the River Sutlej in Himachal

Pradesh, from 1931 to 1934 or 35, and finally a briefer visit in 1948. He visited all the major places of pilgrimage of Buddhism in India, such as Bodh Gaya, Nalanda, Rajgir, Sarnath and Sanci, besides mTsho Padma (Rewalsar) near Mandi. He also visited Varanasi, Haridwar, and Amritsar.

During his second stay he was active as a missionary in Kinnaur, where he acquired many followers and is still remembered. He was also active as a publisher of books; it is clear that he soon discovered that books could be produced much more quickly and cheaply in India than by the traditional xylographic method in Tibet, and he had large numbers of books printed in Delhi and sent to Tibet, an activity which was carried on by his disciples until conditions in Tibet in the early 1950s made this impracticable.

His activities in Kinnaur would merit a separate and detailed study, as the sources for the history of the religion of this region seem to be particularly meagre. Here we can of course only touch on this theme. Returning to Tibet in 1935 he founded a monastery in Khyung-lung in the Kailash-Manasarovar region of western Tibet, and the remaining twenty years of his life were spent in this monastery, apart from the visit to India in 1948 referred to above.

Our main source for the life of Khyung-sprul is a two-volume biography written by the Bonpo scholar dPal-ldan tshul-khrims (1902–73).[3] dPal-ldan tshul-khrims was a disciple of Khyung-sprul from the early 1930s and certainly knew his master intimately. On the basis of this biography, I shall give a brief presentation of the life of Khyung-sprul, with special emphasis on his travels in India, present some information on his activities in Kinnaur, and deal only very briefly with his career as a much respected lama in Tibet. Although this text is, strictly speaking, not an autobiography, it is nevertheless clearly to a large extent based either on notes which Khyung-sprul kept or on direct dictation by Khyung-sprul himself. The narrative is frequently in the first person, so that I shall often refer to it as if it were an autobiography.

Khyung-sprul was born in 1897 into a powerful and well-to-do nomad family in Khyung-po, the Ga-rgya clan, which originally came from Amdo. His grandfather was Ga-rgya Tshe-brtan grags-pa who was the chief minister (*blon-chen*) of the king of Hor (Hor spyi-khyab rgyal-po), 'a man skilled in dharma (*chos*) as well as worldly affairs' (vol. I, p. 55). His father, Ga-rgya bSod-nams brtan-dar, was the oldest of three brothers. He, too, was 'brave, able, rich and energetic', and became the minister (*mdun-blon*) and treasurer (*hyag-mpdzod*) of Hor.

Khyung-sprul took his first monastic vows (*rab-'byung*) in 1911 (lcags-mo-phag) from sGo-ston Nyi-ma rgyal-mtshan (p. 132). Somewhat later he met the lama whom he refers to as his 'root-lama', sPa-ston Nyi-ma 'bum-gsal (p. 160) who was born in 1854.[4] Khyung-sprul wanted to go on an extended pilgrimage, and proposed three alternative routes. This passage is interesting, as it shows rather precisely which pilgrimage tours seemed attractive to a Bonpo at the time. The first would take him to Ri rtse-drug in Khyung-po, Kha-ba dkar-po, Bon-ri in rKong-po,[5] and rTsva-ri[6] (p. 163). The second began with the major Bonpo monastery of sMan-ri[7] and other places of pilgrimage in gTsang, then continued to the stupas of Nepal, Mount Kailash[8] and Lake Manasarovar (Gangs-ri mTsho Ma-pham), and finally Khyung-lung dngul-mkhar, the ancient site on the upper course of the River Sutlej between Manasarovar and mTho-lding (Tholing), identified in Bonpo tradition as the ancient centre of the kingdom of Zhang-zhung. The third alternative was to go to Derge, visit the lamas Shar-rdza Rin-po-che, i.e. Shar-rdza bKra-shis rgyal-mtshan (1859–1935)[9] and Nyag-gter gSang-sngags gling-pa (b. 1864), and then proceed to rGyam rDo-ti gangs-dkar, rMa-chen pom-ra, mTsho Khri-shog (i.e. mTsho-sngon), and rGya-nag glang-chen etc., 'in order to meditate'.

The lama answered that while all three circuits were excellent, he advised him to go to sTod Zhang-zhung mNga'-ris, because 'although this was the region where Bon had originated, nowadays not even the name of Bon existed there' (pp. 165–166). Khyung-sprul was thus set on a course which was to combine pilgrimage and missionary activities, and which was destined to characterize much of his career.

He accordingly left his home in 1919 (sa-mo-lug). He first went to sMan-ri Monastery in gTsang (pp. 209–210) where he was installed in the La-dbyil khang-tshan and was received by the abbot Phun-tshogs blo-gros (b. 1876). In the presence of the abbot he took the vows of a fully ordained monk (pp. 221–222). He received the monastic name of g.Yung-drung rgyal-mtshan dpal-bzang-po, and sent his servants and pack animals back to his home country with the message to his parents that he would leave on pilgrimage.

First Journey to India (c. 1920–1925)

After about a year, he set forth on his first journey, which first of all took him and a companion, another disciple of Nyi-ma 'bum-gsal, to Bhutan (Lho-'brug) (p. 314). The following episode can serve as an example of the lively style of the narrative:

'One day, near Phag-ri, they met a group of about twenty traders who had many horses and mules, and who had halted to boil tea. When the two monks asked for *tsampa* this was willingly given them. An old man then asked where they came from and where they were going. They replied that they were from Khyung-po in Khams and that they were on a pilgrimage without any fixed destination, but at the moment they were on their way to Bhutan. Another trader from the group then jokingly said: "In Bhutan two monks like you can obtain a good living, and you can obtain good women!" – and everybody laughed. Another one said, "Don't talk like that! Not all monks are the same. Although monks who go to Bhutan generally take wives, these two do not seem to be like that, so don't gather the sin of empty talk!"' (p. 315). Khyung-sprul then sang to them a religious song about not needing a wife, after which they all prostrated and asked for his blessing (317), and gave the two monks gifts of tea and butter (318).

On reaching Bhutan, the two monks went to sTag-tshang in the sPa-gro valley. This place, otherwise associated with Padmasambhava, is described as 'a great holy place of Bon treasure' (p. 319) as treasures were deposited there by Bla-chen Dran-pa nam-mkha'[10] and Khyung-po Gyer-chen Zla-med[11], and discovered (1038) by Khu-tsha Zla-'od-'bar (b. 1024)[12]. While they stayed there in retreat, they received food and other gifts from the king of Bhutan (pp. 322–323). The king in question, although not mentioned by name, is the first king of Bhutan, Ugyen Wangchuk, who reigned from 1907 to 1926. They stayed for a week in a cave at sTag-tshang and thereafter two months at Chu-mo-phug (p. 323) which is also in the Pharo Valley[13] – the latter is a holy place connected with the Bonpo *dakini* Thugs-rjes kun-grol and said by Khyung-sprul to have been particularly excellent for meditation.

When the king of Bhutan heard that they were planning to leave, he called them to his palace. He said that if they would stay in Bhutan, they could build a new hermitage at sTag-tshang or stay wherever they wished, if only they would impart religious instruction to himself or to whoever requested it (pp. 330–331). Accordingly they stayed for five months in Nyams-med lha-khang, reciting the Buddhist Kanjur (*rgyal-ba'i bka'-'gyur chos-pa-can*) (p. 331). One day, however, not feeling well after the midday-meal brought by an old woman living close by, they understood that poison had been mixed with the food. So, composing a poem for the king 'in the fashion of Nagarjuna's "Letter to a Friend",' they secretly left Bhutan one evening in the direction of Jo-mo lha-ri (p. 332).

Thereupon they reached Gro-mo (Lho Gro-mo; the Chumbi Valley), where they stayed forty days in Pad-ma-dgon. The monks and lay people of Gro-mo came to him to ask for advice concerning the conflict between Bon and Buddhism in Gro-mo (p. 347) caused by the recent Gelugpa proselytizing efforts in the valley.

They then crossed the rDzi-li-la (Jelep-la) on the border between Tibet and India and came down to Kalimpong (p. 354). Here they seem once more to have been the butt of good-natured banter: 'While descending to Kalimpong, they met a group of Tibetans, men and women, coming up towards the pass. They asked the two monks where they were going, and they replied, "In the direction of Kalimpong. Is it far?" "No, it is very near, you can reach it today". One of the Tibetans said: "Today two girls in Kalimpong will each obtain a suitor" – and everyone laughed. Khyung-sprul and his companion were apparently not amused, and in reply Khyung-sprul again sang one of his spiritual songs.

From Shiliguri they travelled by train and visited Nalanda, Rajgir, and the Vulture's Peak (p. 364). They then continued to Bodh Gaya and the various holy places in that vicinity, before travelling on to Gaya, Sarnath and Varanasi (p. 364). From there Khyung-sprul went to Kusinagara, Gorakhpur, and Raksaul, where he entered Nepal. He remarks that up to that point, he and his companion had spent twenty *rupis* each on train fares. From the border he reached Kathmandu (Bal-yul mchod-rten) in seven days. There he prostrated and cicumambulated Svayambhunath, Bodhnath and other holy places (pp. 365–366).

I have discussed his itinerary so far in detail – in fact he mentions scores of other places which he passed through en route – to show the extent of his travels and that he was well aware of all the Buddhist sites of pilgrimage. I do not know to what extent his pilgrimage was planned in detail at the outset, but he certainly quickly learned how to find his way around in India, in spite, as he explicitly states, of not being able to speak any Indian language (p. 433).

Apparently he stayed two years in Nepal, as his biography informs us that he returned to India in 1924. In Nepal he stayed in a place of meditation called A-su-ra'i brag-phug (p. 372) in Yol-mo (Helambu) on the border between Tibet and Nepal, famous as the spot where gSang-ba 'dus-pa,[14] in Bonpo tradition the name of a *siddha*, subdued the host of haughty gods and demons (*sde-brgyad g.yen-dgu*). I shall not go into further detail now concerning his stay in Nepal, as this is a terrain which at all times has seen Tibetan pilgrims, and instead concentrate on his travels in India where he returned, as already mentioned, in 1924 (shing byi lo) (p. 426).

Khyung-sprul now entered India for the second time, at Raksaul, proceeded to Gorakhpur and Kaunpur, and reached Delhi (p. 432). For each stage of the journey the exact times of departure and arrival are given, so that it is difficult to imagine that he did not keep some form of diary. For example, he says that he left Delhi at nine o'clock in the evening and arrived at Kalka at six o'clock in the morning (p. 432). Clearly he must have gone by night-train, by the Kalka-Howrah Mail which has almost exactly the same schedule today. He notes that from Raxaul to Kalka the train fare for each person was forty rupis. From Kalka he walked to mTsho Padma (Rewalsar), which took five days (p. 433).

After having spent a week at mTsho Padma and circumambulated the lake many times, they continued on foot and reached Rampur, the capital of Kinnaur, in five or six days.

It is not clear to me to what extent Khyung-sprul regarded his travel to Kinnaur as an actual pilgrimage, although he does refer to Kinnaur (Khu-nu) as somehow connected with Zhang-zhung. He certainly, as we shall see, regarded it as a missionary venture. As such, it was rather successful, and he is still remembered and revered in parts of Kinnaur today.

In Rampur he was met by the lay-patron bSod-nams zla-ba. Whether this was a person he already knew, or whether his reputation was already so great that people from Kinnaur, who were generally followers of Tibetan Buddhism, would come down to Rampur to meet him, is not known. From Rampur he travelled – on foot, of course – for one week and reached the village of Lid in Kinnaur, where he met the lama bSod-nams 'brug-rgyas. This lama, a native of the village of Lid where his descendants still live, is famous as the author of a calendar (*lo-tho*) which is still updated and reprinted each year by his descendants. Khyung-sprul stayed with this lama for two months, studying astrology (*rtsis-skar*). In 1928 Khyung-sprul, too, became the author of a work on astrology and calendrical calculations.[15] He also performed rituals in the homes of these two Kinnauri patrons (pp. 433–434), as well as giving long-life initiation (*tshe dbang-bskur*) and sermons to about 800 people there. Thereupon he did the same in A-sa-rang and sPi (p. 434). He also offered tea to the monks in the monasteries in these three districts. He then left Kinnaur and, entering Tibet, reached Tholing (p. 436).

We shall not dwell on his travels in Western Tibet. One event, however, was to be of particular importance for his future life. He relates that he planned to travel with his companion to Ladakh, Kashmir, Swat (O-rgyan), Gilgit (Bru-sha) and so on, in order to meditate 'in a place where not even the name of Tibet was known, much less that of their home country; a lonely spot in the mountains or forest where there was no-one to see them, no doctor to treat them if they became ill, no lama to attend to them if they died' (p. 453). This radical ascetic project was however not to be carried out, for his companion died, and he abandoned the project.

Second Journey to India (1930–1935)

His second stay in India began in 1930 (lcags-rta-lo) (p. 579). In this year he circumambulated Mount Kailash, as this was a particularly auspicious year for this pilgrimage, being a Year of the Horse (gnas-chen gangs-dkar Ti-se'i dus-bzang 'gyur-chen yin). He describes the various sacred places connected with Mount Kailash (pp. 579–581). It was at this time that he met dPal-ldan tshul-khrims, who was one of a group of monks coming from Hor (p. 587) and who thereafter remained continuously with him (p. 588).

Khyung-sprul had at this point made Khyung-lung his base, and had many disciples and lay patrons in the surrounding region. However, he now left once more for Kinnaur, which he now refers to as Zhang-zhung rong-pa Khu-nu'i yul (p. 589), so there must by now (if not before) have been to his mind a definite connection between Kinnaur and Zhang-zhung. He mentions a number of places where he gave long-life initiations, blessings etc., including Pu, Ka-nam and Lid-thang. He also gives the various stages of his itinerary to Rampur, where he had an audience with the Rajah, whom he refers to as 'Khu nu rgyal po'(p. 589). This was Padam Sing (1914–1947), the last Rajah of the hill state of Bushahr,[16] with its capital at Rampur (p. 608).

Khyung-sprul thereupon sent most of his disciples off to mTsho Padma, while he himself continued to Shimla accompanied by only a few disciples. From Shimla he went by train to Kalka, Ambhala, Saharanpur, and Haridwar where he had a bath in the Ganges (p. 589). He continued to Muradabad, Lucknow, and Varanasi; then to Bihar, including Gaya (p. 590), Bodh Gaya (with the temple, which he refers to as a *stupa*, and the tree of Enlightenment), and all the various Buddhist places of pilgrimage in the vicinity which he had already visited in 1922.

He then returned via Gaya, Varanasi, Allahabad, Kaunpur, Agra, and Delhi, where he stayed for about a month, in order to have 500 copies of a text printed there. I imagine that he must have been one of the first, if not the first Tibetan monk to have religious texts printed outside of Tibet by modern techniques, a procedure which he obviously had realized was much quicker and cheaper than having them printed in Tibet in the traditional manner.

He then went to Amritsar, where he caught up with the disciples whom he had sent off on pilgrimage to mTsho Padma. In Amritsar they circumambulated and made offerings at the Golden Temple, which Khyung-sprul somewhat inaccurately refers to as 'Guru Nanak's palace' (Gu-ru Na-nig-gi pho-brang). It is interesting to compare his brief and matter-of-fact description with the lyrical but entirely imaginary interpretation of the Golden Temple provided by the otherwise unknown Bonpo monk rKyang-btsun Shes-rab-rnam rgyal who visited the spot a few years later and who states that as for the worshippers at the temple, 'Their principal *gshen* is the Subduing *gshen* with the "bird-horns".' His secret name is Guru Nanak. His teachings were the Bon of Relative and Absolute Truth. He holds in his hand the Sword of Wisdom . . . At this holy place the oceanic assembly of the tutelary gods and buddhas . . . gather like clouds" – and so on.[17]

From Amritsar the group went by bus back to Mandi and mTsho Padma. By now we are in 1931 (lcags-lug). Khyung-sprul returned to Rampur and performed a special ritual for the queen in order that she might have a son[18] (p. 591). As a matter of fact she subsequently gave birth to a son, who later became a prominent political figure in Himachal Pradesh.

From Rampur, Khyung-sprul followed the Sutlej to upper Kinnaur (Khu-stod) and again reached Lid-thang. This was the beginning of an extended stay in Kinnaur lasting four years. Besides teaching and performing rituals, his main activity during these years was to suppress the custom of worshipping the local mountain gods (*yul-lha*) with animal sacrifices. He first stopped such worship in the village of sPang, where the *yul-lha* was styled bSam-grub dbang-rgyal (p. 592). In all he bound sixteen *yul-lha* of Kinnaur in an oath not to demand animal sacrifices and made them promise to be protectors of Bon (p. 593). A graphic account, as well as photos, of such a sacrifice, dating from a visit to Kinnaur in 1926, is provided by the Dutch geologist W.G.N. van der Sleen.[19]

As mentioned, this missionary activity certainly would merit detailed study, but as it is somewhat peripheral to the theme of the present volume, viz. pilgrimage, this will have to be a task for the future. Among the many details provided, I must nevertheless point out a particularly detailed description of the cult of the local deity (*yul-lha*) in the village of Morang (Khu-nu Mu-rang) (pp. 624 ff). Here, we are told, the villagers used to sacrifice no less than nine hundred goats and sheep every year to the two local *yul-lha*. They also had a temple devoted to this practice, which is described in detail and which seems to have been a particularly fearsome place, covered by blood and pieces of flesh. However, some of the villagers said that if the Tibetan lama could stay there during the night without being harmed, they would abandon the practice of animal sacrifice, so Khyung-sprul entered the temple and practiced *gcod* there, and, as we might expect, left the temple next morning entirely unmolested (p. 629).

There is a minor but interesting piece of information relating to the year 1933 when he sent two of his disciples to his home country in Khyung-po to obtain books. The books were sent by mail from Gyantse to the 'capital of Kinnaur' (Khu-nu'i rgyal-sa) Cin (i.e. Cini) via India (p. 633). Khyung-sprul as we see was fully aware of the advantages of well-organised postal services.

A prominent Western scholar who visited Kinnaur in the same year, viz. 1933, was Giuseppe Tucci. Tucci and his companion, Captain E. Ghersi, visited many of the villages where Khyung-sprul was active. However, there is no mention of Khyung-sprul or of his activities. There is, however, an interesting remark concerning the missionary activities of Tibetan monks in Kinnaur at the time:

> The Hindu dynasties of Bashahr favoured the revival of local traditions more or less coloured with Hinduism; now there is a notable tendency to return to Lamaism, due, above all, to the the apostolic propaganda work of certain missionaries and "Incarnates", particularly of the sects *rNin ma pa* and *dGe lugs pa* . . . who are establishing themselves here with a continually increasing following and are making converts here . . . and, which is strange, they are almost all from Khams, on the borders of China.[20]

As mentioned, Khyung-sprul's second stay in India lasted five years. At the end of this period he accepted an invitation from laypeople in Khyung-lung. He accordingly returned to Tibet in 1935 and founded a monastery in Khyung-lung at a place called Gu-ru-gyam.

In the course of the following years this monastery was built with the help of various lay patrons and donors, including his family in

Khyung-po. Thus we learn that his father was still alive, and supplied complete sets of the Kanjur and the Tenjur, though whether the Bonpo or the Buddhist version is meant, is not clear. We are, however, told that the texts arrived loaded on 35 yaks driven by four men (vol. II, p. 36). We are also told that the abbot of sMan-ri monastery in gTsang, the most prestigious of all Bonpo monasteries, visited Khyung-sprul's monastery in the summer of 1936, and that Khyung-sprul requested an affiliation to sMan-ri for his monastery. This abbot was bsTan-pa blo-gros, who declared that Khyung-sprul was the incarnation of the eighth century Bonpo sage Dran-pa nam-mkha' (p. 39).

Another episode, which would merit further investigation, occurred in the late summer of 1940 (lcags-'brug-lo) (p. 50), when about 800 'border barbarians from the north' (*byang-phyogs-kyi mtha'-mi*) identified as Kazakh (ha-sag-kha) descended on the monastery and pillaged it, taking whatever had any value, including animals, food and clothes, taking even the cloth and wooden boards in which the Kanjur was wrapped (p. 52). However, the Kazakhs were chased into Ladakh by the Tibetan army, where most of them died of disease, hunger and cold during the winter (p. 53). As for Khyung-sprul and his disciples, they spent the winter collecting the scattered pages of the Kanjur and trying to put together the volumes once more.

In 1948 (sa-pho-khyi, erroneous for sa-byi) he met the 16th Karmapa (b. 1924)[21] – in fact, we are constantly reminded of Khyung-sprul's ecumenical attitude: Bon and Buddhism seem to have been equally valid in his view.

Third Journey to India (1948)

Khyung-sprul's third and final journey to India took place in 1948. We are told that in the autumn he wanted to go to India once more, partly to buy paper etc. for printing books, and partly in order to go on pilgrimage. Accordingly he left his monastery at Gur-gyam in Khyung-lung on the 27th of the 8th Tibetan month together with several monks (p. 90). He entered India by the Niti-la (Nyi-ti) and descended through Garhwal via Joshimath, Chamoli, Karnaprayag, Shrinagar, and Pauri, reaching the Ganges at Haridwar (p. 90). From here he went by train to Amritsar via Saharanpur, Ambala and Ludhiana. In Amritsar he visited the Golden Temple once more (p. 91). From Pathankot he then went to Mandi and mTsho Padma before going down to Delhi where he made arrangements to have more books printed (p. 95).

From Delhi he then travelled south to Mathura and Agra, and on to Sanchi where he circumambulated the stupa of Sanchi (p. 95), which he notes was built by Emperor Ashoka as 'the chief of the ten million *stupas* of the world'. Then he went north again by train to Jhansi, Allahabad and Varanasi. Continuing east, he visited Bodh Gaya for the third time, and, as before, the various places of pilgrimage in the surroundings. From Patna he reached Raksaul (p. 96) where he entered Nepal and went on foot to Kathmandu with its two famous *stupas* which he duly worshipped. He then returned as he had come, visited Kushinagara and Lumbini and travelled via Gorakhpur to Muradabad, then north to Ramnagar, and from here he again entered Tibet by the same route that he had come (p. 97). Why he did not choose to visit Kinnaur again, is not explained.

Although this was Khyung-phrul's last visit to India, he sent his disciple dPal-ldan tshul-khrims across the Niti-la in 1949 to Delhi to print books, which he brought back to the monastery on horses and mules in 30 boxes (p. 99), and again in 1953 (chu-mo-sbrul), when he had texts printed in Delhi (p. 125). Among the texts of which he organised the printing during his last years was the gSung-'bum of Shar-rdza bKra-shis rgyal-mtshan in thirteen volumes. He established a fund (*mchod-rgyun rten-rtsa*) to continue the teaching activities in the monastery, for which purpose he set aside 4,000 sheep and 100 head of cattle (184), appointing brTson-grus Rin-po-che (1914–1985) from the monastery at Ri-bo rtse-drug in Khyung-po as the teacher and authorizing eight monks to be his students (p. 143). brTson-grus Rin-po-che had been a disciple of Shar-rdza Rin-po-che; he eventually escaped to India where I met him a number of times. His passing away in 1985 is believed by many Bonpos to have been accompanied by miraculous signs such as rainbows and relic pills.[22]

We have at least one independent source describing Khyung-sprul's monastery in Khyunglung, viz. the extraordinary spiritual autobiography and travelogue of Anagarika Govinda, *The Way of the White Clouds*. Anagarika Govinda visited the Kailash region in September 1948. He tells how he arrived at a monastery which was evidently recently built, but which was strangely deserted, except for the abbot, a caretaker, and, he was told (although he apparently did not see them) some nuns living in caves above the monastery. The German pilgrim only gradually realized that he had come to a Bonpo monastery. He had two brief audiences with the abbot, whom he does not name, but whom he describes as 'a simply clad, middle-aged man with an intelligent face and dignified bearing'.[23] This meeting must have taken place just a month or two before Khyung-sprul's departure for India. Govinda provides a number of details concerning the monastic buildings: he was particularly impressed by a row of latrines by the main entrance to the monastery, built for the convenience of pilgrims – a most unusual structure in Tibet.[24] The idea of building latrines must have occurred to Khyung-sprul during one of his visits to India. He also describes Khyung-sprul's room in which he was received as having the walls entirely covered by innumerable small paper colour prints, producing a pleasing, fresco-like effect. This unexpected decoration was, Govinda was told, the result of the abbot's printing activities in India, and the abbot in fact showed him a number of texts which he had printed there. As Govinda notes, 'Although the titles seemed familiar to me, the texts contained curious names and mantras, which led me to doubt that they really could be Buddhist texts',[25] it is clear that Khyung-sprul at no point explicitly told his visitor that he was a Bonpo.

In general, Govinda says that he was impressed by the 'cleanliness and solidity of the buildings', which had a 'fortress-like compactness and reflected the planning and determination of an intelligent and determined personality'.[26] An indication of the highly venerated status of the lama is perhaps the fact, which Govinda notes to his surprise, that on entering the main prayer hall, he did not face an image of a deity, but the throne of the abbot standing against an empty wall.[27]

Finally, Govinda gives a highly dramatic account of the recent pillaging of the monastery by Muslim robbers, to which I have already referred. His informant was the Tibetan driver of his caravan of yaks, and according to this source – whom we may perhaps suspect of slightly exaggerating events – all the monks had been either killed or abused, and the abbot himself beaten, stripped and left for dead,[28] – none of these details being mentioned by Khyung-sprul himself in the biography.

Khyung-sprul passed away, as we have seen, in 1955 (p. 153) (shing-mo-lug) (not, by the way, as is sometimes stated, in 1956). During his final illness, he was attended on by his disciple dPal-ldan Tshul-khrims, and he entrusted him with the task of writing his biography. He had frequently been requested by his disciples to write his autobiography (I: 27), but his various religious activities had never left him with sufficient time. The master copy (*dpar-rtsa*) of the biography was accordingly written by dPal-ldan Tshul-khrims (and another monk, whom he refers to simply as 'mkhas-mchog') in 1957 (me-bya-lo) (pp. 181 and 193). A monk was thereupon sent to Delhi, and 300 copies of the *rnam-thar* printed there. Including producing the master copy and transport, more than 4,000 *rupis* were spent in printing the biography (p. 181). In the following year (sa-khyi-lo) the lama's remains were enshrined in *stupas* made of silver and gold (ibid.).

Summing up, there is perhaps not much to add on the topic of Khyung-sprul as a pilgrim, although I hope I have succeeded in indicating that his biography would repay further study. He was a gifted scholar, and in particular he was the author of an important medical treatise which Samten Gyaltsen Karmay has characterised as 'the most comprehensive Tibetan medical work yet to appear'.[29] As already mentioned, he composed a work on astrology, and he also wrote a treatise on grammar.[30]

There is no doubt that Khyung-sprul was profoundly committed to the Bon religion and tradition, and the only photo I have been able to find of him, shows him wearing the typical *pad-zhwa*, "Lotus-hat", of a fully ordained Bonpo monk.[31] On the other hand, it is equally clear that in many situations he was very discreet about his Bonpo identity, as we have already seen in connection with Govinda's visit to his monastery. In one of his numerous spiritual songs, he refers to himself as 'a tiger cub ... who is striped, for he has no preference for either Buddhism or Bon; joyfully the tiger cub roams the hills and valleys of non-attachment and impartiality, leaping through the forests of India, Zhang-zhung and O-rgyan' (vol. I, p. 511).

Notes

1 For a penetrating study of dGe-'dun chos-'phel, see Stoddard 1985, *passim*. The guide-book in question is *rGya gar gyi gnas chen khag la 'grod pa'i lam yig. Guide to Buddhist Sacred Places in India*, Calcutta (Maha Bodhi Society), 1939.
2 Ramble 1995, *passim*.
3 *The Biography of Khyun-sprul 'jigs-med-nam-mkha'i-rdo-rje ... together with the Zal gdams and Nams mgur of Khyun-sprul. Reproduced from a lithographic print published in Delhi in 1957*, two vols., Tibetan Bonpo Monastic Centre, New Thobgyal, P.O. Ochghat, H.P., 1972. Tibetan title: *Khyab bdag 'khor lo'i mgon po khas grub 'Jigs med nam mkha'i rnam thar dad brgya'i rma bya rnam par brtse ba*.
4 His biography has been published a few years ago in India (no date or place of publication indicated): *sKyes bu chen po Nyi ma 'bum gsal dbang*

gi rgyal po'i rnam thar nor bu'i phreng ba, by Rig-'dzin Ka-dag mthong-grol.
5 On the sacred mountain rKong-po Bon-ri, see Karmay 1992.
6 On the monastery of sMan-ri, see Kværne 1970.
7 On Kailash, see Filibeck 1988 and Snelling 1990.
8 On Shar-rdza bKra-shis rgyal-mtshan, see Karmay 1972: xv–xvi, and Dixey 1993: 17–29.
9 On gSang-sngags gling-pa, see Karmay 1972: 189.
10 On Dran-pa nam-mkha', see Blondeau 1985: 113–115, and Kværne 1995a: 119.
11 On Khu-tsha Zla-'od-'bar, see Karmay 1972: 145–148.
12 Aris 1979: 337.
13 *Op.cit.*: 157.
14 On gSang-ba 'dus-pa, see Karmay 1972: xxi, and Kværne 1995a: 118.
15 Listed in Karmay 1977: 147–148.
16 Samkrtyayan 1990: 244.
17 Ramble 1995: 110.
18 The son was Virbhadra Singh, who is currently (1997) serving as Chief Minister of that state.
19 van der Sleen 1927: 85–91 (with photos). I wish to thank Dr W. van Spengen for kindly bringing this interesting book to my attention.
20 Tucci & Ghersi 1935: 66–67.
21 On the 16th Karmapa, see Douglas and White 1976: 107–122.
22 On brTson-grus Rin-po-che, see Dixey 1993: 137.
23 Govinda 1969: 337.
24 *Op.cit.*: 340
25 *Op.cit.*: 338.
26 *Op.cit.*: 342.
27 *Op.cit.*: 341.
28 *Op.cit.*: 336.
29 Listed in Karmay 1977: 150.
30 I wish to thank Dr Peter Verhagen, Leiden, for bringing the existence of a grammatical treatise attributed to Khyung-sprul to my attention. The text in question is entitled *dByangs can sgra mdo'i 'grel pa rgyal yum bZang bza' rin btsun gi dgongs bcud dpyod ldan bye ba'i mgul rgyan srid gsum dga' ba'i snying nor*, 2 vols, Delhi 1974 (lithographic ed., Delhi 1955).
31 I do not know when this photo, in a private collection in India, was taken. Judging from the features, I would guess that Khyung-sprul was in his late thirties or forties when the photo was taken. There is a photo of "The Lama of Gurugem Bonpa (*sic*) Monastery", i.e. of Khyung-sprul (shown in profile) in Li Gotami Govinda, *Tibet in Pictures. A Journey into the Past*, vol. 2, Berkeley (Dharma Publishing), 1979, p. 121.

Chapter 5

On Pilgrimage for Forty Years in the Himalayas

The Female Lama Jetsun Lochen Rinpoche's (1865–1951) Quest for Sacred Sites

Hanna Havnevik

In the Buddhist Himalayan cultures pilgrimage has been a salient feature for centuries, but has been severely disrupted in Tibet by the Chinese occupation. Due to the Chinese presence, however, pilgrimage has in the last decades taken on new significance and become part of a process of religio-cultural revitalization and political protest in Lhasa and in other areas of Tibet.[1]

Tibetan pilgrimage is an inclusive religious activity where lay and clerics, women and men, young and old participate, although gender differences are often sharply marked.[2] In spite of the fact that a large proportion of pilgrims in the Himalayas are female, their participation has received little attention in the scholarly literature until recently. The religious practices and pilgrimages of women are poorly documented in Tibetan sources too, but we are fortunate to have a small number of texts written by or about female pilgrims in traditional Tibet, and these are valuable in order for us to understand all aspects of Tibetan pilgrimage. The material presented here is based on Jetsun Lochen Rinpoche's autobiography (*rnam thar*).[3] She was a famous Ris med[4] master active in Tibet up till the Chinese occupation; she died in 1951. This paper attempts to give an account of her pilgrimages during a period of around forty years, from 1865 to 1904.

Lochen Rinpoche was presumably born in 1865[5] and in 1904, when she was 39 years old, she settled more or less permanently at Shugseb, near Longchen Rabjampa's (Klong chen rab 'byams pa, 1308–1363) cave at Gangri Thökar (Gangs ri thod dkar)[6] south of Lhasa. From then on she only sporadically left for shorter trips. In order to organize this very rich and detailed material (approximately the first half of the autobiography), I have chosen to present her very long pilgrimages in three periods:

1 Her childhood years, up to the age of 13, when Lochen travelled with her parents, 1865–1877.
2 The pilgrimages with her root lama, Pema Gyatso and his disciples, 1877–c.1890.
3 Independent pilgrimages, c.1890–1904.

Lochen Rinpoche summarically mentions places of pilgrimage by name in the *rnam thar*, but seldom describes the sites, e.g. which buildings they consist of, which statues they contain etc. She is not at all concerned with giving a guide to pilgrimage-sites and apparently assumes this to be known by her followers and the potential readers of her autobiography. Lochen's interest is rather in the sanctity of places and people and how her own nature communicates with what she conceives as sacred. As her descriptions of holy places are scant and as most pilgrimage routes and sites in the Himalayas have been dealt with in detail by others, I will restrict myself here to giving only a very general overview of the places visited by Lochen, with tentative dates. The emphasis will be more on contextualizing Lochen's travels by focussing on social and economic factors, e.g. who Lochen travelled with, their number, their clothing, how they made a living and their religious focus and functions.

I am interested in the 'process of sanctification,' how the sacred accumulated over time in this remarkable woman and made her a saint in her own right. This sacrality accrued from a number of meritorious religious acts of which pilgrimage is but one, but closely intermingled with other "sacred" activities. In my reading of Lochen Rinpoche's *rnam thar* I pay particular attention to gender and try to discern gender-specific experiences related to the pilgrimages, such as whether gender is relevant when it comes to choice of sites of pilgrimage, the exclusion of women at holy places, the gender of the deities worshipped, of her companions, teachers and lamas and finally Lochen's and her nun friends' self-conception and how they are regarded by the larger society.

Lochen Rinpoche's story covers large geographical and cultural areas. Her closest relations during the first half of her life were with her Nepali mother,[7] her father from the Chongye Valley in Central Tibet[8] and a Lama from Amdo.[9] While the *ram thar* was put into writing by a nun from Central Tibet,[10] whom we must presume had a rudimentary education, it was edited by a lama from Kham, who was more learned, but not to very high standards.[11] Thus it is sometimes hard to identify places from the spelling and there is frequent use of abbreviations. We also come across very general geographical references like "the snow mountain" (*gangs ri*), "the valley-areas" (*rong mtshams*), "the market place(s)" (*khrom (sa)/tshong(s) sa*) etc. Lochen also visited a number of small, local sanctuaries, such as nunneries, which are poorly described both in Tibetan and Western works. Further difficulties arise when local sites of pilgrimage are known under several names.

Childhood pilgrimages with her parents 1865–1877 [Tsopema]

Lochen was born at Tsopema/Rewalsar[12] in India, presumably in 1865. Before her birth, her Nepalese mother had a vision of her desceased husband, the Drukpa Lama Kaliwa ('Brug pa Bla ma Kha li ba),[13] telling her to wander without direction through the kingdoms (*rgyal khams*).[14] The mother was apprehensive as she did not know other than her native language, but decided to exchange her household-life with that of an intinerant pilgrim. For the Nepalese mother, important places of pilgrimage were Kailash, Muktinath, Tsopema and Gasha Khandroling (Lahoul).

It is interesting to note that the mother, Tshentsar (mTshan mtshar) or Penpa Dronma (sPen pa sgron ma), carried stones on her back to or around Tang Phagpa (Tang 'Phags pa) and Gasha Phagpa (Ga sha 'Phags pa),[15] statues of Avalokiteśvara in Lahoul, in order to become pregnant with a son. The stones carried on her back are referred to as *bu rdo*, 'boy stones' or 'son stones.'[16] Thereupon the mother had various visions and dreams, miraculous things happened and she was certain that she would give birth to a lama-tulku or a fine boy (*bu legs pa*).[17]

The daughter was born at Tsopema in 1865. This holy lake and nearby mountain(s) are connected with Guru Rinpoche and Mandharava and the area is described by Lochen in Buddhist cosmological terms,

> The mountain is filled with medicinal fruit such as *a, bar, skyur*[18] and so on. At its foot, in the direction of the place where Ogyen Rinpoche's treasury *tsha tsha* (*gter tshwa*) was, it was as if there were seven golden mountains and seven enchanting lakes.[19]

We learn that many Gyagar Khampas were there and they and Lochen's father went to circumambulate the holy mountain(s). We do not know whether they were joined by women, but both genders certainly circumambulate the lake. Lochen says that all the women stayed at a great plain connected with Mandharava, and when the birth took place the lords of the lake (*mtsho bdag*), or the *nagas* (*klu*), presented offering gifts.[20] We sense gender distinctions here, mountain and men vs. plains, waters, underground, birth and women; and an analysis of Tsopema as a place of pilgrimage focussing on gender may reveal new insights.

For several years Lochen and her family stayed at Tsopema during winter and at the Kanika (Ka ni ka) *stupa* in Sani Monastery[21] in Sanskar during summer, and, if the family had a home in Lochen's childhood, it would be Tsopema, where Lochen tells us that people were helpful and friendly, and there was lots of fruit.[22] Lochen's family roams the valleys of Lahul, Spiti, Kulu, Rampur and Sanskar. They went to places named Shaog (Sha 'og), Changlau (Byang la'u), Tshongsarong (Tsong sa rong), where Lochen says that the Dharma did not flourish. Possibly these are places in the Garwal area of Uttar Pradesh. They go to Ladakh and Peldug (dPal 'gdugs)[23] to see religious dances (*'cham*) and made pilgrimages to the Vairocana murals of Alchi (Ab ji),[24] Mangyu (Mang rgyud)[25] and Sungda (gSung rda).[26]

They also went to Tibet proper, to Guge, which is described as a place where Buddhism thrived, to Barga Tasam (Bar ga rta zam)[27] to recite *mani*, and to pay homage to the Avalokiteśvara statues in Khorchag ('Khor chags/Khu char)[28] south of Taklakot.[29] The mother also takes her daughter to her birthplace Yolmo (Helambu), north of Kathmandu, and they proceed through Muktinath and Kyirong visiting sites of pilgrimage on their way. The only sacred site mentioned in the Kathmandu valley is the Takmoluchin *stupa* (sTag mo lus sbyin) near Dhulikhel, east of Kathmandu. After Helambu they quickly visit the pilgrimage sites on their way down to Kyirong to find the girl's root-lama.

From her birth Lochen was carried on the backs of her parents, later she rode a goat, occasionally a donkey, but mostly she moved about on foot. In her childhood she walked bare-foot, sometimes with bark from the Somaratsa tree tied around her sore feet.[30] Steep cliffs, narrow paths, shaky bridges and violent streams were the main physical obstacles during her childhood travels. She almost slipped into abysses more than once and nearly drowned thrice.[31] Every time she says that miracles saved her. I am amazed that Lochen not once, throughout the biography, mentions the icy winds and the low temperatures during winter and how terribly cold she must have been sleeping in tents, grass-huts and caves along their many pilgrimage-routes.

The religious milieu

Most likely in Spiti, Lochen Rinpoche meets Lochen Hangdra (Lo chen Hang sgra), alias Lochen Gokar (Lo chen mGo dkar), the nephew of the *maṇipa* master Dungkar Drugtra (Dung dkar 'brug sgra)[32] who tells her that Avalokiteśvera[33] is the mightiest among gods and that Lochen herself is Drolma or Machig.[34] Lochen Hangdra praises Lochen's voice and tells her that her melody goes back to the *maṇipas* of the past, especially to Ratnabhadra.[35] He also recognizes that Lochen has his own melody and encourages her to recite Avalokiteśvera's mantra. Subsequently the girl learned by heart several biographies, among them *sNang sa'i rnam thar*.[36]

While in Ladakh the father takes her to Tashi Namgyal, the head lama of 'the king of Ladakh,' with whom she studied writing and the biographies of *'das log* Khampa Adrung (Khams pa A khrung, 1508),[37] GyalpoYulha Legpa Döndrup (rGyal po gyu lha legs pa'i don grub)[38] and others. Here she is given a *thanka* and a book (*dpe cha*), part of the ritual paraphernalia of the *maṇipa*.

We also hear that the family proceeded to Western Tibet, to a site for gold-digging (*gser kha*)[39] called Kelsang Drog (sKal bzang khrogs) situated in the area Shungpa Matshen (gZhung pa ma mtshan) and to an old gold-mine called Tramalung (Grva ma lung). Among the gold-diggers were several pilgrims and *maṇipas* and the young Lochen spends time with the three daughters of the *maṇipa* Darpo (Lo chen Dar po) and his wife. Their younger daughter explained the story of Gelongma Palmo (dGe slong ma dPal mo)[40] and Lochen is happy to meet a friend who recites *rnam thar* like herself.[41] Lochen mentions a Mimi[42] Serpön (Mi mi gSer dpon), the head of the gold-diggers. Apparently *gser dpon*(s) were appointed by the Tibetan government to administer taxes on gold-digging. We here come across a cultural milieu we know little about.[43]

All through her childhood pilgrimages, from the age of six, the young Lochen encourages others to the recitation of *maṇis* in a beautiful voice. In Ladakh people were in awe because *dharma* was preached by a child still sucking milk from her mother and everyone wept from compassion.[44] Once, presumably in Spiti, she tells us that a crowd of about 1,000 gathered to listen. Her most prominent lay patron, Khampa Tashi, erected a throne for her in front of which he offered a *maṇḍala*.⁴⁵ Once in Rampur (Ram spur) she is invited by the king⁴⁶ who had heard of her fame. She is placed on a high throne and requested to give a recitation of *maṇi* for a large crowd.⁴⁷ Because Lochen was so small and not visible in the crowd, she had to carry a long cane (*mkhar ba*)⁴⁸ in her hand. She also recites *maṇi* for 'the Ladakhi king' and became his favorite and she says that faith was generated in everyone who heard her.

Lochen conceives of her childhood activities as one consisting of propagating the Doctrine and spreading the worship of Avalokiteśvera. She says that she planted the seeds of liberation in the minds of all the people she met, heard, remembered and touched in the *rong mtshams*, which here means Lahoul, Spiti, Kulu and Rampur. Wherever she sings *maṇis*, Lochen is offered gifts in abundance, such as food, woolen and cotton cloth and sometimes silver. In nomad areas she is occasionally given sheep and goats and these are brought along on their pilgrimages. We get acquainted with the "intelligent" female goat Lhakhen (Ra ma La mkhan) which Lochen rides when small. Animals brought on pilgrimage accumulate merit too, perfectly consistent with the Buddhist conception of existence. Ransomed sheep are called *tshe lug* in Central Tibet, and there are other observations of *tshe lug* with bells around their necks belonging to "the entourage" of *maṇipas*.⁴⁹

The *maṇipas* thus seem to be a group of professional reciters whose repertoire not only contained the *mantra* of Avalokiteśvera, but also autobiographies of saints and particularly of *'das log*. They also taught basic religious doctrines and lead itinerant lives. Jetsun Lochen informs us that her title 'Lochen' has nothing to do with the great '*lotsavas*' of the past, but is rather the title for humble '*maṇi-beggars*' in Western Tibetan dialects.⁵⁰ It is also clear that *maṇipas* and reciters of *'das log* belong to both genders, although it seems that women predominate. Lochen Hangdra who teaches Lochen the skills of the *maṇipa* describes himself as 'nothing but a poor beggar' and this is also Lochen's self-conception and how she is described by others.

Pilgrimage with her master Pema Gyatso, 1877–1890

The time spent with her root-lama Pema Gyatso, alias Chime Dorje (1829–1889/90),⁵¹ sets the next stage for Lochen's pilgrimages and her religious vocation. Pema Gyatso was probably born in Amdo in

1829,[52] and he was a personal disciple of Shabkar Tsogdrug Rangdrol (Zhabs dkar Tshogs drug rang grol, 1781–1851) who was firmly based in the Nyingma tradition, but strongly influenced by 'the Eclectic' 'Ris med'- movement.[53] Ricard refers to him as Shabkar's 'heart son,' but he is not mentioned the latter's autobiography.[54] It is possible that Pema Gyatso met the great master in Amdo after Shabkar returned there from Central Tibet in 1828.[55]

Kyirong, Nupri, Mustang/Thak and Kailash

Lochen met her lama in Kyirong in the late 1870s, where he stayed near Okar Drak (O dkar brag) with his disciples. Here the mother and daughter settle in one of the numerous caves nearby. Other holy places visited by Lochen and her companions while staying in the Kyirong/Lende area are, the 3rd Karmapa's site of birth,[56] three monasteries situated on Riwo Pelbar (Ri bo dPal 'bar),[57] the Milarepa cave Ragma Changchub Dzong (Rag ma byang chub rdzong),[58] Milarepa's most important hermitage in the latter part of his life, Drakar Taso (Brag dkar rta so),[59] Milarepa's birth-place Kyangatsa (sKya rnga rtsa) and the Milarepa cave Zaog Phug (Za 'og phug).[60] Significant people met during this stay were Langdrang Gomchen (Glang 'phrang bsgom chen), two nuns who were personal disciples of Shabkar, Tsumla Lama (Tsum la bla ma)[61] and a lama called Mimi Pema Namgyel (Mi mi Padma rNam rgyal).

We do not know how long Lochen stays in Kyirong, but from the context it seems to be about a year. After Kyirong the group proceeds to the He or Heri (He ri) hermitage in Nubri.[62] Lochen states that by Heri there is a hidden valley blessed by Guru Rinpoche which resembles Tsari. In this hermitage, which was situated on the face of a mountain, Lochen did a sealed meditation retreat for three years. One of the religious practices she focussed on was a Guru *sādhana* of Milarepa.

The hidden valley mentioned by Lochen is probably the one called Kyimolung (sKyid mo lung) situated in a side-valley to the east in Kutang and described in more detail by Michael Aris.[63] According to Aris, Milarepa was the first historical figure associated with this *sbas yul*, and its reputation was spread by the Garwang (Gar dbang) incarnations at Drakar Taso.[64] Drakar Taso was one of the last sites visited by Lochen and her company before proceeding to Nubri and Kutang. When Lochen is 16 years old (1881), Pema Gyatso and his group stay for some time near Pradun Tse (Pra dun rtse)[65] in the Saga

(Sa dga') District in Ngari, while Lochen returns to Nubri, where she nearly died from food poisoning in a small nunnery in Nubri Kok.[66]

Pema Gyatso and his followers proceed to Thak,[67] and due to various incidents here, Pema Gyatso finds Lochen to be self-conceited and punishes her by stamping the word dog (khyi) with a hot iron on her forehead.[68] Then Lochen is banished from the group and sent to Pokara. The lama stays in Tshoro gonpa (mTsho ro)[69] and he is invited here a second time in 1881. During their time in Mustang and Thak they perform pilgrimage to Tö Ngari Panchen Pema Wang gi Gyalpo's (sTod mnga' ris Pan chen Padma dbang gi rgyal po,1487–1542)[70] 'Seat of Learning,' to Chongshi Rangchon (Cong zhi rang byon),[71] and to Kutshab Denga (sKu tshab sde lnga).[72] They stop at Tilri Anigonpa (Til ri a ne dgon p)[73] and stay in an empty monastery in Muktinath.

Pema Gyatso then received a message from his lama Dharma Senge[74] in Lhasa, informing him that Shabkar's incarnation[75] was planning to come in the direction of central Tibet and Kailash.[76] Pema Gyatso was told to go there to meet him. The group proceed via Khuchar/ Khorchag[77] and Purang (Pu rang)/Taklakot.[78] Pema Gyatso stays alone by the shore of Manasarovar while the disciples circumambulate the lake. They visit Trugo (Khrus sgo) and reside for some time at Gonzur Gon (dGon zur dgon) which used to be Shabkar's disciple Chinpa Norbu's (sByin pa nor bu)[79] residence. Thereupon many of the students start a meditation retreat in Dzutrul Phug (rDzu 'phrul phug) situated on the circumambulation path around Kailash.[80] Here they practice yogic breathing, eat nettles to survive (which turns their urine blue) and taste tea for the first time.

Apparently Shabkar's incarnation never turned up, and by way of Pretapuri (Pre ta pu ri)[81] and Gyanyima (rGya nyi ma)[82] the group proceeds once more down into Nubri and stay for some years at Nubri Nagtshel Gonpa (Nags tshal dgon pa).[83]

The Kathmandu Valley, Labchi and Dingri

In the year of the bird (1885), when Lochen is 20 years old, they proceed to the Kathmandu valley,[84] where they white-wash the three stupas and print their guide-books (dkar chag). Then they proceed towards Dingri, and stop some months at one of the famous Milarepa retreats, Potinyima Dzong (Po ti nyi ma rdzong) at Dragmar (Brag dmar).[85] They also visit a number of other sites connected to Milarepa in this area. Here they encounter many statues of Shabkar and his disciples and Pema Gyatso stays with a personal disciple of Shabkar known as Nangdze Dorje (sNang mdzad rdo rje),[86] while the disciples were sent on pilgrimage to Labchi (La phyi).[87]

Lochen herself does not go to Labchi, but heads towards Dingri Langkor (Ding ri glang 'khor),[88] the residence of Padampa (Pha dam pa, d.1117),[89] Latö Gyel gyi Sri (La stod rgyal gyi śri), Tsibri (rTsib ri),[90] Gramtsho (Gram mtsho),[91] and Lho Dechen Phug (lHo bde chen phug).[92] Then the group is gathered again and they gradually come to (a place) called Phuma Partsho's island (Phu ma bar mtsho'i do)[93] where they reside for a few months with a great benefactor of Shabkar. Lochen says that in all the directions in this district, Shabkar's image protruded (*'bur*) on the stupas and even the *man thang*[94] were full (of his image).

Central Tibet and Woka/Loyul

Thereupon Pema Gyatso and his group head towards Lhasa, via Sakya, Tashilhunpo and Gyantse. They visit the Drolma temple in Nyethang[95] and on the 22th day of the ninth month, the day of Buddha's descent from the gods, possibly in 1887, they reach Lhasa, where they have an audience with the young 13th Dalai Lama (1876–1933).[96] Pema Gyatso stays in Drib Tshechogling (Grib Tshe chog gling)[97] with Dharma Senge, while most of the disciples go on pilgrimage to the south. Lochen went to Phenpo (north-east of Lhasa) to beg, to Potowa's (Po to ba) 'Seat of learning,' to Tagchen Shawa Bumpa (rTag spyan sha ba 'bum pa),[98] then to Ganden and other sites. She goes to see the Monlam Tshogchö (sMon lam tshogs mchod)[99] in Lhasa and has another audience with the 13th Dalai Lama.[100] While her companions make pilgrimage in Tö (sTod), Lochen is left behind because of a bad ankle, but attends the Curd Festival at Drepung ('Bras spung zho ston),[101] which was celebrated on the 30th day of the 6th month (the year may be 1888).

After arriving in Lhasa, Pema Gyatso wants to find a permanent residence for his group and sent Lochen off to seach for it. The Padmasambhava cave Sangyag Drag (Zangs yag brag)[102] on Riwo Tsenga, Tibet's Wutaishan, sacred to Mañjuśri, attracts their attention, and the lama settles there for long meditation retreats. Gangri Thökar, connected to Longchen Rabjampa, is considered suitable for a permanent hermitage.

While Pema Gyatso is in retreat at Sangyak Drak, Lochen wanders around and proceeds, apparently alone, on pilgrimage and to beg, as far east as Woka ('Ol dkar) and Loyul.[103] She also goes south of the Tsangpo, to E-yul, to the Shagyang (bShag byang) estate.[104] She makes pilgrimage to the many cliff-caves by Samling Ritrö (bSam gling ri khrod),[105] and then she returns to Sangyag Drag and alternates between Lhasa and Sangyag Drak for some time. Shabkar Rinpoche's incarnation arrives in Lhasa (c.1888–1889) and is invited to Sangyag Drag, where he stays some months with Pema Gyatso and his group. From him, Lochen receives empowerment and oral transmission of *rTa phag yid bzhin nor bu*[106] and the complete volumes of Shabkar's writings[107] and she is given the name Rigdzin Chönyid Sangmo (Rig 'dzin chos nyid bzang mo). The religious teachings received now were to become crucial for her later religious practice and her status as a Nyingma master. On his way to Lhasa, Pema Gyatso becomes ill and dies on the 17th of the second month, possibly in 1890.

The Group

The group of diciples who gathered around Pema Gyatso in Kyirong are referred to by Lochen as religious companions (*mched grogs*), which seems to refer to the immediate group of fellow disciples, but also to a larger group of adherents of Shabkar. It is difficult to estimate their number, but Lochen speaks of them as many. She names about twenty, but the group must have been considerably larger. They are both men and women, but it appears that the majority was female.[108]

Lochen's description of Pema Gyatso fits very well with what we know about lamas in the Nyingmapa tradition. He is described as humble and clad in ragged sheep-skin and although not explicitly mentioned, we may assume that he kept his hair long, as did his master Shabkar and several of his own disciples. When he stayed in Kyirong in the late 1870s he had a consort, she is mentioned twice, but never by name. Rather than in monasteries and institutions of learning, the lama stays with his entourage in caves and pilgrim-sites mainly associated with Padmasambhava, Milarepa and Shabkar. He emphasizes meditation and retreat for his students and keeps strict discipline. We never hear of lavish contributions to the lama (as in the case of Shabkar), although large crowds seem to have gathered when he taught. Lochen informs us, doubtless with some exaggeration, that once when he offered empowerment on *The Seven chapters of the Guru (Le'u bdun ma)* in Nubri, around 100,000 people attended.[109] Pema Gyatso's entourage moved about as a group, occasionally they split up into smaller units to perform meditational retreats, pilgrimages or to beg (*so sbyong*).

When she met her lama, Lochen was clad as a beggar, but after receiving instruction on yoga and breathing-techniques in Thak in the late 1870s and until her ordination as a Buddhist nun in the early 1890s, her standard outfit was a 'single piece of cotton'. She made her yoga outfit, meditation trousers and meditation ribbon from her mother's bedding, which she dyed in the appropriate colour, and she bought a cotton shawl (*gzan*) for six *paise* (*pad shag*). While in Nubri/ Thak word spread rapidly of her qualifications and people were puzzled that one who was so famous looked like an undernourished beggar.

When the group arrived in Lhasa around 1887, she still wore her cotton cloth and had to buy a felt *chuba* from a friend to be allowed an audience with the 13th Dalai Lama.[110] During a pilgrimage to Ganden she tells us, 'Because I was wearing only a piece of cotton, it was said that I was a *tsar mo*[111] and many people gathered to watch.'[112]

It seems that this group of mountain-dwelling hermits was a relatively rare sight around Lhasa and the nearby Gelugpa establishments. We also hear of unconventional behaviour by some of the members of the group. Yamdrok Thrulshig Rinpoche ('Khrul zhig Rin po che), another of Lochen's main lamas, tells her to tie her hair on top of her head and circumambulate the Barkor naked.[113] We also learn that Lochen's friend Ani Tsultrim made prostrations for the preliminary religious practice naked. Apparently Pema Gyatso's disciples were not ordained as we know that the Vinaya contains minute regulations for hiding the body, particularly the female. Lochen always kept her hair long, even after being ordained in the early 1890s. This was also true for at least one of her companions, Ani Changchub, and people gossiped saying they were laywomen in monastic robes.

Lochen was faithful to her root-lama Pema Gyatso until his death, and with him, her religious practices change direction. From being a *manipa* and reciter of '*das log* stories, she now professes a more defined Nyingma orientation. There seems to be no conflict here, all through her life Lochen continues her activities as a *manipa*, but other religious practices are integrated in her repertoire, mainly those of the Nyingma school and its *terma* tradition, with emphasis on *siddha* practices and transmissions of teachings which originated from Padmasambhava, Longchen Rabjampa, Shabkar and other great teachers of this religious tradition. The side-stream of *gCod* from Machig Labdron (1049/1055–1155) receives special attention all along, as also does Mind-training (*blo sbyong*) with its root in the Kadam/Geluk tradition.[114]

Motives for Travelling

The sites of pilgrimage Lochen pays homage to with her lama are mainly connected to Padmasambhava (Henang, Sangyag Drag), Milarepa (Kailash, Kyirong, Labchi), Machig Labdron and Padampa Sangye (Dingri) and Longchenpa (Gangri Thökar) and various hierarchs and saints of the Nyingmapa school. They also visit great "national" monasteries and monuments of other schools like, Sakya, the Gyantse Kumbum, Tashilhumpo, Sera, Ganden, Drepung, Potala and the Jokhang. On their pilgrimages to Kailash, Mustang, Kyirong, the Kathmandu Valley, Labchi, Dingri and Lhasa, they follow in Shabkar's footsteps. With the exception of Nubri, Shabkar made the same tour of pilgrimage a generation earlier.[115]

The main purpose of Pema Gyatso's and his retinue's travels was to make connection with places sanctified by great religious masters in the past and to perform prolonged meditations at such "powerful" sites. When Lochen was about 14 years old she started a three-year retreat in Nubri and another one at Sangyag Drag at the age of 25. In between she performed meditations lasting for several months at the time, some were sealed and some performed in total darkness. The lama gave religious instructions to his group and to the general public and Lochen too taught and sang *manis* along her way. They practiced *gCod* at cemeteries and fearful places (*gnyan sa*) to turn back obstacles such as illness and epidemics. This was their explicit purpose for going both to Nubri and Mustang. Once in Nubri, we hear that an illness said to have been caused by black magic nearly wiped out the group of fellow devotees. Lochen says that even the dogs turned mad. As they were *gCod pas* called on to cure diseases, we are not surprised that they were infected. In fact illness was conceived as a major threat and we hear of unidentified diseases, fevers and small-pox. Food-poisoning caused her lama's death and nearly took Lochen's and Pema Gyatso's consort's lives.[116] All through the *rnam thar* long life rituals (*zhabs brtan*), warding off obstacle rituals (*bsun bzlog*)[117] and *gCod* are performed to control sickness believed to be caused by disorder of the elements, inauspicious times, black magic, and various other obstacles.[118]

Lochen's Status

Lochen was harassed during the first phase of her stay with Pema Gyatso as the self-confidence of this child-*maṇipa* who had been celebrated as a saint ever since her birth had to be broken. Despite being physically abused and ostracised by her lama, the young girl stubbornly continues her religious practices. Large crowds gather when she sings *maṇis* and preaches the Dharma and words about her fame spread rapidly. As their relationship develops Lochen becomes Pema Gyatso's closest disciple and she follows him everywhere as his servant. Lochen's physical condition in her youth must have been remarkable. When travelling with Pema Gyatso in Central Tibet in the late 1880s she was called 'the Tantric Lama's donkey.' She states,

> Without fear or embarrassement I carried the burden of the Lama's *tsampa*, the weight of five *khal* of barley, besides mother's and my own luggage, to Lhasa and other places, near and far, day and night, wherever we went.[119]

At another occasion Lochen again talks about her strength and says that she could carry seven loads of sheep (*lug rgyab*),[120] and later, when her mother became sick on a pilgrimage in Yarlung and Chongye in the mid-1890s, Lochen and her nun friend alternately carry her on their backs. No wonder that Lochen's legs fail her after numerous slips on narrow paths with enormous loads on her back.

As time goes by Lochen also acquires a prominent position among her fellow disciples, and we hear that she sends them here and there. Once at Tshechogling when she asks Pema Gyatso for religious teachings, she is placed in the centre while her companions sit around her in a circle. In Lhasa she is asked to read Prajñāpāramitā in 8000 verses for the Lhalu (lHa klu) family[121] and receives a full bucket of grain per day as a fee. She also functions as house-lama for the Lady Shagyang when on pilgrimage in E-yul in the late 1880s and when Pema Gyatso is seriously ill, she is told by Shabkar's incarnation to perform the warding off obstacle rituals all by herself.

Independent Pilgrimages

After Pema Gyatso's death, Lochen alternately spends the winters in Sangyag Drag and the summers at Gangri Thökar. She is advised to take ordaination and immediately afterwards sets out on pilgrimage with her friend Changchub. She performs a strict three-year retreat and some shorter meditations at Sangyag Drag before she sets out on a combined begging and pilgrimage tour to Lhoka, possibly in 1894. This trip was to last for several years. She stops at Dorje Drag (rDo rje Brag) and pays homage to the shrines there, crosses the Tsangpo to Dophung Chökhor (rDo phung chos 'khor)[122] with its talking Tārā (sGrol ma gsung byon ma). Again she proceeds north of the Tsangpo to pilgrimage sites in Dragyul connected with Padmasambhava and Yeshe Tsogyal, Dragda Tshogyal Latsho (sGrag mda' mtsho rgyal bla mtsho),[123] Dragyang Dzong (sGrags yang rdzong),[124] Ngadra (rNga sgra) Monastery[125] and Dzong Kumbum (rDzong sku 'bum).[126] She proceeds gradually, begging along the way and arrives at Samye Chimphu (bSam yas 'chims phu),[127] Samye Sangri (bSam yas zangs ri)[128] and Machig's residence Sangri Kharmar (Zangs ri mkhar dmar).[129] She is invited to Shagyang, southeast of Lhagyari (lHa rgya ri) in E-yul, and makes pilgrimage to Sangmo ri and Ogyen phug (O rgyan phug) on the way. She performs a six month *rDzog chen*[130] meditation retreat at Sangri, builds a large *mani*-wall at Sangri Kharmar and repairs a *mani*-wall at Densathil (gDan sa mthil).[131]

Together with the Lady of Shagyang, Lochen plans to head towards Tsari (possibly 1896),[132] but they change their minds and go on an extended pilgrimage to the south. They proceed to Tradrug (Khra 'brug)[133] in the Yarlung valley, Tsering Jong (Tshe ring ljongs)[134] Chongye Pelri Monastery (dPal ri dGon)[135] and go as far as Yarlha Shampo (Yar lha sham po).[136] They visit to Dargye Chöling (Dar rgyas chos gling) or old Mindroling, and Chasa Lhakhang (Bya sa lha khang),[137] and then return to Sangri and to Langlung (Glang lung) in the district of E, where Lochen performed rituals together with many nuns from the house of Lhagyari. Then she returns to Samye, she goes to the top of Hepori (Has po ri),[138] to Chimphu and Yemalung (g.Ya' ma lung)[139] before she goes back to Lhasa, possibly in 1897/98. The following years she spends at Sangyag Drag where she performs dark meditation. She stays in a cave at Chagpori (lCags po ri), goes to Nechung, spends a couple of months in Lhodrag and wanders around in Nyemo. When the Younghusband mission soldiers arrive in 1903–1904, she collects her things at Sangyag Drag and settles at Shugseb.

During the period after her Lama's death and until she settles permanently at Shugseb, Lochen Rinpoche's religious status is further enhanced. She now combines the role of the recluse and that of the ordained monastic. It was Kham Lama Sangye Tendzin (Bla ma Sangs rgyas bstan 'dzin),[140] a personal disciple of Peltrul Dorje Chang (dPal sprul rdo rje 'chang, 1808–1887),[141] who advises her to become ordained. It seems that Lochen now comes more directly under influence of the Gemang (dGe mang) movement from Eastern Tibet,[142] with its emphasis on Nyingma monastic scholasticism and the Vinaya. Lochen continues, however, to receive impulses from "crazy" *siddhas* like Thrulshig Rinpoche and Taklung Matrul Rinpoche (sTag lung Ma sprul Rin po che) that pull her in another direction. At times we sense a conflict here and she tries to keep the crazy lamas at a distance, but Lochen herself manifests saintly madness and her mother and friends fear for her sanity. They discuss whether she has acquired the *siddhas* of clairvoyance (*mgon shes*) and the ability to move without hindrances.[143]

Gender related issues

Throughout her life Lochen has a strong connection to saintly women of the past and highly qualified female religious specialists of the present. Her first encounter with a great female spiritual master was the Amdovan nun Lobsang Drolma, who became the head lama for the king of Mandi because she was said to have secured the sonless king an heir. It was Lobsang Drolma who prophesied Lochen's spiritual connection with Pema Gyatso and Shabkar. In the mid-1880s Lochen meets one of the Sakya Jetsunmas and is greatly impressed and she has close contact with the Ragshag Jetsunmas (Rag shag rje btsun) in Lhasa. In the early 1890s Lochen goes twice to meet Gyagari Dorje Phamo (rGya gar ri rDo rje phag mo)[144] at Gangthö and wants to stay with her.

The connection to "the female"[145] is clearly manifested during her independent pilgrimages starting in the 1890s. Now she increasingly plays her own role as a female hermit-nun, and there are no male lamas with her to direct her their way. She seeks out pilgrimage sites connected to holy women like Yeshe Tsogyal and Machig Labdron and during her travels she stops over at nunneries and associates with nuns, e.g. in Lab in E-yul she stays in a nunnery which followed Shabkar's tradition called Gongla Lame (dGongs bla bla med).[146] Her main patron during this time is a noble woman, the Lady of Shagyang.

An interesting episode occurs while the group of fellow devotees stays in Kyirong in 1877. Pema Gyatso is 49 years old and becomes ill and Lochen is 13 year old. Both ages are considered inauspicious, as is every twelfth year in a person's life cycle. The young girl is made to perform warding off obstacle rituals for the lama. She puts on a flower bonnet which she offers and then she is sent as the Lama's ransom-offering (*sku glud*)¹⁴⁷ to Mangyul Champa Drin (Mang yul Byams pa sprin).¹⁴⁸ The ransom-offering brings us back to pre-buddhist religious practices. The ritual performed resembles the *mkha' 'gro bsun bzlog* rituals performed to turn back *ḍākinīs* who come to take dying persons to their realm. We wonder if Lochen is dressed as a *ḍākinī* in order to pacify these female beings and whether the temple has some special connection with *ḍākinīs*.

Because she is herself a woman with great spiritual power, she is approached to perform rituals to goddesses. When on pilgrimage to the talking Tārā at Dophung Chökor, she is requested to recite Tārā prayers for a week and is offered around 165 kilos of grain as payment. When on pilgrimage in Dragyul, she arrives at a place where a lama is making a Khandro statue and Lochen's arrival is regarded as a good omen. Lochen obviously has some special connection to Sangri Kharmar. She can move miraculously to a large rock in the middle of Tsangpo which had auspicious signs of being Machig's residence. She is inspired by visions and stays in retreat during the day, but at night she practices *gCod* at a charnel ground and dances *gCod cham* with a dog in the middle of a field.¹⁴⁹ Because of her special "affinity" with Machig, she also starts a major building project at Sangri Kharmar, a *maṇi*-wall around the Tsuklakhang, a very meritorius activity it seems, because gods, lamas and people in the Sangri area are said to assist willingly and the auspiciousness of the *maṇi*-building is so great that it produces rain in this arid area.

As Lochen's fame spreads she is also called on to perform specialized religious rituals. She is called on to assist the Abbot at Sangri and reads the *Bardo Thödol (Bar do thos grol)*¹⁵⁰ for him when he is dying. At Sangri Kharmar she is called to perform a ritual that no-one else there knew how to perform, while a master of *Zhiche (Zhi byed)*,¹⁵¹ Nedo Chöpa (gNas mdo gcod pa), maintains that Lochen is the wisdom *ḍākinī* Machig Labdron and as such she becomes known to everyone present.

There thus seems to be a number of specific religious functions and roles to fill for a woman religious practitioner and we see that femaleness is considered an asset in certain situations. It appears that the Nyingma school of Tibetan Buddhism has greater scope and more willingly accepts female religious talent through their close association to what may be termed "folk-religion." Special roles for women, like the *maṇipa*, the *'das log*, and the *sku glud* are integrated into the religious role-repertoire and women also have important roles as hermits and consorts.

Apart from the few female role-models Lochen Rinpoche was able to identify with, all the Rinpoches, lamas, *siddhas*, abbots and mediums she came across on her pilgrimages were men and we get a definite impression that Lochen's way to mastership was not an easy one. At times her female gender was a strong impediment. Once when Lochen has visions (*dgongs gter*) of ritual texts in Thak and a local deity supplies her with birch bark and ink so that she can write it all down, the male teacher Chösang kicks her head and burns her writings telling her that such compositions are not allowed for her. Another time in Lhasa, monks from Kyetshel (sKyed tshal) Monastery in Sikkim are jealous because she functions as the house-lama for the noble Lhalu family and they try, unsuccessfully, to defeat her in a debate. Crestfallen, they have to admit that she is indeed learned. Also when Dharma Senge is dying, his disciples do not allow her an audience, nor do they hand over to her the religious objects Dharma Senge bequeaths her. When she wants to offer gold for his statue, the physicians at Mentsikhang (sMan rtsis khang) do not accept it saying that her gold is of an inferior quality.[152] When she wants to settle at Shugseb together with Semnyi Rinpoche (Sems nyid Rin po che) and fellow female companions at the turn of the century, they are told that only the lama and his attendant are allowed to stay.[153]

Lochen is not concerned with issues like "the exclusion of women" and seems to accept this as an established fact, although she mentions it here and there. At several of the larger monasteries she visited, such as Tashilunpo, Gyantse, Ganden and Tsechogling, only her lama and his male companions are allowed to stay, while Lochen and her '*ani*' friends have to find alternative housing. When at Sangri in the mid-1890s, she goes to the Sangri *btsan khang*,[154] but is thrown out by the caretaker who tells her that women are not allowed to enter. The question of exclusion of women at sites of pilgrimage needs more research, but there are numerous indications that women were considered inferior religious practitioners and that they may even bring defilement to holy sites. This pertinent remark on gender made by the Nyingma master Kathog Situ Rinpoche may serve as an illustration. Kathog Situ visited one of Lochen's and her companions' main site for meditation, Sangyag Drag in 1918–19, he describes the Padmasambhava caves, the statues and the surroundings in great detail, but concludes, '(. . .) there are all these wonderful and splendid sites, but due to (all the) nuns staying there the area is not a suitable/happy place.[155]

Notes

1 In Lhasa, during Sakadawa in 1994, a large number of people were circumambulating the *gling skor* before day-break, and I was amazed to find a large number of young people there. According to informants the participation of young people in religious festivals and pilgrimages is presently increasing in Central Tibet.
2 Huber 1994b.
3 Abbr. *rJe btsun rnam thar*, see bibliography. The material presented here is based on the prose part of the autobiography. See also Havnevik (forthcoming).
4 See Smith 1970: 5–36 and Samuel 1993: 344–355, 463–465, 537–543, 546–551.
5 For a discussion of the dates of Lochen Rinpoche, see Havnevik (forthcoming).
6 For Klong chen, see Karmay 1988, for Gangri Thökar, see *KaSi* (see Tibetanbibliography) p. 146, cf. Chan 1994: 470, 488, 491, 492; and Dowman 1988: 139, 143, 169, 206, 293.
7 She was born in Yolmo probably of mixed Tibetan and Sherpa/Tamang ethnicity. See *rJe btsun rnam thar*, 19, 62 and Havnevik (ongoing).
8 From the Khe smad family, *rJe btsun rnam thar*, 17.
9 See below.
10 rGan or sKu zhabs 'Phrin las chos sgron from Tselna, see *rJe btsun rnam thar*, 393, 561 and Havnevik (ongoing).
11 Drubchen Dawa Dorje Rinpoche came from Nangchen Kham, see *rJe btsun rnam thar*, 440, and Havnevik (ongoing). He authored the poetical songs inserted in *rJe btsun rnam thar* and his level of education is evident by e.g. a corrupt Sanskrit.
12 Francke 1914: 122, 123; Cantwell, 1989, 1994, 1995. For a photo of Tsopema, see Dudjom Rinpoche 1991, vol. 1, plate no. 51.
13 Brug pa may either refer to 'the Bhutanese lama' or 'lama belonging to the Drukpa school of Tibetan Buddhism.'
14 *rJe btsun rnam thar*, 20.
15 For the Gasha 'Phags pa (also called Chenresig Phagpa), see Stuchbury, E., 'Pumo Kuluta: the Story of a Contested Site', paper delivered at the Leiden "Pilgrimage in Tibet" conference, September 1996.
16 *rJe btsun rnam thar*, 20. Tibetans also carry stones on their backs while on pilgrimage, see Buffetrille 1996a.
17 *rJe btsun rnam thar*, 21.
18 Medicinal fruit, see *Tshig mdzod*, vol. 3: 3122.
19 *rJe btsun rnam thar*, 22. Based on Buddhist cosmological notions, see Snelling 1990: 48–60; Brauen 1992: 49–67; and Sørensen 1994: 44–48.
20 *rJe btsun rnam thar*, 22.
21 Snellgrove & Skorupski (1977) 1979: 6, 7, 9, 38, 61 (vol. 2).
22 *rJe btsun rnam thar*, 31.
23 Probably Spitok Monastery, see Snellgrove & Skorupski (1977) 1979: 106–109. (vol. 1).
24 *Ibid.*: 23–80, see also Francke 1914: 32, 43, 78, 86, 88–94, 97. (Part 1).

25 Snellgrove & Skorupski *op.cit.*: 22, 80 (vol. 1). See also Francke 1914: 93, 94. (Part 1).
26 Possibly the large murals of Vairocana at the Alchi gSum brtsegs temple, see Snellgrove & Skorupski *op.cit.*: 44, 53, 54, 55, 56, 61–64, 79–80 (vol. 1).
27 Chan *op.cit.*: 292, 293, 617, 952, 957, 966.
28 Tucci (1937) 1989: 71–79 and Chan *op.cit.*: 936, 957, 959, Vitali 1996. Several different spellings, see below.
29 Today Purang is called Taklakot, see Francke (1926) 1972: 93–94, 96, 105, 110, 133, 137, 168–9, 273, 276 (part 2); and Chan *op.cit.*: 28, 292, 435, 444, 617, 621, 936, 943, 950, 955, 957.
30 *rJe btsun rnam thar*, 49.
31 *Ibid.*: 32.33, 117–118, 191–192.
32 *Ibid.*: 37.
33 For the origin of and the cult of *Avalokiteśvera*, see Snellgrove 1987: 454–455; Kapstein 1992; and Samuel 1993: 226, 234, 484–485, 539.
34 *rJe btsun rnam thar*, 37. This is the first time Lochen is mentioned (the songs not considered) as Machig Labdron's emanation, see also *rJe btsun rnam thar*, 378, 394, 458.
35 Possibly mKhas grub Nor bzang rgya mtsho (b. 1478) who might be the founder of the *maṇipa* tradition in the 15th century or alluding to king Nor(bu) bzang(po) of the biography of Padma 'od 'bar. Stein maintains that the *maṇipa* tradition goes back to the 12th century; Stein (1962) 1972: 174.
36 *rJe btsun rnam thar*, 38. Cf. *BDTT*, vol. 4: 528–530. For the biography of sNang sa 'od 'bum, see *Rigs bzang gi mkha' 'gro ma snang sa 'od 'bum gyi rnam thar bzhugs so*, Dharamsala 1976. There is a huge amount of literature on sNang sa 'od 'bum including many articles in Tibetan, see *Bod kyi lha mo'i 'khrab gzhung*, Lhasa 1989: 44–132.
37 *rJe btsun rnam thar*, 45. See *'Das log dkar chag thar pa'i lam ston gsal ba'i sgron me / Visionary experiences of a return from death experience by the Rdzogs chen Stag bla Dkon mchog rgyal mtshan*, Paro Bhutan 1983: 279. See also Epstein 1982: 82, cf. Pommaret 1989: 83.
38 See *rGyal po gyu rna ral pa'i rnam thar bzhugs so* by Konchhog Lhadrepa, Delhi 1990, *Rare Tibetan Texts from Lahul. Native accounts (rnam thar) of Rgod tshang pa Mgon po rdo rje, Chos rgyal G'yu sna Legs pa'i don grub and Sras Guru Chos kyi dbang phyug*, Dolanji 1974.
39 There may have been prohibitions against digging in the earth and 'site for gold-winning' or 'gold-ore' may be better translations of *gser kha*.
40 See Gelongma Palmo's *rnam thar*, a photocopied handwritten manuscript in *u chen* 58 folios, LTWA (acc. no 1602).
41 *rJe btsun rnam thar*, 56–57.
42 Old people are called by the honorific *mi mi* in Western Tibet and Ladakh.
43 See Huber 1991: 16.
44 *rJe btsun rnam thar*, 46.
45 *Ibid.*: 38.
46 For Rampur kings, see Francke 1914: 124. (Part 1).
47 Every November thousands of people from as far as Kinnaur, Spiti and Lahoul gather for a market in Rampur, which is one of the largest in northern India.

48 rJe btsun rnam thar, 42. For photos of maṇipas see MacDonald 1967: plate i and «Le Conteur Ambulant» in *Voyages dans les maches Tibetaines*, Musee de l'Homme, 1989: 51.
49 Tseyang Changngopa observed maṇipas with ransomed sheep in Lhasa during Sakadawa in 1993.
50 rJe btsun rnam thar, 472.
51 His dates are tentative, see Thondup 1996: 252 and Havnevik (ongoing).
52 Havnevik, (ongoing).
53 Ricard 1994: xv, xviii, 547–548. See also Ehrhard 1990.
54 Ricard *ibid.*: 576 n26,
55 *Ibid.*: 485.
56 Douglas and White 1976: 47.
57 rJe btsun rnam thar, 99. See Chan *op.cit.*: 925, 934.
58 rJe btsun rnam thar, 101. Chan *ibid*: 934.
59 Aris 1975: 80, 1979a, Chan *ibid*: 924, 925, 932, 934.
60 Chan *ibid*: 930.
61 The lama may come from Mu dgon pa, also called Tsum dgon pa, see Snellgrove (1981) 1989: 260, 280.
62 He ri khrod, Heri or Henang are not mentioned by Aris (1975) or by Snellgrove (1981) 1989 in their surveys of Nubri and Kutang.
63 Aris (1975, 1979)
64 The first one was born 1580, see Aris 1979: 3.
65 Pra dun rtse, a mTha' 'dul temple, see Aris 1979a: 16, 23, 33, 53, 294; Chan, *op.cit.*: 44.
66 There is a place called Kok situated on the west side of the Buri Gandaki in Kutang, see Aris 1975: 56, map following 76. Snellgrove marks it Gak, (1981) 1989: 300.
67 rJe btsun rnam thar, 110. See Snellgrove (1981) 1989: 174–188, 298, Ramble 1984, Vinding (forthcoming) and Sørensen and Vinding, (forthcoming).
68 In Amdo thieves were marked with a scar on their forehead (S. Karmay, personal communication), see also French 1995: 323.
69 I have not been able to identify Tshoro Gonpa. It could be Tshe rog, south of sKu tshab gter lnga or Dzar Monastery, near Muktinath.
70 Dargyay 1977: 156–160, 240, 246, Dudjom Rinpoche *op.cit.*: 805–809, Jackson 1984: 18, 21.
71 rJe btsun rnam thar, 136. See Snellgrove 1979: 111–112, 132, and Snellgrove (1981) 1989: 189.
72 See Snellgrove 1979: 74, 76, 84–101, 106–128, and Snellgrove (1981) 1989: 183, 186–187.
73 Locally pronounced Tiri (in local documents spelt Ting ri/gTing ri), situated 2½ hours walk up the Kali Gandaki from Jomsom. The Lama Ngag dbang thog med may have been the tutelary lama of the Tiri nuns, many of whom came from the neighbouring village Kag. (Ramble, personal communication).
74 Alias Khams smyon, see Havnevik (ongoing).
75 Two successive incarnations were recognized in Amdo, Ye shes bstan pa'i rgyal mtshan and Theg mchog bstan pa'i nyi ma, see Ricard *op.cit.*: XVn7. According to Tashi Tsering (LTWA) the name should be Jigme Tenpa

Nyima, see *Rang bo dgon chen gyi gdan rabs rdzogs ldan gtam gyi rang sgra zhes bya ba bzhugs so*, Kokonor 1988: 644–647.
76 There are a large amount of publications on Kailash and its surroundings, see e.g. Tucci (1937) 1989; Snelling (1983) 1990; Filibeck 1988; Namkai Norbu 1989; and Buffetrille 1996a.
77 Tucci (1937) 1989: 71–81.
78 *Ibid.*: 47–63, 81–85; Chan *op.cit.*: 28, 292, 435, 444, 617, 621, 936, 943, 950, 955, 957.
79 Shabkar's main disciple in Western and Central Tibet, Ricard *op.cit.*: 591.
80 According to Snelling there used to be eight monsteries surrounding Lake Manasarovar: Chiu, Cherkip, Langpona, Bönri, Seralung, Yerngo, Trügo, Gösul and five of the eight (Langpona, Seralung, Trügo, Gösul, Chiu) still exist today, Snelling (1983) 1990, cf. Tucci (1937) 1989: 121–128, 167–172, see also Chan *op.cit.* and Buffetrille 1996a.
81 sPre zla spru ri is also called Thirtapuri, see Tucci (1937) 1989: 177–181.
82 Gyanyima was the largest market in Western Tibet, Snelling *op.cit.*: 96, 102, 131, 159, 163, 224, 248, 251, 260, 272.
83 See Snellgrove (1981) 1989: 247, 248, 252, 281, 300 and Aris 1975: map following p. 77.
84 *rJe btsun rnam thar*, 145.
85 sPo mtho nam mkha rdzong, one of Milarepa's caves, see Ricard *op.cit.*: 434. Chan *op.cit.*: 261–262.
86 He is not mentioned in Ricard's list of Shabkar's disciples.
87 See Filibeck 1988; Huber 1989; Ricard *op.cit.*: xiv, 5, 9, 10, 389, 395, 442n.1, 434, 443 n.9, 479, 493; Dowman *op.cit.*: 106, 265. Shabkar reached Labchi in 1819 (Ricard *op.cit.*: 443).
88 gLang 'khor or Ding ri glang 'khor was Padampa's residence from 1098, see Aziz *op.cit.*: 17, 24, 25, 83, 206, 208; Ricard *op.cit.*: 447, 480n, 4.
89 Aziz *op.cit.*: 17, 24, 25–26, 83, 96, 27–28, Kollmar-Paulenz 1993 and Lo Bue 1994.
90 Gyel gyi shri is also known as Tsibri, see Aziz 1978: 25, 206, 207, 217–219, 215; Ricard *op.cit.*: 448, 450, 480 n.6: & Buffetrille 1996a: 112–137, (vol. 1).
91 Situated to the west of Shel dkar and the rTsib ri range, see Aziz 1978: 97, 207, Wangdu/Diemberger 1996, map section.
92 Possibly close to Dechen teng in Nyanang, Aziz *op.cit.*: 207 (map).
93 Cf. Ricard *op.cit.*: 546. Situated in Latö, but I have not been able to find the exact location.
94 *man thang* is possibly the same as '*maṇi*-wall.'
95 See Everding 1993: 234–35.
96 *rJe btsun rnam thar*, 179.
97 *KaSi*: 142.
98 *KaSi*: 274, Wylie 1962: 86, 162 n.446; Dowman *op.cit.*: 82, 86, 87.
99 Celebrated in the 2nd lunar month, see Richardson 1993: 60–61 and *Tshig mdzod*: 2290.
100 *Je btsun rnam thar*, 210.
101 Celebrated in Lhasa (Norbulinka) 1st–5th day of the seventh month, see Richardson 1993: 103–107, cf. Chan *op.cit.*: 1053. Chan states that the

Shotun was celebrated on the 8th day of the 7th month at Drepung. (*ibid.*: 149).
102 Or Zangs yag Nam mkha' brag, *KaSi*: 149, cf. Dowman *op.cit.*: 145, 293.
103 Dowman *ibid*: 245, 247.
104 Cf. *rJe btsun rnam thar*, 190. Yuthok Dorje Yudon writes that Shagyang was one of three *sger pa* families in E. (1990: 306), see also Chan *op.cit.*: 220, 225.
105 Samling is probably bSam gtan gling, a hermitage connected to Gampopa and Tsongkapa, see Dowman *op.cit.*: 253.
106 *rTa phag yid bzhin nor bu*, 'Wish-fulfilling gem, Hayagriva and Vajravarahi' revealed by Kunsang Dechen Gyalpo, see Ricard *op cit.*: xxii, xxiii, 44, 50, 125, 211, 569, 587.
107 Ricard *ibid*: 577–589.
108 Lochen names c. 12 female companions and 6–8 male.
109 *rJe btsun rnam thar*, 110.
110 *Ibid.*: 210.
111 A female ascetic (from Skt. *Acarya*).
112 *rJe btsun rnam thar*, 182.
113 *Ibid*: 330. Her friends stopped her however. There are a few other references to female religious specialists and nakedness, see Hanna 1994: 7–8 and the improbable story about Alak Gongri Khandro by Forman 1936: 172–186.
114 Sweet 1996, cf. Ricard *op.cit.*: 547.
115 Lochen read Shabkar's collected works in the late 1880s (*rJe btsun rnam thar*, 185).
116 *Ibid.*: 100, 107, 195.
117 'Warding off' rituals in order to drive back obstacles, particularly *ḍākinī*s who have come to take the person to their land.
118 Unfavourable *karma* is seldom referred to explicitly to explain illness.
119 *rJe btsun rnam thar*, 193. If one *khal* is c. 30 lb/13, 6 kg (Jäschke) this means that Lochen says that she could carry c. 68 kg.
120 *rJe btsun rnam thar*, 110. *lug rgyab* = *lug khal*, e.g. c. 95kg. The exact weight of a *khal* and a *lug rgyab* is uncertain, but she no doubt carried heavy loads.
121 The name of a noble family, see Petech 1973: 19, 20, 22, 6n, 39–49, 70n, 102, 105, 136, 149, 156, 157, 182, 214. The house is situated north of the Potala and the whole village is called Lha klu.
122 Chan *op.cit.*: 470, 481, 482, 599, cf. Dowman *op.cit.*: 136, 147, 156.
123 *KaSi*: 217, Dowman *ibid.*: 205, 214, 215 and Chan *ibid.*: 319, 320.
124 Chan *ibid.*: 37, 45, 317, 318, 321, 483, 522, 595, 598.
125 Chan *ibid*: 319, 320.
126 *Ibid.*: 317, 318, 321, 325, 483, 595, 598, cf. Dowman, *op.cit.*: 205, 213.
127 Chan *ibid.*: 45, 114, 295, 338, 339, 631–3, 522.
128 Wylie 1962: 116, 171, 210.
129 *KaSi*: 246, Wylie *ibid.*: 91, 92, 171, Chan *op.cit.*: 517, 635, 636, Dowman *op.cit.*: 173, 245, 246.
130 E.g. Karmay 1988.

131 *KaSi*: 247. She also visits the sacred sites Terkyil (gTer dkyil), Terchung (gTer chung), Ogyen Phug (O rgyan phug), Drungtshel ('Khrung tshal), Ludeng (Klu ldeng).
132 *KaSi*: 526. Every twelfth year (the year of the monkey) is considered particularly auspicious for pilgrimage to Tsari, see Huber 1993.
133 Ferrari 1958: 49, 50, 108, 124, 125, 128; Sørensen 1994: 275–6, 563–567; Dowman *op.cit.*: 103, 173, 177–179, 289, 293.
134 Founded by Jigme Lingpa (1729–98), Dowman *op.cit.*: 196, 202.
135 Dowman *ibid*: 196, 200, 202, 232, cf. Chan *op.cit.*: 528.
136 Sørensen 1994: 139, 142; Dowman *ibid.*: 15, 184, 294.
137 *KaSi*: 244; Ferrari *op.cit.*: 54, 131; Tucci (1956), 1987: 144; Dowman *ibid.*: 162-163.
138 Has po ri is the hill from where Padmasambhava went to meet king Kri srong lde brtsan, see Ferrari *ibid.*: 45, 114; Tucci (1956) 1987: 115n. 140, 161; Dowman *ibid*: 223, 225; Chan *op.cit.*: 295, 298, 624, 629, 631.
139 *KaSi*: 216; Dowman *op.cit.*: 167, 217, 233, 293; Chan *ibid*: 316, 318, 380, 511, 513, 550, 624, 627, 631, 710, 938.
140 The father of the 6th Dzogchen Rinpoche, see Havnevik (ongoing).
141 dPal sprul O rgyan 'Jigs med chos kyi dbang po, see Dudjom Rinpoche *op.cit.*: 871, 875, 958 and Thondup 1996: 198–202, 222–227, 362–365.
142 Started by the monastic reformer rDzogs chen rGyal sras gZhan phan mtha' yas (b. 1740), see Smith 1970.
143 *rJe btsun rnam thar*, 215.
144 See Havnevik (forthcoming).
145 The relation between gender symbolism and the status of women is very complex and needs to be investigated for each religous group we study. It is not so that elevated female symbols are necessarily paired with high status for women, see Bynum *et.al.* 1986.
146 *rJe btsun rnam thar*, 251.
147 For ransom offering, see e.g. Karmay 1991; Richardson 1993: 9, 61, 64, 66, 70.
148 Aris 1979a: 16; Chan *op.cit.*: 45, 925, 935, 936.
149 *rJe btsun rnam thar*, 246.
150 The Tibetan Book of the Dead, "discovered" by Karma gLing pa (14th century), see Dargyay 1979: 151–153.
151 See Kollmar-Paulenz 1993.
152 *rJe btsun rnam thar*, 202, 492,
153 *Ibid.*: 366.
154 Temple of a protective deity.
155 *KaSi*: 150.

Chapter 6

On the way to Kailash

Winand M. Callewaert

If you are looking for research information about pilgrimage to the Kailash, you may not need to continue reading now. This is a personal account of my travel in the Kailash region, as a student of Indian studies for more than 30 years. Throughout that period Kailash, particularly as the seat of Shiva in meditation and as a faraway 'extraordinary' site for my Hindu friends, has been beckoning me. I had the chance to go there in June 1996, and in this article I would like to share some of my experiences, my thrills, and my disappointments. I clearly went there as a pilgrim from the Indian perspective. I was well aware of the belief that your sins are expiated if you do the *parikrama*, but I had to disappoint my Hindu friends when they asked me what it felt like to be there.

We were a party of eleven Belgians, travelling [on the northern route via Gerze] with one passenger "bus", a supply truck, four Tibetans and one Chinese "companion". You may not travel without that "company", but the fellow himself felt miserable, having to live in Lhasa, without understanding Tibetan and having as much difficulty in breathing as we had. He spoke English well enough, but he became the symbol of the sad side of our pilgrimage: the Chinese presence. Even he stood with bowed head in front of the administrators who once in a while on the road checked our papers. I am sure he sometimes cursed us for wanting to do this tour, because that meant he had to leave Lhasa and sleep in tents. Why an earth do people want to do this?

We travelled from the Bridge of Friendship near Zhangmu for ten days, a total of 2,167 kilometres, before we reached Dharchen, sitting in a Dakar-Dakar truck for more than 80 hours (several times 10 hours a day). We swallowed heaps of dust and after one week in Shiquanhe we found water in the hotel. A brave lady who could stand the cold water washed her hair and remarked afterwards, "the whole of Tibet went down the sink!" I do a lot of exercise and until now have not had excessive fat on my thin frame; but on the tour I lost 10 precious pounds, not because of sickness, but because the tour operator was too stingy with the food; and let me not complain anymore now.

It was a pilgrimage of hardship alright, but we travelled through the most spectacular scenery I have seen anywhere. For me it was a pilgrimage, but I also had an academic interest. Kailash and Manasarovar are abundantly mentioned in the Indian scriptures (you can read about this elsewhere in this book). The sixteenth century 'Hindi' poet Tulsidas describes these sites with great emotion in his *Ramcharitmanas*, but I realise that he did that from hearsay: he had not been there because I did not see all the birds and trees he mentions.

There is more. When I studied the Hindu *Vasta-shastra* or Scriptures about architecture, I entered into a way of thinking that was totally alien to me. It is less alien now: the macrocosmic order is to be imitated in the microcosmic world of my environment and of my personal feelings. Central in that relation between the macrocosmic and the microcosmic order is the *axis mundi*, the vertical shaft that links both worlds. This notion of the *axis mundi* is very much present in the plans of buildings, both sacred and civil in India, and I saw it symbolically in all the *chörten*-s on the way. That *axis mundi* is Mount Meru in ancient mythology, shaped like a mushroom, on top of which all the Hindu gods, including Brahma, Indra, Shiva, Vishnu, Kuber and so on, have their paradises. Agni, the Vedic god Fire, is the forerunner of the symbolical *axis mundi*, that links our microcosmic world to the macrocosmic harmony. That Mount Meru, many Hindus will now say, is identical with Kailash, and that is why a pilgrimage there is auspicious. You can imagine the very strong vibrations of anticipation when I started on this journey. All my Indology was focussed in one place. I was ripe to go on pilgrimage to Kailash.

Of course, I had been on pilgrimage in India, to Pandharpur, joining a crowd of half a million Varkaris, or to Benares, doing the Panchakroshi *parikrama* that goes around the centre of the universe which is the Vishvanath ('the golden') temple. If that is the centre of the universe, I thought, how much more should Kailash be, where Shiva himself resides.

Those who know me well will testify that I am very committed to my research, but when everything is said and published, I consider all my publications only as *lila*; as a play. It is an exciting *lila* alright, but of little value when compared to the endeavour of searching for That which the eye cannot see, in two traditions. For me, no doubt, the pilgrimage to Kailash was a personal pilgrimage, but I shall come back to that later, when I share some personal experiences, without any academic pretense.

Let us first look at the itinerary which we followed to reach the Kailash. (The A in e.g. 1770A, etc., stands for Altitude)

13 May 1996 Kathmandu (1350A) to Kodari (1770A) 7.30–12.00am; 117km to Zhangmu (2300A): 1700: (12.00am Nep. = 2.15pm China).

14 May Zhangmu (2300A) to new Tingri (4200A; km 255) 9am–8pm; 255km via Nyalam (3600A), Milarepa cave (3900A), La Lungla (5010A; km 94) and Old Tingri (4260A; km 195).

15 May New Tingri (4200A) to 'creek campsite' (4300A; km 424) 9.15am–5.45pm; 169km via Chacho La (5090A): km 310) and Lhatse (3950A: km 326) and Brahmaputra ferry (3800A).

16 May 'Creek campsite (4310A) to lake campsite (5000A; km 643)9.30am–6.30pm; 119km via geysers (4915A; km 613) and pass. (5100A).

17 May Lake Campsite (5000A) to lodge (4920A) km 979; halfway between Tsochen and Gerze) 10am–9.30pm; 336km, via a pass (5370A at 13.45) and Tsochen (A?; km 832; 16.00).

18 May From lodge (4920A) to campsite near lake with fresh water springs (4365A; km 1,228); 9.15am–7pm; 249km, via Gerze (with *chörten*; 4310A; km 1,128).

19 May From Lake campsite (4365A) to Shiquanhe (4135A; km 1,603; 10 km E. Of border with Samskar); 9.30am–8.30pm; 375km.

20 May From Shiquanhe (4135A) to campsite near the Indus river after a vain attempt to short-cut across the mountains; (4235A; km 1,685) 2–6pm; 82km.

21 May From campsite (4235A) to Thöling (3615A; km 1,877); 10am–6.30pm; 192km via passes (4875A and 4980A).

22 May Visiting Thöling and Saparam [Tsaparang] (Sutlej 3475A; at gate 3585A; highest point 3725A); 40km.

23 May Thöling (3165A) to Dharchen (4480A; km 2,167); 8.30am–9.00pm; 250km via pass 4800A.
24 May Day One; 9.15am–4.45pm; 4480A to 4820A.
25 May Day Two; 9.15am–6.15pm; 4820A via 5350A (most guidebooks give 5600A or more!) to 4,580A.
26 May Day Three; 9.15–12.15 (Dharchen) and to Manasarovar (3–4.30pm; 4410A); 35km at km 2,202.
27 May Manasarovar (4410A) to a lovely campsite (4720A; km 2,313); 2.30–6.30pm; 111km.
28 May Campsite (4720A) to Paryang (4475A; km 2, 484); 10am–6.30pm via Maryum La pass (5030A; km 2,338).
29 May Paryang (4475A) to Saga (4345A; km 2,730); 10am–8pm; 246km.
30 May Saga (4345A) to last (and beautiful) campsite near river (4455A; km 2,886); 11am–7.30pm; 156km. (Across the Brahmaputra at 11.15 and along the Paiku tso).
31 May Campsite (4455A)to Zhangmu (2300A) km 3008); 12.15–18.00pm (15.45 Nep); 122km via La Lungla (5010).

One should *not* do what we did on the second day; from Zhangmu at 2300A, across the La Longla (pass) at 5010A, and go to Tingri at 4260A to spend the night. Half of our party were sick or had a terrible headache when we reached the (rather fine) hotel in New Tingri. On the way there, we stopped in the Milarepa cave and I noted with great interest in the murals the conspicuous presence of Bhairav, who is a form of Shiva as policeman of Benares, and the patron of Nepal. (Incidentally, Bhairav was also present in the Chiu *gompa*, near Manasarovar).

On the third night – this was even more stupid – we made a detour to see the spectacular geysers, but had to spend the night near a lake at 5000A. Majushri, god of wisdom, was definitely not in the office of the agency at Lhasa when the beginning of our tour was organized. It was the next day, before reaching Tsochen, that we had an experience that was very disturbing to me (this was my first tour in Tibet). I was in ecstasy contemplating the exquisite beauty of the desolate plateau we were driving through; a desert road with agriculture up to an altitude of 4,500 metres, gigantic cloud formations against the backdrop of a dark blue sky, and a horizon of snow-clad mountains more than 7,000 metres high. All of a sudden, in the middle of nowhere, we had to stop for five hitch-hikers. Five young Chinese soldiers, hardly bearded, in green uniforms, carrying automatic rifles and electrical batons most probably used to torture people. The elated atmosphere in our bus vanished in the thin air of the Tibetan plateau as they 'politely' occupied a seat in our bus. We realized that we were in an occupied land, where even the young Chinese military hated to be. This experience was repeated several times on the northern route, and was each time in a very strong contrast to the jolly character of the Tibetan people we met, or who travelled with us; two cooks and two drivers.

On the fourth day out of Zhangmu we did not find a suitable camping place – no water! – and we drove for a total of eleven hours, 336 kilometres of rough road, through a land of indescribable beauty. The road was very dusty in the month of May, and that is where my personal problem started. My nose got clogged and at night, at an altitude always above 4500 metres, I had no air, because I did not want to breathe through my mouth. It was a frightening experience. After that long day, in a pitch-dark night, all of a sudden we found ourselves in front of a Tibetan house (I imagine now that of course the driver knew where he was heading for), somewhere halfway between Tsochen and Gerze; 4290A. Possibly the only house for more than one hundred kilometres in any direction. There we found four generations of people in one room. They put us up for a splendid night. No tents, no wind, no freezing cold.

The northern route is hard, but very rewarding. One unique site is the row of about 25 *chörten* just outside Gerze. They are built in an immense open space, and beautifully preserved (at a 'low' 4300A). One could see from the well-trodden path in the sand that pilgrims come here frequently to circumambulate the *chörten*. However, when we did our tour in the month of May 1996, I do not remember having seen one truck with pilgrims on the route from Tingri to Shiquanhe. I saw several such trucks on the southern route from Manasarovar going west to Tingri (and Lhasa).

Like most townships on the way, Shiquanhe is a Chinese settlement, at about 10 km from the border with Sanskar. Satellite dish, Chinese shops and restaurants lining the filthy square, powdered Chinese prostitutes and plenty of soldiers looking very bored. The Chinese guesthouse had an unpleasant drunken official, but good food. Shiquanhe, a place to fill our petrol tanks and our supply truck and to go away from. Soon we found ourselves on the banks of the Indus river, back in Tibet, 1,685km out of Zhangmu. Having in me 50 years of Chinese and Hindu spirituality, I wrote that evening in my diary:

> *You, highest in the universe,*
>   *we call on you with many names.*
> *Only with human words,*
>   *with human images,*
>   *we stammer to say something about you.*
> *I know that you are full of compassion,*
>   *Lord of Kailash,*
>   *for every human, for every being.*
> *Where are we going to?*
> *To another body, or*
>   *to an intimate union with you?*
> *Or shall I disappear like one of the*
>   *billion specks of dust on this immense desert road?*
> *I do not know.*
> *Yet I know that I am not a mere speck of dust,*
>   *and that you present yourself to me.*

Anticipation increased, as the Kailash was approaching.

> *The road to Kailash,*
>   *the road of life with all its variety.*
> *I sometimes forget Kailash,*
>   *in the intensity of experiences,*
>   *of work, of relations,*
>   *in fatigue and exultations,*
>   *admiring the overwhelming beauty*
>   *along the road of life.*
> *Kailash goes on beckoning, invisible.*
> *On the road to Kailash,*
>   *on the road of life,*
>   *we drive through sands and rivers,*
>   *across the endless plateau and impossible tracks.*
> *We see the yaks in the hot sun of summer*
>   *eating what is not there.*
> *Hundreds of sheep with a lonely shepherd.*
> *Of what does he think in this immense silence?*
> *What happens in his life,*
>   *except for the comings and goings of generations?*
> *On the road to Kailash,*
>   *on the road of life,*
>   *there is our Tibetan driver*

faultlessly taking us across mountains
and through rivers,
there are the Tibetan cooks
ever so friendly and strong,
there are the Chinese officials,
unfriendly and bored.
We see it all as we spend hours with ourselves,
on the way to Kailash calling.
Dust, dust, dust.

When we finally approached the mountains we had to cross in order to reach Thöling, somebody (who had travelled in all continents) remarked: "One should not make this (northern) tour at an early age. If you have seen this beauty of nature, you have seen everything that can be seen on this planet" (except for Antarctica of course). Another said: "Yes, man can never create the pieces of art nature has produced here, but of course it took a very long time to do it!"

On the night before Thöling we got stuck again trying to make a short-cut across the mountains. Luckily we got stuck, because it was a beautiful campsite. A hundred yards away there was a tent of nomads, and their fierce dogs really attacked us. We chased them away with stones and eventually they agreed on a compromise. Ostentatiously, they passed in front of me, three yards from where I sat on a boulder, writing, and they pissed to mark their and our territory.

During the night I had the first experience of what Kailash would actually mean to me. After all my expectations, it was sheer emptiness. Because of my clogged nose, I had little input of oxygen and frequently I awoke, in panic. I tried to stay awake to control my breathing, and I tried to pray for strength and confidence. I prayed my favourite Sanskrit *mantras*, but no peace came. I tried my familiar Christian lines. Total darkness. I prayed to Krishna, to the Guru of the Sikhs, and to Shiva, Lord of the Caves, with all the lines in my memory, but He kept not only his third eye closed. All eyes of the divine were closed to me. It was an experience I shall and should never forget. Finally I concentrated on the mountain I had not yet seen. A piece of rock covered by a glacier, that much I knew. No words, no priests, no traditions. Pure transcendence. I continued to look and fell asleep, solidly. In the morning I awoke with the vision of the Vaisakhi temple in central Bali, dedicated to the Trimurti, or the three Hindu gods. In the central courtyard of the temple you can see the three seats sculpted from the rock on which the three gods are seated. They are invisible, they have no representation, the seats are empty! When I folded my tent in the morning, it was − 8 Celsius.

After 1,877 km we reached Thöling, a major goal of the trek and a very saddening experience. Or were we worn by fatigue? A dusty village without toilets, a couple of temples: that is what remains of the glorious centre of nearly one thousand years ago. Was it because of lack of rain that the region turned into a near desert from *circa* 1850 onwards?

We had glorious predecessors here: the Jesuit Father Andrade in 1625, Tucci in 1936 and Lama Govinda in 1948. They left fine descriptions of what was then there. The once famous White chapel (Lakhang Carpo) with an entrance flanked with two tree trunks, (probably carried all the way from Kashmir one day, across high mountain passes), was now a storehouse for wood and stones, on a floor of cobblestones. But the walls are covered with splendid paintings, dating back to the 15–16th centuries. Those on the right side are in excellent condition; life-size male images of peaceful tantric *yidams*. On the left side, slightly damaged, are the female counterparts. Among the most striking images are cemetery scenes that show various stages of sky-burial: improbable figures representing the spirits of the dead, wild beasts devouring corpses, ascetics in meditation, deities presiding over the cemetery. The Yesho ö chapel, dating back to a Guge king of the 11th century, was now a heap of rubble, destroyed by "young Buddhists at the time of the cultural revolution", we were told! The nice *maṇdala*-shaped ground plan was the main attraction of the ruin, along with the four elegant *chörten*, shaped like minarets, surviving on top of the perimeter walls.

In sharp contrast with the depressing visit to Thöling, was the sight of Tsaparang, which made our bodies climb to 3725A and our spirits soar even higher. From the top of the 'palace' we had an unforgettable eagle's eye view of the surroundings. In Hall number 1, I noticed in the paintings even figures of Ganesh dancing, of Varah and of Brahma. The paintings were playful – didn't some of the gods smile at us? – and a section of the exquisite wooden ceiling had been restored. In the wall-paintings of Hall 2 I admired among the Buddhist figures also acrobats and Persian horse-riders. Especially a 5 metre high figure of a black Buddha drew my attention: I remained sitting in front of it for 15 minutes and the penetrating eyes and peaceful face have not left me ever since. Excellent reading for the days in Tsaparang and Thöling was the description given by Lama Govinda in his work *The Way of the White Clouds*.

Coming to the vast valley from the east, the first view of Kailash is disappointing. Is that all? And why should this one peak among so many have been selected to become so special? I honestly still do not yet have an answer that satisfies me. The trekking around the sacred mountain I personally did not find difficult, except for the lack of air at night, but that had to do with my nose again. Most of us were awed or shocked by the sight of the pilgrims who did the *parikrama* kneeling down, for whatever reasons, in twenty days. The atheists in our group remarked: "If God wants this to wash away sins, I do not believe in God". They did not realize that even the Buddhist pilgrims did not believe in God. More striking was the remark of the anti-clerics; "If a religion can get people to do this, let this religion disappear!" I thought: "If divine energy is *in* man (and woman), what an amount of energy you gather and you will have access to if you get yourself to do this exercise. Nothing can hurt you anymore in this life, if you go around Kailash with such determination. No doubt your sins must thus be washed away, not by an external power, but by the sheer divine energy within you". It reminded me of the extreme powers Indian ascetics, in the myths, are said to acquire through *tapasya* (lit: heat of ascetic prowess); it makes them even more powerful than the gods. With that power they even cursed Shiva and made his Lingam drop! Asceticism and 'divine' energy, a topic neatly avoided in our modern society.

When I came back to Delhi and Belgium, my Hindu friends asked me enthusiastically if I had been to heaven, and back. "Was it a wonderful experience to see Kailash?" I had to disappoint them, saying that it had been a wonderful trek, in splendid scenery, but that it had been a religious experience of nothingness. Perhaps Kailash had one message for me: "Let go of all that you are holding on to".

I should like to conclude with a quotation from my notes written a few days after Kailash and Manasarovar:

> *We have seen the extraordinary beauty of nature,*
>   *ruins of a once flourishing*
>   *with exquisite murals in a setting I saw never before.*
> *We have seen Kailash,*
>   *but what above all stays in my memory is*
>   *the seemingly carefree generosity,*
>   *the readiness to help and*
>   *the lack of complexity*
>   *of the Tibetan people.*
>
> *They are worthy to live in this land.*

Chapter 7

The opening of the sBas Yul 'Bras mo'i gshongs according to the Chronicle of the Rulers of Sikkim

Pilgrimage as a metaphorical model of the submission of foreign populations

Brigitte Steinmann

After vainly searching British libraries for a copy of the *History of Sikkim*, written in 1908 by their Highnesses the Maharaja of Sikkim, Sir Thutob Namgyal, 9th Chogyal of Sikkim (1860–1914) and Maharani Yeshe Dolma,[1] I finally obtained a manuscript from the family of Captain Yongda.[2] The text comprises 175 pages, typewritten in the English language on 35cm. lengthwise pages.[3] The most interesting feature of this work is that it provides us with an example of a historiographic and hagiographic work, which illustrates how a dynasty of twelve rulers created and propagated the sanctity of their cult through the creation of pilgrimage places. The manuscript covers events up to 1908.

The beginning of the Chronicle, in eulogistic style, is devoted to salutations to 'the Blessed Lord Sakya, Saviour of all sentient beings', to 'Vimalamitra, the crown jewel of the assembly of 500 panditas and Siddhi Purusha', and to 'Namkha Jigmed, Ngadag Sempa and Kahtog Kuntu Zangpo'; the three Lamas who opened the sBas Yul 'Bras mo gshongs and consecrated the first Chogyal. Extracts from Tibetan *gter ma* constitute the bulk of the early part of the text, which relates a history back to the origins of the Tibetan people. The authors (Thutob Namgyal and Yeshe Dolma) rely on excerpts from Bu sTon to describe the first mythical kings of Tibet, with Vedic and Tibetan cosmological visions of the world intermingled.

Cosmologies, stories, legends, anecdotes and excerpts of *gNas yig*, *gter ma* and Tibetan historical corpus, constitute the bulk of this text, which we cannot classify only as a 'History of the Sikkimese kingdom', or as simple extracts of *gNas yig*. To consider it as a chronicle or a historiography allows us to realise the writer's concern

Depiction of the Holy Sites in West Sikkim according to the "Neysol Text". Representation of the Hidden Land, diffused by the family of Captain Yongda. Collection of B. Steinmann.

with giving a coherent description of successive events, dated or not, which define how a physical centre – the country with its mountains and people – became a religious centre where Buddhism could spread and monasteries could be built as centres of pilgrimage to assure the process of diffusion of the Dharma.

It is only from the 17th century, with the consecration of the first Chogyal, that dated events make this text resemble the history of a dynasty. It describes how an organized body of priests (real Lamas or flying *arhats*), promoted the idea of the sanctity of this sacred site. The royal authors describe the specific methods employed by the priestly caste to promote this sanctity, although it was only a part of Sikkim which became a prestigious pilgrimage place, viz the Western part, dominated by the Kanchenjunga range. This region became the seat for the foundation of the kingship in 1642. Subsequently all the history of the kingdom is related to this event, at the core of a vast spatial model linking Sikkim to Tibet, and especially to Minyak in Kham and to Sakya monastery.

This manuscript also shows how different populations were knitted together into one religious society. We can decipher, through many stories retold by the writers from oral traditions, the history of the domination and conquest of the Lepcha and Limbu minorities who had first settled there. This model of propagation of the sanctity of a chosen dynasty linked to the universal aspect of a doctrine, is built on a single idea; that the importance of pilgrimage places does not come from their geographical situation within the actual limits of the settlement of strongholds destined to become a kingdom. Rather, their importance comes from the fact that it is these pilgrimage places which delimit the kingdom and its sanctity.

Among these pilgrimage places, there are the mountains with their lakes and caves, controlled by the hermits and the flying *arhats*, the circle of monasteries, surrounded by natural gardens, controlled by the bodies of priests in relation with the king's palace, and the inner core of the monastery, controlled by the deities resident there. From this scheme, we can infer the model of pilgrimage instituted by the Lamas. The country of 'Bras mo'i gshongs is described as a high-level sacred place[4] or a *sBas Yul*, one described in the esoteric literature as being inaccessible to the mass of future pilgrims. At this point, the local populations are not yet involved; they remain dwellers of the forests.

The kind of pilgrimage which is suggested in the text corresponds to the Indian schema of the *yatra*. Such a pilgrimage, to Tibet and to

Chumbi Valley, was frequently undertaken by the Chogyals during their long attempt to settle in their own country, under pressure as they were from Bhutanese or Gurkha invaders. This pilgrimage model also comprises the classical *pradaksina*[5] and all the actions which are required from the pilgrims, such as the *darsana*[6] of the deities.

But, according to the characteristics of a Holy Place, as they are found in the Tibetan records, it was a religious elite, composed of small groups of lama's or king's attendants, which were allowed to invest these places in order to acquire the corresponding merits. It is clearly defined that the religious aim of pilgrimages is to visit places where an event of supreme religious significance may be happening because it has happened in the past. The place is likely to be connected with an ancient legend which relates the high origins of the Bhotia-Sikkimese king, as well as the high powers of the Lepcha king. But the Lepchas have been reduced to the role of providers of shamanic seers or caste services.[7] By comparison to high-level pilgrimage, we are allowed, therefore, to define 'first-level' pilgrimage places: the sacred sites, visited in the past by the Lepcha and Limbu shamans, and where they still go to worship their ancestors. A history of these pilgrimage traditions, in dotted lines and in negative, can also be read in this Chronicle.

The geographical outline of the pilgrimages through the mountain passes of Sikkim, following the ways of the lamas or the shamans, is difficult to observe now. Restrictions on the circulation of foreigners and the heavy monsoon rainfalls do not allow travel to the higher parts of the forests. But many individual groups do visit the country and the monasteries throughout the year, while the Lepcha and Limbu shamans, side by side with the retreating lamas, visit the caves and the hidden places, according to the constraints of the seasons.

The history of Sikkimese pilgrimages is rooted in the history of the land and linked to life and agricultural-cycles. Pilgrimages are the occasion for the Lepchas and Limbus, the original inhabitants of the country, to engage in new business contacts and to find some work abroad. In this way, the pilgrimage is also a kind of emancipation. Through several extracts of administrative records included in the Chronicle, the question of the establishment of taxation in the kingdom sheds light on the slow process of the setting up of the borders, which was closely linked to the land-revenues of the king and to the assimilation of Lepchas and Limbus. The Lepchas revolted several times against their servitude, which consisted mainly of being, for their neighbours, the keepers of the wild borders of this mandala-state system.

A mountain regarded as a pacific and resourceful figure by the Lepchas was transformed into a warrior and a guardian of the religious order for the Sikkimese-Bhotias. The model of the peregrinations of the Lepchas is still linked, metaphorically, to hunting activities and to clearing of new patches of jungle. The unsteady and scattered habitations of the Lepchas are generally grouped around a small *dgon pa*, in the middle of irregular fields. The Lepchas follow the shamans (*bongthing* and *mun*) when, in November, they celebrate the *puja* to the spirits (*rum*) in the forest. These shamans are evoked several times in the Chronicle, through the figure of Tehkong Tek and his descendancy. In the text, they are called *bijuwa*, the name of Limbu shamans, and are placed in opposition to the Bhotia *bla ma* and to the hermits converting the country to Buddhist law. The first Tibetan colonists meet them in the forest to obtain resources and progeny from their magical powers, which are supposed to be great. For the Lepchas, all resources, plants and cereals, come from behind the generous Mountain Kanchenbu[8]. In the Lepcha mythology, a hunter who had discovered the path behind the mountain displeased the gods and caused the way to be definitely closed. In the Bhotia mythology, the flying *arhats* came above the mountains, to open the heavenly country and to transform the god of Kanchenjunga, mDzod lnga, into a guardian of the holy kingdom.

We shall examine, firstly, the chronological events of the manuscript, before going through the various fragments of tales and myths put together by the writer of the Chronicle.

The composition of the Chronicle: the modern context

During the period (1875–1905) when this Chronicle was written, Sikkim increasingly came under British imperial influence, and the 9th Chogyal, Thutob Namgyal, the author of this manuscript, was forced to accept British authority. After his death in 1914, two more Chogyals succeeded him before the final annexation of Sikkim to India in 1975.

Sikkim's modern history begins in 1642, with the consecration of the first Chogyal, Puntsok Namgyal. Prior to this event, the Namgyal kings had been ruling over the Chumbi Valley and the Tista Valley for at least three centuries. According to the Chronicle, they claim to be 'scions of the Minyak House' in eastern Tibet, and to have been 'on pilgrimage in Central Tibet at the opening of the 13th century'. It is also recorded that Khye Bumsag, a Namgyal prince, helped in the construction of the great Sakya monastery in 1268. Khye Bumsag married the daughter of the Sakya hierarch and settled in the nearby Chumbi Valley, which became the nucleus of the later kingdom of Sikkim.

The history of the creation of this dynasty starts with excerpts of descriptions of the Hidden Land by different *gter ston*, among them Shes rab me 'bar, also quoted by Nebesky.[9] The images are stereotypical descriptions of the mountains and the lakes, where landscape is the ornamentation of the Doctrine. The whole land is described as 'resembling a vast pagoda, like a natural *kanika* or *stupa*', and 'like a king's throne'. It is said that 'The bearings and situations of different localities where treasures have been hidden are to be measured from there':

'The most suitable place of devotion, where the Di-ki-mas congregate without being involved. In Da-ki Yang-rDzong. The Vakas (words) retreat is Sam-ye Chen-po. (. . .)

Several hidden countries have been mentioned in the prophecies and apocalyptical books of Avalokitesvara and the Omniscient Guru Padmasambhava and other Jinas who have blessed these places and sanctified them by consecrating them as devotional retreats, and each of them have been indexed and each have their guide books, which give instructions and clues to locating the hidden treasure, and all of these have been hidden in safe places. Out of all such hidden sacred lands, Sikkim is said to be most sacred and sanctified. It is said to be the king of all sacred places equalling paradise itself. Its situation and description as given in the guide book of the gter ston Shes rab me 'bar runs thus:

Situated in the North of India[10] and to south of Tibet there lies 18 large tracts of land sloping southward, in the midst of these, there is a tract with its hill tops in the north and the base of hills extending southwards. The peaks of Kanchen Junga called mdzod lnga sTag rTse appear (. . .) as if hung round with a white silk curtain. At the top of the valley the five perpetual snow clad peaks look like a crown, or the mitred points of an image crown. Seven crystal lakes in the front, looking like a set of water offerings, white cliffs on the right and left, looking like lions rampant towards the skies, adorned with vulture nests on their necks, the middle of the country looks like a bow containing gums, set down with lid raised, the valley like a hand with the fingers stretched out, the arms of the ridges and spurs of hills look like a big wish-granting tree fallen down. Mountains adorn the upper parts of the valleys and rivers issue from the base of the hills. These waters having medicinal virtues like nectar, the left banks always extend in grassy flats or slopes; the entire country is richly wooded with caves, ravines and gorges covered with dense jungles. Immense forests of big trees cover all the hill sides, the banks of lakes extending into an immense plain. The grassy ridges and hill spurs resemble sleeping (mongooses), the hill tops look like rampant lions springing up towards the skies. The largest and the longest ranges are running out like tigresses rushing forward, spurs like leopard cubs jumping forward. The currents of the rivers look like swords sliding downwards, the smaller brooks and rivulets like strings of pearls cascading, while the falls resemble white silk curtains spread out. The sound of the falls mixing with the sounds of forests produces a rhythmic sound like that produced by the repetition of mantras. The whole resembles a vast pagoda with a heart shaped natural kanika (*stupa*).

Right in the centre of this country, there is the stone of auspiciousness. There is a valley resembling a scroll of chinese paper, with a big rock looking like a king's throne. The bearings and situations of different localities where treasures have been hidden are to be measured from there. All the guides and keys to the sacred and inner treasures have been hidden underneath the rock. The directions are to be known from there. There are five trees which are the prince of all drugs and which can cure all combinations of diseases. There are countless varieties of fruits of different colour and taste.'

Dorje Lingpa describes four passes on the four cardinal points, and four middle passes, with 'four unchangeable doors'. He employs the same metaphors as above to compare the landscape to different animals and to a necromancer's triangle.

The text continues in a historical style, describing three periods of expansion of Buddhism:

'*The first one* (. . .) refers to the origins of the Tibetan people, issued from the Bodhisattva Avalokitesvara. Three hundred years later, the celestial king Indra is said to have come down on the highest peak of Kanchenjunga, the Tiger Peak. Five incarnations of Chenrezig named the different mountains and valley and compiled the art of astronomy. Three thousand three hundred and four years later, Padmasambhava exorcised the land and rid it of every obstacle. He compiled the nine apocalyptical works called 'Phrul med sDe kyi lungs ('the nine texts of unerring prophecies'). Then King Khri srong lDe bTsan compiled the Gyal po'i Ga' lungs ('the king's secret prophecy'), to confer benedictions on the land. Finally, the consort of Padmasambhava, Ma chig Ye shes mtsho rGyal and She sa rGron compiled the sKye lo 'Dren pa gnas kyi lung ('the text on the power of places to save people').

These books (. . .) are called the seven apocalyptical works. When the Guru was returning to Urgyen, these were hidden by him in the Zang zang brag'. For Ratna Lingpa, Sikkim is 'the best of all the sacred places of pilgrimage, as it will come to be resorted to in the end of the evil times. (. . .)

The middle period of the expansion of Buddhism was when the Great Incarnate treasure extractor gter ston Rig dZin rGid kyi ldem phru chan came miraculously and obtained the images of Guru Drag-po and mThing kha from the top of the Kanchenjunga's peak, and spent long periods in devotion and seclusion in the northern and western passes, and blessed those places by doing so on several occasions. He twice made his discoveries of these sacred places known in Tibet by attaching letters to the neck of vultures. The great Rig dzin Chenpo of 'Ca-ri established a monastery on the north pass called the gold country. He performed several rites to render the mountain ranges issuing from the mDzod lNga auspicious and favourable for devotional purposes.

The foremost Karthok La, named U wod Ye-shes 'Trum, met the famous Sakya Maha Pandita who had been invited by the Tartar Emperor, at the place called Dzing. He performed the miracle of turning the temple inside out, which excited the admiration of the Sakya Panchen, who thereupon condescended to receive the text of the Gya khrul zhyi khro along with the proper ceremonies. This saint also being directed by a prophetic injunction from the Dakinis, came down to the western pass named Mar rDjong, where he performed the rites of the bDe 'Dus mandalas. He went down to the gZah dMar rJa ri. The Kartok Lama Sonam Gyaltsen came from the eastern pass and trod over the entire length and breadth of hill and dale of the dbang lag thang. The incarnation of Kartok Lama Ye shes 'Bum took rebirth in Kang-ba Chan under the name Gyal-wa rNam-grol bZangpo and coming to this land he did great many useful things.

Then at the time of the last growth and spread, it was the four prophesied brothers who came and took actual possession of this land. One of the above quorum came to be the ruler of this land. In the time of former Maharajas of this land, who were well educated and cultured, there must have been some authentic historical records as to the origin of their caste and creed, but owing to the incessant raids and inroads of the Bhutanese and Gurkhas, which prevented the growth of Sikkim, such records must have been destroyed or scattered to our irreparable loss. But from some old writings and documents, the present ruling family of Sikkim are mentioned as having been descended directly from Guru Padmasambhava.'

In the next section, Tuthob Namgyal retraces the genealogy of his ancestors, beginning with some hypothesis about the gNyans', ancestors of the Sikkimese people, or a group of Nagas, in a human shape and driven by Se hu yi Rgyalpo, who had intercourse with a witch. Their progeny came from the mountain Mon Shri and became the ancestors of the Sikkimese. Another recurrent theme invokes a relationship between the first inhabitants of Sikkim and the Minyak kingdom in Tibet, and a history of the Minyak family is given.[11]

The Tibetan chief, the Bhutanese athlete and the Lepcha sorcerer

Different representations of the first contact between populations are schematized in legends and mythology. One such account, widespread in Sikkim, describes the encounter in the forest between the Bhotia chief, Khye Bumsag (hero of Sakya) and The Kong Tek, the Lepcha wizard, near Kabi Lonstok, north-east of Gangtok. This meeting is preceeded in the Chronicle by another one between Khye Bumsag and a Bhutanese athlete, who wrestle together:

'Gyad-'Bum-bSags himself also proceeded slowly southwards (. . .) down to Chumbi, where he built a masonary house and lived for some time. At about that time there was another athlete named nGa-Wang Gyadpa'i-pal-bar in Bhutan, famous for his strength. There was no one who could compete with him in a wrestling match, nor in any game of strength throughout the whole of Bhutan and he was bursting with pride. Hearing that another man noted for his physical strength had come to Tromo, he came there anxious to arrange a wrestling-match with Gyad-'Bum bSags (. . .) Pal-bar asked Gyad-'Bum to wrestle, at which Gyad-'Bum asked his wife to bring up three pathies of mustard seeds for grinding and oil pressing. Then he called for the oil bowl, which being brought, he pressed with bare hands the mustard seeds and extracted oil out of them. Nga-wang Pal-bar was also anxious to do the same, and called for a similar quantity of mustard seeds etc (. . .) One *pathi* of mustard seeds were given to him, but he only succeeded in grinding them to powder in his hands, and could not get a single drop of oil out of them. At this he was provoked, and challenged Gyad-'Bum to a trial of strength out in the fields. Gyad-'Bum [was] reluctant, and ask Nga-wang Pal-bar to eat and drink and feast away to his heart's content, and to spare him the trial of strength (. . .) But Gyad-'Bum at last went out and, presenting his right hand to Nga-wang, challenged him to hold it tightly. On Gyad-'Bum's wrenching his hand, Pal-bar could not restrain it and had to let it go, because Gyad-'Bum gave such a strong twirl and pull that Pal-bar measured his full length on the ground on his back. Next he rose up and offered Gyad-'Bum his right hand to grasp, which he did with such a firmness and strength that Pal-bar, in making excited efforts to pull his hand free, had the whole arm torn out of the shoulder blade, while he himself sprung off a distance of 5 to 6 paces, leaving his torn out arm in the hand of Gyad-'Bum. Such was his excitement that he himself was not aware of the injury and was boastfully saying "how, now, have I got free or not?" But the next moment Gyad-'Bum held up the detached arm before him and said "whose is this?" On this he went back crestfallen to his own country, bewailing the loss of his arm. He sacrificed a yak to his local family deity (the spirit of the Ma-sang peak called Ma'-sang Khyung-dus, and asked him to go and kill Gyad-'Bum). But Gyad-'Bum was spiritually superior to such local spirits, as he was physically superior to other man. So when this spirit came to Gyad-'Bum, in the shape of a person of blue color with an iron-grey horse and dog, he was interrogated by Gyad-'Bum as to where he was bound. The spirit answered: "Nga-wang Pal-bar has invoked me and sent me to take your life." Gyad-'Bum said with a sneer: "what are you, I would not care for an entire host of such spirits like yourself, better get back to him who directed you." Ma-sang said, "to go back without having obtained so much as a propitiatory puja is indeed very hard upon me. So you must give me something in return." Gyad-'Bum replied that: "I have no wine to give you as an oblation", but Ma-sang said: "if you fill a big vessel with barley, put some water and the fermenting drug on the top of it, that will propriate me." So Gyad-'Bum sacrified a yak with white heels and with some rice cakes etc . . . performed a propitiatory puja to Ma-sang, who then returned back. After the puja was over, Gyad-'Bum asked his wife to throw out the water and wash out the drug from barley and dry it in the sun. On doing so, it was observed that the barley had been sucked dry. So the puja to Ma-sang spirit came in vogue for the Sikkimese, from that time'.

Other versions of this kind of fighting can be found among Tibeto-Burman populations of Nepal, such as the Tamangs[12] and the Sherpas. It is often questions concerning the delimitation of the land which bring about such competitions. In the meeting between Khye Bumsag and the Lepcha chief, the Lepcha chief is presented as a powerful chief with high shamanic powers, who can bestow progeny on the Bhotia chief:

'Although Gyad-'Bum lived three years in Chumbi, he had no issue. Hearing that in the interior of Sikkim there was a great Lepcha patriarch and wizard called The-Kong-Tek, who was reputed to be the incarnation of Guru Rinpoche and who could confer the boon of a progeny, he, after due consultation with his lamas, and divinations, all of which promised success, resolved to pay a visit to the great Lepcha wizard, and started with sixteen followers, carrying various kinds of silk etc . . . They came via Chola to Sa-tha-la, Sedeong Longchok, and thence down through Ring-tsom, where they came upon The-Kong Tek and his wife Nyo-Kong Ngel, who were clearing a patch of jungle for the purpose of cultivation. Gyad-'Bum asked them where The-Kong-Tek and Nyo-Kong Ngel lived, not being aware that they were these persons themselves. Both said they do not know. On asking again, the couple said: 'let your party stay here, while we go find them'. So saying they went away and did not return. After waiting some time, their party saw that they had been given the slip, so they tracked them to the bamboo house. Entering inside they discovered the old gentleman on a raised throne of bamboo. He had washed off the dust and the ashes. He had donned on his feather cap and his garland of teeth and shells. He sat with a dignified mien, while his wife Nyo-Kong Ngel was busily engaged in getting food and drink ready. When the strangers entered, a wide bamboo mat was spread on the ground where they sat and instantly were served with tea and wine. Gyad-'Bum, seeing that this was The-Kong, offered him the presents which he had brought for him, and asked for the boon of a son, which the wizard promised him. This was at Ringchom, and sure enough, as soon as he returned to Chumbi, in the proper time, Jomo Guru showed signs of conception and gave birth to a son, which event was followed by two more male issues. Gyad-'Bum thought that it was time to celebrate the thanksgiving by offering puja to the local deities of Sikkim. So he came down via Chola and had arrived at the cave just at the foot of Dong-tsa-gong rock near the hill side of Kyachung La. There, he was met by The-Kong-Tek and Nyo-Kong-Ngal, who had come up bringing various fruits from Sikkim upon the same errand: viz- to see Gyad-'Bum and to celebrate the thanksgiving by a puja. So they performed the puja there. That was called Brag-tsan, from which the three sons of Gyad-'Bum-gSangs came to be called the three Brag-tsan-dar brothers. Eternal friendship was sworn between Gyad-'Bum-gSangs and The-Kong-Tek and they agreed that all their male descendants should be considered to be their sons and all the females as their daughters. The friendship was cemented by a ceremony at which several animals both domestic and wild were sacrified and all the local deities invoked to bear witness to this solemn contract of friendship, binding the Lepchas and Bhoteas in an inseparable bond. They sat together on the raw animal-hides, entwined the entrails around their persons and put their feet together in a vessel filled with blood, thus smearing the blood over each other. The-Kong invoked all the Sikkimese local spirits, asking them to stand witness to this solemn contract, invoking blessing on those who observed these faithfully, and curses on those who broke this eternal hereditary and national contract between the two races.'

This tale explains at the same time how the Lepcha bilineal system of kinship prevailed, with male clans related to mountains and female clans to lakes, and how the Lepchas were dominated by the Tibetans. This is stated clearly: 'Therefore, the Lepchas gradually came under the influence of the strangers.'

The last part of the tale is the partition of power between the different sons of the chief, Khye Bumsag, whose youngest son Mi-pon-rab was the only one to show 'noble aspirations.' He became chief, and his four sons "were called the sTong-Du-rus-bShi, meaning the four clans of a thousand each".

The genealogy of the Chogyal: the enrolment of the Lepchas to the service of the king

The domination of the Lepchas is the main feature of the conquest of the Holy Land. It was already complete at the time of the first Chogyal Puntsok Namgyal in the 17th century:

'The son of Guru Tashi was Phuntso Namgyal, the first Maharajah of Sikkim.[13] He was born at Gangtok in the year 1604 A. D., the shing-'brug (wood-dragon) year of the 10th century of Tibetan era. He married a lady of the Bab-tsan-Gyad family residing in Gangtok. The Guru Tashi family became very influential and prosperous. The Lepcha soon came under their influence and power. One Lepcha retainer (Nang-gZan) called Sambar became the favourite of the chief, from among the Lepchas. From that time, the Lepchas flocked to the service of the new chief, and those who proved themselves most trustworthy were appointed to the household establishment of the Raja, while others were entrusted with posts of responsibility and honour in the State. Gradually, as the Lepchas of Tashi-teng-kha and Seng-deng also came under the direct influence and control of the chief, they were called the ministerial Lepchas (Monpas). Those not so much in the chief's confidence or favour were employed as traders to carry goods and were called Tshong-sKyel Monpas, and employed in outdoor services, in building or handicrafts. They were also expected to strike or kill anyone if necessary, (. . .) Besides, they were to contribute the summer Nazar (Yarzal) in the shape of newly gathered crops, grains and fruits, and they were also to carry grains etc. to any market for trade or barter.'

This recruitment of the Lepchas to the service of the king is followed immediately by a 'clerical' tale,[14] centered around the notion of the 'flying body' of the saint.

The invention of the holy place: the flying body of the saint

The invention of a holy body of a saint makes written scripture permanent, it fixes it.[15] The discovery of the body of a saint in a rock or the heavens, equipped with magical powers, usually precedes the invention of relics distributed to the pilgrims. Flying bodies, or petrified shamans in the rock are the basis of the sanctity of pilgrimage places; they are components of the diffusion of the Doctrine. This notion of a 'flying body', abundantly illustrated in the opening of the country of Sikkim, takes sense through the very meaning of the word 'pilgrimage' in western languages. Derived from the Latin word '*peregrinus*', we find the Sanskrit root *parah*; meaning 'sent away', 'far away', 'one who travels abroad'. Under Christian inspiration, *peregrinus* was related to different types of exile and particularly that of the people of the Exodus, the Just ones, the prophets wandering in the Desert. The pilgrim became, metaphorically, the Christian who walked towards the Holy City during his earthly life.[16] The Chronicle illustrates these allegories of far-flung travel. In the biography of lHa btsun Chenpo, who consecrated the first Chogyal, we see the Doctrine spreading up from the top of the mountains and not from the bottom of the Valleys. The flying *arhats* choose the most difficult access to the country:

The hagiography of lHa btsun Chenpo

'Now we come to the great dZog-chen Lama saint, called lHa-btsun-Namkha'-jig-med (the founder of the dZog-chen sect in Sikkim). His advent in Sikkim and his previous lives have been foretold in all the following works, in which he is said to have been the great Khanpo Vimalamitra. He was born in a southern province of Tibet called Jarpa, in a village called Lha-yul Zhi-rab, and was born of the celestial race. His father was one Cho-sKyong mGonpo, and his mother's name was Yig-wang buga.

He was born in the me-bya year (fire fowl) 311 years ago from the present sa-sprel year (1908) or in 1597 AD. He received his instructions under the saints Sonam-Wangpo, Rinzing Jatshon Nyingpo and the learned Pema-legs-grub. Under these gurus he had carried on his studies to a perfect proficiency in hearing, thinking and meditating, until he surpassed all the learned ones of Tibet. He repaired the Sam-yes monastery six times over. He received the revelation or inspiration of mystic texts of the gTer-sar and Dag-sNag dGong-Ter (now texts taken out from their hidden places). In the Thang-lha oracle his appearance is also foretold in these words: that by the grace of Chen-re-zi and Indra a celestial being will be born, named Kunga-nyingpo, who will open the passes of this hidden land. He started from Kongbu and came to Sikkim gradually with about 35 followers, proclaiming that it was the time for serious people to enter the sacred hidden land. He first came to the cave called Mag-blo lDan-phug, where he performed a benedictory ceremony, and then returned. He obtained a vision in the Rong-mo-Ding in the shing-sprel year; the next year he was directed by the great gTer-sTon saint Jatshon Nyingpo to serve humanity and all sentient beings, on the 25th day of the 12th month of the year, at Bang-ri Tashi-wod-bar monastery.

[*Several such prophecies are quoted, all predicting his appearance and advent in Sikkim, as well as his career as a pioneer of Buddhism.*]

In the 3rd month of the same year, the local spirits also appeared to him and invited him to enter Sikkim. Accordingly, he set out on the 13th of the 5th month of the me-kyi year, and coming to the vicinity of Shelkar-Gyaltse, to a lawn, he had a vision of the landscape of Sikkim, pictured in the clouds. He saw himself crossing beyond the pastures and villages of Tibet in quick succession, and at last coming upon these grand sceneries, which delighted him and moved him to a prayerful mood. He offered a mandala mentally by way of thanksgiving and just at this juncture, he saw a white swan-vulture flying up from inside Sikkim. This proved to be a divine being who had assumed this shape and he had a long discourse with the divinity, in the course of which he learnt several things regarding Sikkim and the various places of sacred nature in it. Old people describe the place as being where the ritual of the gNas-gSol, local deities worship, was composed. Then while sojourning at the cave of Nyams-dGa' tsal, the foremost lama of the Kathong sect named Kathong Kuntu-bzangpo came through the Kang-la Nangma pass and around the sPreu-gyab-lag. Not finding any road, he looked towards Jongri, where he saw the rocky cliffs of Kampa Khab-rag, the range which ran down to the west of Kabru and down to the Ratong Chu. But as that range consisted of stiff cliffs and precipices, there was no way along the ridge. Retracing his way back for some distance he came to Nyams-DGa'-tsal, where lHa btsun was then sojourning and they met each other. Kathong Kuntu bzangpo told lHa btsun how he had to retrace his way, seeing that there was no path along the rock cliff of Khampa-Khab-rag which looked like pillars of the heaven. lHa btsun told him that the opening of the northern pass into Sikkim was alloted to him and to no one else, and that the western pass was Kathog's share. So he returned thence. lHa btsun also passed by the Kang-la Nangma, and coming to the same rocky cliffs of the Kampa-khab-rag, stopped there as he did not see any path. Exerting his siddhic powers, he passed across the face of the rocky precipices on the top of Kabru and over the top of the sPreu-rGyab-lag (the back part of a monkey). As he passed beyond the sight of his followers, and did not return within seven days, they concluded that he had perished amongst the precipices. They began to mourn his loss and built a *mendong* to his memory. Having completed it, they were about to return back, when they heard his thigh-bone trumpet sounding and they waited yet another week, praying. At the end of three weeks he obtained the siddhic power necessary to enable him to perform his mission successfully. So he came back as miraculously as he had gone forth, right to the place where the Mendong had been built and his disciples were moved to deep faith and confidence by the wonderful exhibition of this siddhic power. A path was then cut across the face of the cliff and a road towards Jongri was opened.

The search for the king: the Lepchas become 'primitive' people or 'natural' Sikkimese

There follows an account of the search for the king, in Gangtok and Rumtek hills:

'Having assembled there, lHa-btsun Chen-po said "we are all lamas, we want a layman to rule the kingdom righteously" and he quoted the oracular guide-book of Rinzhen Lingpa (one of the eight great gTer-sTon), which stated that "one of my four *avatars* will be like a lion, the king among beasts, he will protect the kingdom by his bravery and powers", and also alluded to the residence and name of the chosen one: "One named Phuntso from the direction of Cang will appear". So he deputed one hermit named Tog-ldan Kalzang Tondup to go to Gangtok and to seek out and invite the person bearing the name of Phuntso. One Pasang led the party (. . .) and at last after several adventures, they came to Gangtok, where they met the same Phuntso Namgyal milking his cows. On their accosting him, he took them inside and rendered the meeting auspicious by giving the ascetic lamas a drink of nice fresh milk as the very first treat, and informed them of his name. On their presenting him the invitation from the lamas assembled at Yuksam, Phuntso Namgyal saw that everything suggested a fortunate development of events. So he started forth with his entire retinue of followers, officers and household establishment.

They stayed at Rumtek for the night. The next morning, when the Lepchas saw the party starting forth on the journey, they all exclaimed, "Along kyyu-sa Rumtek non-pa-o", meaning 'now, our god is going away'. That place came to be called Rumtek. This shows how simple the Lepchas must have been, and also how kind and helpful Raja Phuntso Namgyal must have been to them.

The next stage was bSangs (incense), which was so called because the people there burnt incense by way of reception and welcome. The next day they crossed over the Rag-dong bridge, and proceeded through Yangang, where there were Lepchas and Magars. As the party happened to be riding on ponies and some of their retainers had matchlock rifles, which they fired along the way, the simple natives who had never seen ponies nor firearms said to others that the entire party rode on huge hogs, and some of them bore sticks from which proceeded great sound. In time, they arrived at Yuksam Norbugang and presented vast stores of treasures to the lamas and especially to lHa btsun Chenpo.

Having been brought together by the illimitable merits of countless previous lives, on the present mission of benefitting this sacred hidden land which had been mentioned in the prophetic books, the Maharaja Phuntso Namgyal spared no expenses to render this occasion as magnificent and auspicious as he could. His presents to lHa btsun Chenpo were on a grand scale.'

The text emphasizes the fact that all the gNas yig of Sikkim agreed to state that the royal dynasty of the Chogyal came in a direct line from King Khri srong lde btsan. The enthronment of the first king of Sikkim is compared to the rite consecrating a Cakravartin emperor. It is said that the lamas gathered earth and stone from all parts of Sikkim and built a *mchod rten* with it at Yuksam, called the Tashi 'Od Bar mchod rten. The construction of the monasteries came afterwards:

'On the 3rd day of the 11th month of chu lug (water-sheep) year, the next year after the installation, the mNga bDag lama built the Lhakhang marpo (red temple) and the Kathog lama built the Kathog monastery, while the Maharaja built the palace at Tashiding. Having brought all the Lepchas and Bhutias under his direct power, he selected 12 Kazi from amongst the 12 chief Bhutia clans then existing and likewise he selected 12 Lepcha Dzongpons from amongst the superior families of Lepchas in Sikkim. Proclamations were made promising recognition and emoluments to those who distinguished themselves by loyal and faithful services, and stating that the posts of minister and prime minister (Chag-mZod) would be conferred on them. Those who did not serve well, however, would be classed amongst the common people and required to contribute such services as were required by the Maharaja. Thus they were not allowed to remain master-less as before.

The boundaries of the new kingdom of Sikkim were next fixed. They were: Dibdala in the north, Shingsa Dag pay, Walung, Yangang Khangchen, Yarlung and Timar Chorten in the west down along the Arun and Dudh Kosi rivers, down to Maha Lodi Naxalbari, Titalia in the south. On the east, Tagong La and Tang La in the north. These constituted the boundaries of Sikkim, within which the Raja reigned in righteousness, making the land enjoy such peace and happiness as was enjoyed during the Sateyuga periods of the world. This event confirmed the prophecy of Ratna Lingpa'.

Even the mountain is said to have played a role in the consecration of the place, when a bright stream of light, issuing from the peak of mDzod lnga shone right upon Tashiding and the air was filled with fragrance of incense. The Lepcha shamans were then shown the direction of the hidden places by the saint lHa btsun, an event which was also contained in a prophecy.

The subordination of the Lepcha pilgrimage places by the saint

'The manner in which lHa btsun came into Sikkim, after getting over the afore-mentioned difficulty, is said to have agreed literally with the prophecies contained in the dGong 'Dus. Firstly, The Kong Sa Langpa, a Lepcha wizard, went by divine direction to receive lHa btsun and met him at Chukar Pang Shong. Then lHa btsun, who had opened the pass and was coming down, met him again and guided him past the great caves, Kharg thung rong, Phag mo rong, Lhari nying phug and Yangsang phug, then down to Dechen phug, besides showing him several smaller caves of note. As he came down, lHa btsun composed a book describing the various caves and peaks in Sikkim, after having visited the places on his own feet. The Kong Sa lang is believed to have lived about 300 years and to have possessed supernatural powers, though of a benign type. Hence The Kong Sa lang left miraculous traces at Lhari nying phug, the dent made by the lower end of his bow on the shoulder, his foot print at Khrag thung rong, the clump of bamboo planted by him and the tobacco plant and his own grave. These are still pointed out and visited with reverential interest.

The great lHa btsun at one time even allowed one Yugthing Tishay (a Lepcha and the ancestor of the Barphung Putso) to partake of the initiation into the mystic rites of Rig 'Zin Srong 'grub, at which only the three lamas themselves, the Raja and twenty one persons were allowed in the ceremonies. These persons were hereafter considered as Chos bDag (religious authorities) of the text.'

The Lepcha: at issue between Bhotias and Bhutanese

After the establishment of the religious geography, ordered around the cult of the kings through the Doctrine, the Chronicle gives some precise details about the political geography. 'In the religious and oracular books', it is written, 'these slopes were considered as a part of Tibet politically', and the borders at that time extended to China in the east, to India in the south, and to the country of Nagas in the west. Accordingly, a conch shell, a green pillar and a silver white pillar marked the borders. These mythico-political connections not being enough to distinguish the kingdoms, Thutob Namgyal emphasises the line of transmission of the texts. The Fifth Dalai Lama had 'condescended to regard the brotherhood thus established' with the Raja of Sikkim, sending him some presents and an image of Guru Rinpoche. In Sikkim, lHa btsun and the king continued to rule together, choosing the setting for the Palace of Rabdentse.

The text states that during the reign of the next Chogyal, Tensung Namgyal, a strong connection was established between the hierarch of sMin Grol Ling and the Sikkimese king. In addition, a governor (*gçags mdzod*) was also appointed from amongst the Bhutias and 'eight ministers were chosen from the eight clans of the Bhutias, to hold court below the Rabdentse palace'. It seems likely that the Lepchas at that time had not yet completely submitted to the new religious order and did not participate directly in the government. Their submission, like that of the demoness of Sikkim, needed to be inscribed in the body itself, through direct assimilation.

The Lepchas are always suspected of being on the verge of becoming traitors and dissidents, although they never completely break their alliance with the Bhotias, as was the case with the Tsongs, Limbus and Magars of Sikkim. A dream by the lama Jig med Pa 'bo, the builder of Sangha Choling monastery, reported in his autobiography, is retold by Thutob Namgyal, to show how the Lepchas were still regarded with suspicion by the Bhotias because of their magical powers:

> 'Jigmed Poa in his autobiography says that while he was once in devotional seclusion, he had a vision of an evil spirit, which brought in its train ill luck and every untoward misfortune to the Sikkim state in general and especially to the Raja and his connections, had entered in the Rabdentse palace, about the 6th month. He was gradually diminishing the prosperity of the Sikkim state, like the brooks in winter. But being exposed and disgraced, he had betaken himself to Rinchenpong, where he conspired to raise a general insurrection. Having failed in that too, and with his party having foresaken him, he then went to the place whence he had come, viz. Pasak. Here he collected a body of 14 male and female Bijuas and Bijuanis of the Lepcha race called Bonbons. These he employed to work mischief by

means of the black arts, but this produced no effect on the Raja, who was now so incensed that he ordered the men to be arrested and brought up, which was done in the 9th month. The person thus possessed by the evil spirit was not immolated but he was put among the slaves engaged in fetching water, splitting fuel and sweeping the yards, etc . . . Those monasteries which had not been rendered impure by the evil spirit were regarded highly, with thanks and monetary presents.'

Again, the construction of this monastery required fixing down the body of the sorcerers, who repeat their attacks:

'Sometime after his ascent to the throne, five Lepchas appeared, who pretended to be the incarnation of Tashe thing, the great ancient Lepcha wizard chief. They imposed upon the credulity of the Raja, who, knowing the Lepcha language and writing, was rather favourably inclined towards them. These five imposters pretended that they could make the ropes of the Rabdentse Palace and Pemayangtse monastery, tie a fountain into a knot, suspend a stone in the sky, etc. . . . The king was credulous enough to believe them and the Lepchas spoke to the lamas of the Pemayangtse with undue pride in their miraculous powers.

But then when the Lamas and the king were looking down upon Cho chat gong, below Pemayangtse, the Lepchas showed the people a vision of the tops of the monastery and the palace meeting together. The Raja, being under their influence, saw the sight as they wished he would, but the lamas saw that they had only two empty baskets. From this, they knew that the Lepchas had no miraculous powers, so they insisted that the Lepchas show their miraculous powers. But the Lepchas said that the time had not yet arrived for that. Then the *trapas* of the Pemayangtse monastery threatened that unless the Lepchas showed their miraculous powers they would show the Lepchas their physical powers; and they took each a piece of stone from their pockets and began to belabour the imposters with them. In spite of their attempting to run away, the Lepchas were pursued and killed (. . .) The raja himself was convinced of their imposition and trickery, and that he had been duped by heretical imposters.'

During the reign of this Raja, a Lepcha subject of Sikkim living on the frontier plains, who was called Tishe Bidur, pretended to be the incarnation of Guru Rinpoche (. . .) He exhibited some miraculous powers in the way of necromancy and divination. He acquired such a notorious fame that he collected around him several followers, until he thought himself powerful enough to stop the Raja's revenues from the plains with impunity; he also sought the aid of Mangar Raja and tried to raise a rebellion, upon which Yugthing Desit was sent with a force to quell it by arms. He accomplished this successfully and killed all the Tashes at Chakhung. Yuthing was seriously wounded by a poisoned arrow shot by the Tashe. Upon this Yugthing was exalted to the rank of Chikuap. Changzod Karawang was appointed Tenang Dzongpon in Tibet.'

Religious topography and taxation charts

The Chronicle states that while the Lepchas engaged in shamanic actions against the conquerors, the Limbus and Magars, (or Tsongs), who were constantly employed in building fortifications for the Sikkimese Rajas, were 'driven in disgust' and left the country. That was the begining of the alienation, and finally the separation, of this Limbuan land from Sikkim, preparing the ground for the settlement of Nepalese populations. The opening of pilgrimage places as limits of the sacred kingdom closely links a religious topography with a chart of taxable areas. The writer of the Chronicle explains, immediately after discussing these examples of revolts by the Lepchas, how the first taxes were instituted in the country:

'The young raja was once taken over to Bhutan when the Kazis or Dzongpons of Lepcha extract obtained the upper hand in Sikkim. This was about the year 1740 A. D., when the usurper Gyalpo Tamding fled to Tibet and submitted a representation to the Tibetan government (. . .) In the me yos year (1747), the Tibetan Government deputed one Rabdan Sherpa into Sikkim to act as Regent. On his coming to Sikkim, Rabdan Sherpa at once restored the people to their homes and gave them some feeling of security. He built *rdsongs* in Karmi and Mangsher. To every subject who came to pay him respects, he gave a present of a plate full of salt. As salt was a very rare thing then, it induced everyone to come to him so that they might secure the *bhakshish* of a plateful of salt. The Regent had all the names of the recipients of this *bakshish* noted down, and the next year the first assessment of taxes were made according to the above roll. Thus the Regent's generosity was actually a means of obtaining a reasonably correct census. This was the beginning of the collection of annual rents from the people of Sikkim.

(. . .) The regent Rabden Sherpa and Karwang convened a vast assembly of all the subjects of Sikkim at Mangsher and made a proclamation, which came to be called the Mangsher Duma, at which all the lamas and laymen, headmen and raiyats, signed the constitution then drawn up. The powers and privileges, duties etc., of the Lepcha headmen called Tu myangs and the Bhutia Jongpens were defined therein. A regular source of income to the ruler, called Zolung (handle of manufacture) meaning a sort of tax, and a duty on trade, was thus fixed. (The regent then omitted to honour the Mangar chief after his death by sending some representatives to the funeral rite. The Mangars were offended and sought the patronage of the Dev raja of Bhutan. Thus the coalition failed).'

The opening of the most secret part of the country, the area of Tolung where the relics of lHa btsun Chenpo are kept, is then described. The king recalls, once again, how the annual collection of grain taxes was definitely settled in the kingdom at that time. It was a question of an annual collection "realised from the *rajyat*", the *rajyat* being the patron of "the *rajya* or inner core region under the direct authority of the Raja",[17] an important concept for the formation and the legitimation of the cult of the kings in southeast Asia. Under the Bhotia headmen and the *rajyats*, the Lepchas became the first subjects of the king, in this pre-modern mandala-state system originally conceived as chieftaincies controlled by *rdsong dpon* and *gçags mdzod*.

Concluding remarks

This Chronicle illustrates how a place endowed with particular and desirable features for the inhabitants of the High Tibetan Plateau becomes, in clerical literature, a Paradise for the spread of the Law under a dynasty of kings who promote the modes of the cult. The growth of the Law is shown as being based on the lamas's creation of pilgrimage places centred around descriptions of hidden sites.

In the Chronicle, the modes of these pilgrimages rest on the conquest, the submission and the conversion of the indigenous people, mainly the Lepcha sorcerers. The Saint lHa btsun guides the Lepcha shaman to the cave of lHari Nyimphuk and shows him the new way of worshipping the place: the cult of the king as a sacred body and the imprint of the Buddhist deities in the rock will replace shamanic demontrations of their power. Magical phenomenon do not surprise the monks of Pemayangtse monastery, who make fun of the sorcerers who try to knot together the tops of the temples. The sorcerers are then lynched by the crowd.

If we consider the narrative order of the text, we can see that great authority is given to Tibetan corpus references. Popular tales are recorded when it is question of reassuring the legitimation of the new religious order. This order is grounded, in the text, on the demonstration of the supremacy of the magical powers of the flying *arhats* over those of the shamans and hunters: Khye Bumsag easily overcomes the Bhutanese athlete and his Masang spirit; the Lepcha who is thrown into the dungeon is also easily put to the service of the Bhutanese king.

According to the Indian model of the Cakravartin emperor, it is the relation between the king and the lama which fixes down the temporal and spiritual orders. lHa btsun, flying *arhat* and hermit, is progressively invested with the role of wordly advisor to the king; the holy legislator who still bears the virtues of the ascetic. The founding event of this new order is not inscribed in the apocalyptical books but in the popular narrations and the elements of hagiographies which are interspersed in the text: however, the concern for enlightening the people, which we can observe through the demonstration of the magical powers of the *arhats* opening the passes, can be acceptable to the popular mind only with the concurrence of the indigenous shaman. The Kong Tek bestowing progeny upon Khye Bumsag the conqueror is a metaphorical image of the real establishment of the temporal order in the Lepcha country. Some elements of the universal and popular narrative have been caught by the clerical narrative, in what looks to be, above all, a didactic elaboration to the glory of the kings of Sikkim.

The legitimation of the holiness of the Chogyal ascendancy is illustrated through a process of domination of landscape and people; the widespread religious model of this pacific domination in the Himalayas being the conversion of the mountain-gods to Buddhist law. This manuscript of the king also illustrates the social and political aspects of such a model.

Another important point raised in the manuscript concerns the question of how awareness of the sanctity of a holy place can be spread beyond the field of interlinkage between priests and pilgrims. Pilgrims may then visit a place known only from the records of religious literature, without having any trading or commercial concerns. One example is by the writers of the Chronicle, who diffuse religious ideas through a reconstructed history of their dynasty, and in the English language, during the period of British domination in Sikkim. Another attempt is being made at the present time, by the family of the Sikkimese guard of the late king, the keeper of the traditions of Pemayangtse, who tries to diffuse the hidden *gNas yig* by way of press and newspapers, in order to bring the attention of the public on the next destruction of the holy site. The construction of a huge dam in the Yoksum area, in the core of the holy land, not only threatens the religious site, but also the temporal order of the monastery. The new 'openers' of the country are now the Bihari workers, brought into this Tibetan area in their thousands by the Indian colonialists.

Notes

1 I have been doing some field research in Sikkim for five years and I discovered the existence of this *History of Sikkim* two years ago, in Gangtok, during the festival of Pang lHa bsol. I give here large extracts of the first third of the text, without any corrections. The titles of the different paragraphs are my own. [Editor's Note: Copies of the manuscript may now be found in the Oriental and India Office Collection (Formerly the India Office Library and Records); London, under reference MSS Eur E 78, and in the manuscript department library of the School of Oriental and African Studies (London University), ref: MS 380072.]

2 Captain Yongda is the heroic chief of the private guard of the last Chogyal of Sikkim, who resisted until the end the annexation of the kingdom by India in April 1975. He was jailed and became, for a time, a charismatic leader in Sikkim. A copy of the manuscript was kindly given to me by Captain Yongda's brother in law, who was himself engaged, in 1995, in legal action against the Indian company who are building an important dam in the Yoksum area. Situated at the feet of Mount Kanchenjunga, it threatens to flood the ancient sacred site and to destroy the ecological equilibrium in the area.

3 Parts of this manuscript were cited by Joseph F. Rock (1953: 925–48); Rock was mainly interested in the genealogy of the Sikkimese family. Nebesky-Wojkowitz also mentions this Chronicle (1956: 218): where he states that 'Some informations about the cult of Gangs chen mdzod lnga can also be gathered from the Chronicle of the rulers of Sıkkım'. He takes excerpts of the *gter ston* Shes rab me 'bar and Rig 'dzin rgod kyi lden phru can and seems to have had access to the Tibetan sources of the Chronicle. E. Sperling 1994: 807, note 39 refers to another copy of this manuscript,

owned by Michael Aris, and cites a passage related to the fame of the Tangut state in Tibet and its links with the Sikkimese rulers. Finally, Chantal Massonaud 1982: 125, also refers to this chronicle. I intend to publish this manuscript in its entirety.

4 Bhardwaj 1973: 148.
5 Blondeau 1960: 205–208.
6 Bhardwaj, *op.cit.*: 154, describes, for India, the *snana*, sacred bath, the *sukhna, mannat, anauti*, or 'vows', the *mundana*, 'tonsure ceremony', accomplished largely and for general purification purposes, at regional and subregional level shrines, to some specific-purpose oriented aims (afflictions and problems of daily-life).
7 According to Indira Awasty 1978: 28–29: 'The French Fathers who tried to enter Tibet through Burma (19th century), say that they found a number of instances of Lepchas, Mishimi and Lushai tribals as sort of slaves of Tibetan Lamas'.
8 See Steinmann 1996.
9 Nebesky-Wojkowitz 1975: 218.
10 Rock *op.cit.*: 926, gives a slightly different text, quoting excerpts of the mss. from 'situated in the north' till 'image's crown'.
11 Rock *op.cit.*: 929.
12 See the story of the fight for land between two kings (Gyising and Golma), among Tamangs in: Steinmann *op.cit.*
13 The first part is cited by Rock *op.cit.*: 930.
14 This term of 'clerical narration' is used by A. Bourreau, (1983: 41–64). The author tries to classify a hagiographic legend among the different popular narrative styles; the clerical hagiography would be more developed in a urban centralized area: 63.
15 See the example of the pilgrimage of Rocamadour, in France, and the invention of the body of Saint Amadour 'the lover of the rock' (after the 6th or the 7th century), in Montaigne 1991: 27.
16 Rey 1992: 1465.
17 See the definition given by Kulke 1993: 323.

Chapter 8

On the Sacredness of Mount Kailasa in the Indian and Tibetan Sources[1]

Andrea Loseries-Leick

Beyond the 'Site of Eternal Snow' (*himalaya*) and beyond the Chang Tang (*byang thang*) plain, emerges a luminous crystal dome, the holy mountain Kailasa. All the mountains around it seem to bow to its gleaming peak, although at a height of "only" 6,714 metres it is not the highest of them. Four of the greatest Asian rivers have their source within a range of hundred kilometers: the Indus in the north, the Brahmaputra in the east, the Karnali in the south and the Sutlej in the west.

To the south of Kailasa, 36 km away, lies like a giant magic mirror, the holiest lake of the world, Manasarovar. Situated at 4,558 metres, it is the highest freshwater lake on earth. Together with its neighbour, Lake Rakshastal, it has been venerated as holy for 3,000 years. Uncountable myths and an uncountable number of sages have been attracted to these holy surrounds.

A particular spiritual attraction surrounds Kailasa, for thousands of years the most highly esteemed goal for pilgrims of different religions. Whether orthodox Hindus, ascetic Jains, pious Buddhists, Tantric Yogis or Tibetan shamans, these pilgrims all expect that by the spiritual merit of circumambulation (*parikrama*) of the sacred sites they will attain spiritual purification, strength for contemplation and last but not least, the actual awakening of their innate being; the ultimate liberation.[2]

The potential for enlightenment which, according to Buddhist beliefs, all sentient beings possess, should be activated and developed by the mere sight of Mount Kailasa. It is regarded by the different religions as the "World Mountain", the centre of the macrocosm, the centre of one's own being, the actual nature of our as-yet-unrevealed mind. Here the net of myths woven by the religions of India and Tibet is revealed.

On the value of a pilgrimage to Mount Kailasa

In the Vinaya, the spiritual importance of circumambulation, prostrations and making offerings is mentioned.[3] These actions are to be performed every day, as well as on special occasions such as pilgrimages. On certain auspicious days, the merit thus gathered may be a hundred or thousand times greater.[4]

All pilgrims express their veneration by the act of circumambulation, and, according to Tibetan beliefs, the circumambulation of Mount Kailasa will bear great fruits. It is said that a single circuit will purify the defilements of one life time. Ten will purify the defilement of one Kalpa. And after a hundred a pilgrim will attain Buddhahood in one life time.[5]

During circumambulation, which may also be performed by prostration, the pilgrim is supposed to recite the secret *mantra*s of their meditation deity, or contemplate on the *mantra* of the All-compassionate, *Om Mani Padme Hum*. Each and every pious act on the pilgrimage should be dedicated to the welfare of all sentient beings. This accumulation of merit, together with the accumulation of wisdom, will lead finally to full enlightenment. Those pilgrims rooted in folk-beliefs expect from a pilgrimage a better fate in this life, good health and wealth, as well as a favorable rebirth here or in a Buddha field.

For thousands of years pilgrims of different religions have travelled to this sacred mountain, often risking their life on the emptiness of the high plain, exposed to robbers, wild animals and the forces of nature, although only a few Europeans were able to reach Mount Kailasa before the forceful occupation by the Chinese. The first were the Jesuits, Ippolito Desideri and Manuel Freyre, who came from Kashmir in 1715 on their way to Lhasa. Their travel accounts are limited to listing the hardships they endured, such as 'a high, cloud hidden mountain of ice which is abhorrent, infertile, steep and extremely cold'.[6] The first European who circumambulated the sacred mountain in the traditional way was Sven Hedin, but only a few foreign visitors were true pilgrims, such as the Japanese Buddhist monk Ekai Kawaguchi (1897).

In 1962 the stream of Kailasa pilgrims was suddenly stopped and all religious activity forbidden by order of the Chinese Central

Government. Only in August 1981 were the first Tibetan and Indian pilgrim groups permitted to resume pilgrimage to the Kailasa. Within a few years they were followed by the Toyota land cruisers of international tourism.[7]

Since then the mythical divine mountain seems to have been swept over by worldly ambition: used in advertisements by travel agents promising 'real' adventure, or misused for publicity by Reinhold Messnier. For the Chinese government the sacred Kailasa is now an important means of earning foreign exchange and thus marketed as much as possible. Yet, being officially open again to pilgrims, the old tradition has been revived and many thousands of pilgrims have again breathed the enlightened atmosphere of Kailasa, nourished by countless sages.

KAILASA IN INDIAN SOURCES

Mahameru: Great Universal Mountain of Ancient India

According to Indian mythology, the golden Mount Meru is at the centre of the world, surrounded by the universal ocean.

The earliest Indian sources on Kailasa we find in the *Mahabharata*, which originated over a period of eight centuries (4th cent. B.C. – 4th cent. A.C.). In the earlier Vedic texts, Kailasa is not mentioned, although the geographical area which is acknowledged in the *Rigveda-Samhita* is fairly large, and there are references to the mountains and streams of the Indus system. While we may assume that the Aryan peoples came via the Western passes of the Hindukush and the Punjab towards the East; we cannot ascertain whether they had any knowledge of the Kailasa region beyond that range of mountains.[8]

In the *Mahabharata*, however, it is stated that Vyasa, the legendary systemizer of the Vedas, had visited Kailasa.[9] We may assume that the codification of the Vedas attributed to Vyasa was terminated by around 600 B.C., but the oldest parts of the Vedic hymns, the *Rigveda*, may have existed well before that in oral transmission.[10] Thus, although the name Kailasa is not found in the *Rigveda*, Kailasa might have already had sacred significance some 3000 years ago.

However, Kailasa is mentioned as Mahameru in connection with mythological ideas on the creation of the world, perhaps because according to the Vedic view the outer material world was not of major interest; the texts centre around the question of life and the hereafter.[11]

The question of the creation and destruction of the universe is treated later in the system of the Samkhya. Here in the *Samkhyakarika* by Isvakrisna (500 A.C.), we find hints of a possible connection of Kailasa with Mahameru. According to the Samkhya system, in the middle of the earth is the round disc of Jambudvipa. Crossed by seven mountain ranges, the continent is separated in zones of which the furthest southeast is India, separated from the north by the range of the Himalaya. Beyond that, in the fourth zone, resides the giant divine mountain Meru.

Meru itself is described as consisting in all four directions of precious materials: in the east silver, in the south beryl, in the west crystal and in the north gold. The wonderful blueness of the sky which we perceive is but the reflection of the lustre of its southern side. Its peak is the pleasure grove of the thirty-three god-realms headed by Indra. Sun, moon, planets; all circle around Mount Meru.[12]

The sacred Kailasa – abode of the Indian gods

According to Puranic texts, there are seven cities on Mahameru.[13] In the north, the abode of Kubera Mahodaya is situated. Kailasa is also called the abode of Kubera in the *Mahabharata*, where a legend recounts how Kubera, in his earlier existence as a thief, broke once into a Shiva temple. As there was no light, he lit a candle and this attempt to illuminate the temple made him a god in the next life. Originally Kubera is depicted as residing in Sri Lanka, but demons, with the help of Ravana, turned him out. Brahma then erected a new temple for Kubera on Mount Kailasa, from where he protects the treasures of the earth.[14]

According to the *Mahabharata*, the Pandava Bhimasena saw the golden lotus tank of Kubera on the forested hill-slope of Kailasa.[15] It also states that King Sagara, Baghirati and the wishfulfilling cow Kamadhenu, all practiced asceticism (*tapas*) on Mount Kailasa. They enriched the Kailasa with their spiritual power and made it into a *tirtha*, a sacred pilgrimage place.[16]

The most famous Kailasa legends focus on Shiva and his wife Parvati, who are believed to reside on Kailasa. Their existence is reflected in the wonderful poetry and monumental arts of ancient India. Shiva (who has 1008 names), is one of the oldest Indian gods. In his wrathful aspect he is the god of thunder, in his peaceful aspect he is a healer. Under the name of Rudra he was venerated as the non-Aryan god of thunder and storms who, after his marriage with Sita, the daughter of the Aryan god Daksa Prajapati, became integrated into the Aryan pantheon.[17]

The legend of Shiva marrying Uma, the daughter of Himavat, is mentioned in the *Brahma Puranas*, the oldest part of which may date to the pre-Christian era (according to orthodox Hindu tradition, the texts are attributed to Vyasa). But later Puranas also contain a number of accounts of Shiva at his divine abode, Kailasa. In general, all of the Puranas which concern Shiva, such as the *Matsya-, Karma, Linga, Shiva, Skanda* and *Agni Puranas* belong to the system of Samkhya.[18]

In the *Brahmapurana* we read a lengthy description of how Daksa was infuriated with the unconventional manner of Rudra, who roamed about on the burning *ghats*, highly intoxicated with *bhang* and *datura* and smeared with ash and wearing human bones. In consequence, Daksa did not invite his son-in-law to the sacred horse-sacrifice which he had arranged. This enraged Shiva and in revenge he manifested out of his head two monsters, Virabhadra and Bhadrakali, who destroyed the sacrifice ground and killed Daksa. Uma, ashamed of her husband's and her father's behavior, committed suicide by fire, but was later reborn as Parvati, the daughter of Himavat. Shiva, however, was totally distraught and retired forever into the loneliness of Kailasa, where he spent his time in deep contemplation. Parvati, the daughter of Himavat, then came to follow Shiva, and finally won his love after demonstrating her will-power by asceticism. Since then she has lived by his side on the throne in a cloud palace situated at the peak of Kailasa. Shiva as Kailasanatha, playing chess with Parvati while the demon king Ravana tries to lift the mountain with his divine force, has become a reknowed subject for art; as in cave No.19 in Elephanta, the Umasahitamurti (5–7th cent.), and at Ellora Kailasa temple caves No.16, 14 and 30, which also features the sacred mountain (8th cent.).

Another favoured subject for artists is the illustration of Shiva as Gangadharamurti, when Shiva held the goddess Ganga in his locks.[19] This legend tells of a time when the earth was nearly destroyed by a drought, and the Rishis of the Himalaya begged Ganga to descend on earth.[20]

In literature, the 5th century poet Kalidasa created several wonderful masterpieces of Kailasa-related poetry. such as his unfinished epic *Kumarasambhava*. This tells of Kumara, the god of war, a son of Shiva and Parvati, and the poet made the gods come alive with his lyrical description of their love-making 'which hinders the sun to rise'. Thus the fame of Kailasa is also contributed to by Kalidasa.

Shivalingam – Kailasa as a tantric symbol

The most popular form of Shiva worship is the phallus (*linga*) cult, where aniconic symbols such as hand-formed phalli and phallus-shaped stones are venerated. The luminous snow peak of Kailasa is also worshipped as Shivalinga. It symbolizes the unshakable power of universal consciousness (*purusa*), just as does the world-egg Brahmanda. This form of the Shiva cult we find in the *Linga Purana*, which describes in 12,000 verses the 28 forms of Shiva as well as the Linga symbolism. The *Varaha Purana* also mentions a Linga cult which shows strong Tantric influence.

The Tantras directly follow the Puranas, which are differentiated according to the school they belong to. They show a strong affinity to the Vedas, as some Tantric rites are rooted in Vedic practices. They are also influenced by the Upanisads, the Epics and the Puranas, as mentioned above, and reached their full development in the Middle Ages. Originally an oral tradition, the writing down of the Tantra doctrines began in the first centuries A.D. and continued until the 18–19th century. Most Tantric texts are composed as 'divine' dialogues, and Tantric texts in which Shiva speaks to Parvati are known as Agama. Of the three original Tantras, the *Shaiva Agamas*, *Vaishnava Agamas* and the *Shakta Agamas*, only the *Shaiva Agamas* are connected to the Linga cult. The origins of the Linga cult seem to be found in Kashmir, while the mother cult oriented *Shakta Agamas* derive from Bengal.

The main subject of these Tantric doctrines is the wisdom to realize reality as undivided unity; which is Shiva-Shakti. Shiva is symbolically presented as Linga in sexual union with Yoni, the female organ representing Shakti. The fundamental dualism between consciousness (*purusa*) and *prakriti*, which we find also in the Samkhya philosophy, is to be transformed by means of Tantric contemplative rites for attaining full development of one's capacity for enlightenment.

The nature of *purusa* is described as being unshakable like the world mountain Mahameru. Prakriti is Shakti, untamed, destroying energy like the floods of the Ganga, before Shiva (*purusa*) caught her in his matted locks. The union of Shiva and Shakti, *purusa* and *prakrti*, being the highest Tantric goal, became a favoured subject of early Indian medieval art. The erotic *mithuna* sculptures on temples in Khajuraho (11th/12th centuries), and Konarak (13th century) are wonderful examples of this.

In the *shakta* cult of Bengal, there are images in the temples depicting the blood thirsty Kali, who in her ecstasy of love threatens to destroy the whole world. Only when Shiva falls under her trampling feet, corpse like, does Kali stop – and put out her tongue, ashamed!

This popular account is interpreted more deeply in the yoga tradition: the corpse-like Shiva is consciousness (*purusa*) in contemplation (*samadhi*), free of any sense activities, while Kali is the untamed play of nature (*prakrti*), only to be bound by Yoga and contemplation. The stretched out tongue is actually a yoga technique (Khecharimudra). This very moment of existential awareness of unity, *so'ham* and *sa'ham*, 'I am him' and 'I am her', 'as there is no difference between you and me' is the foundation, as well as the goal, of the Hindu Tantras.

In folk beliefs, women expect that by worshipping Shiva they will be blessed with a Shiva-like husband and healthy sons. Particularly during the 'Night of Shiva' (Shivaratri), after the ritual bath and fasting, they anoint the Lingam in the temple with butter and milk, flowers and grains, incense and coins. The phallus form dome of Kailasa is venerated in the same way, by circumambulation (*parikrama*) of the mountain, regarding Kailasa and its surroundings as a giant psycho-cosmogramm, symbolizing the all-pervading cosmic space of absolute consciousness – Shiva.

The significance of Kailasa for the Jain religion

Jainism originated in North India centuries before the appearance of the Buddha Sakyamuni and increasingly spread southwards. Between the 5th and 12th century it enjoyed great influence, but was later replaced by Hinduism and Islam. Jainism bears all the characteristics of an Indian religion: the idea of Karma and liberation (*moksha*), and also the cosmogony are quite similar. Of major importance is the ethical concept of asceticism (*tapas*), which is seen as the only means to attain liberation. According to Jainism, the individual soul (*jivah*) is soiled with Karma. Only moral discipline and *tapas* bring liberation from reincarnation and bestow on the soul the state of eternal bliss.[21]

Many Jain sacred sites are situated on mountains. To the Jains, Kailasa is Astapada, 'Spider', the place where the first Tirthankara Risabha attained liberation. All sites where Jains prophets are born or have died are called *tirtha*, pilgrimage place. Tirthankara means 'the one who has cut through the ocean of Samsara towards liberation'.

According to Jain tradition there are 24 Tirthankaras, 12 Cakravartins who each govern a continent, and 18 heroes (Baladevas, Vasudevas and Prativasudevas), who are together called "The 63 Great Men".[22]

Accounts of the first Tirthankara Risabha are mythical, he is described as having lived for 8,400,000 Purva years each measuring 500 bow lengths. The two last Tirthankaras, Parshva and Mahavira, are of more human dimensions and within our time: Parshva is said to have died around 750 B.C. and Mahavira in 500 B.C.[23]

Jain cosmogony is very similar to that of other Indian religions, which distinguish three worlds: the heavenly realms above, the middle world and below, the nether worlds. The middle world, where humans and animals live, is situated on the earth disc, in the centre of the universe. In its centre lies Mount Meru, surrounded by the continent Jambudvipa which is divided in zones (*varsa*). Its detailed description speaks of diamond walls and lotus terraces with wonderful forests and ponds. The walls have a fencing of gold and precious jewels with four big gates protected by gods. Again, the continent furthest south of Jambudvipa, Bharatavarsa, is bordered in the north by the Himavant mountains, from there Mahasindhu and Mahaganga rivers stream downwards. Bharatavarsa is a *karmabhumi*, which the law of cause and effect means is afflicted. In the zones further north the conditions for beings improve. In the next zone, Haimatavarsa, the beings feed on the fruits of the wondersome wish-fulfilling tree.[24]

In the fourth zone, Videhavarsa, is the actual centre of Jambudvipa, with the world mountain Meru in its middle. In the Jain tradition Meru is called Mandara. The mountain is belly-shaped and built up in three levels. The first is made of stone, the second of silver and crystal, the third is of gold. The peak is made of beryl. This detailed description is reminiscent of the account of Samkhya. But the Jains may have thought Mount Meru to be inaccessible, being situated beyond the fourth zone, three mountain ranges north of Bharatavarsa.

The name Mandara is also known from the Hindu myth of world creation from the churning of the milk ocean. This ocean was surrounded by three mountain ranges, with Mount Meru, the abode of the gods, in its centre. Mandara was the name given to the churn stick and Anda the world snake was used as the churn string. On one side the gods pulled, on the other the Asuras, and the mountain started to spin. The spinning motion of Mandara as the churn stick thereby symbolizing the dynamic of cosmic life.[25]

The question of whether the Jains identify the world mountain Mandara with Kailasa has to remain open. In any case, Kailasa, under the name of Astapada, is often mentioned in the hagiographies of the Jain prophets and is, therefore, an important pilgrimage place to them.

Kailasa/Astapada – the mountain of the first liberation

In the extensive Jain hagiographies we find descriptions of the saints and heroes of the different world periods. They describe the first Tirthankara Risabha as having lived in the best world period, called *sushama-sushama*, when the earth was still covered with wish-fulfilling trees (*kalpadruma*). When Risabha was born, the light of these trees had already diminished and humans could not feed on their fruits alone, but started to depend on herbs and plants. Risabha was born in Ayodhya and at the age of two million Purva years he was elected as the first king of human-kind. After reigning for 6,300,000 Purva years he renounced the world and became the first mendicant Yogi of the world period. It is said that he attained enlightenment on Mount Abu and was also called Adinatha, 'the first master'. When he was 8,400,000 Purva years old he retired to the peak of Mount Astapada together with ten thousand monks. There he went into final liberation after having fasted for six and a half days. The gods cremated his body there – Mount Kailasa became the first cremation ground of the world period.

Risabha's son Bharata, considered the first Cakravartin of India, built a temple on Astapada. He also attained his liberation there by fasting to death.

In the next world period, *dushama-sushama*, there were no more wish-fulfilling trees. When the second Tirthankara Ajita renounced the world, his nephew Sagara became the second Cakravartin. Sagara had 60,000 sons. Once they reached the temple which Bharata had built on Astapada. On seeing the richness of the temple, the eldest son Jahnu was afraid that the temple might be robbed. Therefore he built a ravine around the temple and filled it with the water of the Ganga. Yet, by this action, the dwelling places of the Nagas were filled with water. In revenge, the Naga king sent an army who burnt all the sons of Sagara with their poisoned eyes. After the death ceremony King Sagara sent Bhagiratha to Astapada, who again directed the Ganga towards the ocean. This legend shows a strong affinity with the Brahmanic legend told in chapter 106 of the Vana Parva in the *Mahabharata*.[26]

Thus, in the Jain tradition Kailasa is a *tirtha*. The mountain is mentioned in their hagiographies under the name of Astapada as the first liberation mountain. As in the Hindu tradition, a Jain pilgrim prepares himself by fasting, meditation and performing virtuous deeds. During the pilgrimage he should take food only once daily, sleep on the earth, walk on foot and remain chaste. At the holy site the pilgrims are supposed to circumambulate and make offerings. The completion of a pilgrimage to Astapada promises Jain adepts the highest transcendental rewards.[27]

KAILASA IN TIBETAN SOURCES

Snow Mountain Tise – The White Lion Face

The Palace of Cakrasamvara,
one of twenty four sacred sites, is called Himalaya
Great Snow mountain Tise,
or Tise, the body site of the White Lion Face,
the navel of southern Jambudvipa,
where Tise is, the four river vomiting heads,
the palace of Cakrasamvara and his 62 deities –
all that our masters have realized.[28]

In the Tibetan Buddhist tradition Kailasa is referred to as Tise: "Great Snow Mountain" or "Snow Jewel". In the Sutras are prophecies regarding Kailasa and it said that Buddha Sakyamuni himself had visited the place.

According to the Buddhist Tantra transmission, Kailasa is identified with the Mandala of Cakrasamvara and the extensive commentaries on this Tantra cycle are a primary source on the sacredness of Kailasa. During the second spread of Buddhism in Tibet, after the 10th century particularly, the region around Kailasa began to be frequented for meditation by a number of illustrious Yogis, such as Milarepa, and later by practitioners of the 'Brug pa and 'Bri gung pa orders. It was also a 'Bri gung pa, the 34th hierarch (*gdan rab*) bTsan 'dzin Chos kyi blo gros, who, in 1896, composed the most complete pilgrim-guide to Mount Kailasa. This text, *Tise lo rgyus. . .*, describes the creation of the universe with Mount Meru at its centre and also identifies Meru with Mount Tise.

The creation of Mount Meru and its identification with Tise

After the earlier world was destroyed by fire, water and wind, there were 21 Kalpas of emptiness. Then appeared according to the Karma of the beings a white light of ether called 'completely pure thought' which alone was able to support the three thousand-fold cosmic sphere. Then fire which was aroused by red and yellow wind put the air into motion which was of sapphire colour and round in form. Over the wind circles of water assembled as golden rain clouds. On top of it formed a golden land of square shape with mountain ranges, oceans and continents. In the centre was Mount Meru, surrounded by golden and iron mountains. It is said that this is also Mount Tise, the head which unites four rivers, in the navel of Jambudvipa.[29]

In the developing meditation stage of the Cakrasamvara Tantra, the creation of the universe is mentally repeated until the apparition of Cakrasamsamvara on top of the World Mountain Meru is visualised. According to the Tantric sources, this Meru is understood to be identical with Kailasa. In the Sutras *Avatamsaka* and *Smrityupasthana*, Buddha is quoted as describing Tise as similar to Meru in that: "Mount Tise has the form of a five pointed Vajra and is 500 yojanas high." In addition, in the *Abhidharmakosha*, a description of a 'Snow Mountain" suits Tise as well:

North of Jambudvipa, beyond the nine black mountains, lies the Snow Mountain. Behind that, near the 'Smoke Smelling Mountain', is the Lake Manasarovar, from where four rivers emerge: Ganga, Sindhu, Sita and Pakshu.[30]

When Buddha flew towards Tise...

The second chapter of *Tise lo rgyus* describes how the Buddha in his Nirmanakaya body blessed the holy mountain Tise. When Buddha taught at Magadha on the benefits of bodily images, the gods, Nagas and humans asked permission to create his image. He then let appear by the light of his eye-brows the world architect Visvakarma, who created three images of the Buddha representing past, present and future. These were preserved at Magadha. Subsequently, the statue of the future Buddha called "Subduer of Elephants" was stolen by the wisdom protector Benchen and brought to Tise. The Buddha therefore flew with a retinue of 500 Arhats to a rock called "Mandala Peak" at the west of Mount Tise. There he left four foot prints which are still visible. While sitting on the "Buddha Throne" he taught the Lankavatara Sutra and blessed the site in all four directions. Then Buddha entrusted the stolen image to the Naga king, Ma dros pa, with the request that he hand it over to a monk called Ratnashri, who will come in the future together with 100,000 Bodhisattvas.[31]

The consecration of Tise into the divine palace of Cakrasamvara

In the second chapter of the *Tise lo rgyus* the consecration of Tise is described as it is in the commentaries to the Tantra:

> After a long period of perfection the world again fell into quarrelling. At that time, an emanation of Ishvara, 'Jigs byed chen po, reigned in Magadha over Jambudvipa together with his wife Dus ma mtshan ma, an emanation of Parvati. It happened that 24 gods and demons overpowered the 24 sacred sites of the Vajrayana: from heaven four gods and four Gandharvas descended. Out of the earth four Yakshas and four Rakshasas emerged of whom the demon Mig mi bzang fell in the northern direction into the 'Great Snow Mountain Tise'. From the nether worlds four Nagas and four Asuras appeared. At the same time, four Kinnara and four Phra men ma dwelled on the eight fearful cemeteries and threatened to take over the world. In fear of that, the 24 celestial and demonic beings started to worship and invoke Ishvara. Ishvara, in answer, sent 24 emanations of himself in form of stone Lingams to each of these places, where the 24 gods and demons made blood offerings to him. In such a way the passions increased and thus the beings were lead astray by ignorance. At last, the great Vajradhara in his Tusita Paradise realized that the time had come to liberate all beings. He emerged from his state of Dharmakaya and without altering his mind of compassion and voidness he manifested in the wrathful form of a Heruka with four faces and twelve arms on top of the World Mountain Meru. There, Buddha Akshobya to whose Mandala he belongs, built a celestial palace for him. The other Buddhas of the Mandala sent their presents as well. Thus was formed the 62-fold Mandala of Cakra Samavara. Then he trampled Ishvara and Kali under his feet in a dance of joy by which they attained immediate Buddhahood. In the same way,

the demonic beings in the 24 sites were subdued by male and female Bodhisattvas: by blessing them with Mantras, by revealing to them the clear light of enlightenment and by merging them into the blissful state of Samadhi by sexual union. Then the Heruka and his retinue got hold of the war trophies of his enemies. He put on the six fold bone ornament, the tiger skin for a lower garment, the magic stick, the drum and the hook knife, the skull cup and the corpse meditation mat etc. The divinities also confiscated all substances of enjoyment, such as meat and alcohol, sacrificed everything in a Ganacakra and turned them into enlightenment potions.[32]

Kailasa, the sacred meditation site for bKa' rgyud Yogis

*On this Tise, the king of mountains in Jambudvipa,
I, the cotton clad Tibetan Yogi,
have vanquished the Bon po with Dharma
and made the practice lineage of the Buddha into day.*
(Milarepa).[33]

The story of how the great Yogi, Milarepa (1052–1135), subdued the Bon magician, Naro bon chung, and made the sacred mountain Kailasa his meditation abode, is well known. It is said that during their competition in magic powers the Bonpo flew on his drum to the peak of Kailasa, but Milarepa was already there, having magically beamed himself up. In consequence, Milarepa stayed on at Kailasa, while the Bonpo had to retreat to the nearby mountain, Gurla Mandhata.[34]

Later, Milarepa's disciple, Gampopa (1079–1153), ordered Phags mo sGrub pa (1110–1170) to send practitioners to the holy sites of Kailasa, La phyi and rTsa ri. Phags mo sGrub pa transmitted the order of his *guru* to 'Jig rten gSum mgon (1143–1217), the founder of the 'Bri gung lineage, and to 'Brug pa rGyas ras pa ye shes (1161–1211), the founder of 'Brug pa order of the bKa'rgyud lineage. Many 'Brug pa practitioners followed his example. One of them, rGod Tshang ba, meditated there practicing bCud len, 'Essence Sucking', which permitted him to live on the essence of water alone, without any substantial food. Later the Mahasiddha Urgyan pa and other Yogis of the 'Brug pa order came into the Kailasa region and made it their spiritual abode.

In the beginning of the 13th century the 'Bri gung school founded the first monastery in the Kailash region. The history states that 'Jig rten gSum mgon, while meditating in the valley of Tshva 'ug in Central Tibet, once had a vision of the local deities of Tise, La phyi and rTsa ri, who asked him to visit their places. 'Jig rten gSum mgon would not follow their invitations, but manifested his bodily images there. Yet he promised them that he would send his disciples there. Firstly he selected three groups each of eighty realized Yogis and sent them off to the three holy mountains. In the second mission he sent 900 practitioners in each group. The third group 'Jig rten gSum mgon selected at the age of 73 years. Then he sent 5,5000 monks and Yogis in each group.

The Kailasa group was under the leadership of the Vajracarya Ghu ya sgang pa, who quickly won the respect and veneration of the kings of Guge and Purang. Both kings financially supported the Yogi community at Kailasa. Once. in meditation, the Lama Ghu ya sgang pa was offered a lump of gold by the local god Tise, which he refused. But then 'Jig rten gSum mgon himself manifested in the sky, riding on a white lion and ordered him to use the gold for constructing a monastery. In this way the rGyangs grags monastery at the western side of Kailasa, in the valley of Darlung, was built. It became a great centre of learning and there was also preserved there, when the author of the Ti se lo rgyus visited, an image of the Buddha called the "Elephant Subduer".

rGyangs grags has a special connection to the 'Bri gung protectress, A phyi chos gyi sGrol ma. She is regarded as the Nirmanakaya aspect of Vajravarahi (Samboghakaya) and Prajnaparamita (Dharmakaya) respectively. Emerging from a ray of light out of Cakrasamvara, she manifested first at rGyang grags. Later, in the 16th century, the Vajra master lDan ma kun dga' grags pa followed the invitation of the king of Ladakh and founded the Phyang monastery there. He was thus responsible for the spread of the 'Bri gung order to Ladakh.[35]

The pilgrimage guide to Kailasa

The sixth chapter of the *Tise lo rgyus* describes the actual pilgrim's path (*gnas yig*) around the Kailasa.[36] It states that the outer appearance of the mountain depends on the spiritual level of its observer. For Hindus, it is externally a giant crystal Lingam, and internally it is the divine abode of Shiva and Parvati. For practitioners of the Therevada it is outwardly a snow mountain and inwardly the residence of 500 Arhats. To followers of the Vajrayana the Tise and the smaller peak Ti chung are outwardly the embracing figures of

Demchog Heruka and his consort Vajravarahi. Internally it is within the 62-fold Mandala of Cakrasamvara, of which the three surrounding valleys Dar lung, Lha lung and rJong lung are the three psychic nerves (*rtsa*).

The circumambulation path starts at the destroyed castle called the hermitage of Ghu ya sgang pa, and continues in an easterly direction. Passing the retreat places of the 'Bri gung Yogis Nag po and Ghu ya pa, the pilgrim passes by the right of the Mount "Buddha Throne", where Buddha Sakyamuni recited the *Lankavatara-Sutra*. There are foot prints of the Buddha and of the 500 Arhats in the rock. Around this area are several caves of famous 'Bri gung Yogis.

East of Lha lung there is a mountain called "Golden Palace of Shambala" with foot prints of Milarepa and 16 stone images of Mahasthavira Buddhas. After crossing the Lha chu river one reaches a mountain called "Black Palace of Shambala", a meditation cave of Padma Sambhava which has his feet- and handprints in the rocks. The pilgrim then reaches the sGrolma-la. It is said that Lama rGod Tshang pa had once lost his way in the vicinity, when suddenly 21 wolves appeared, whom he recognized to be the 21 emanations of Tara. He followed them up the path until he saw them disappear in a rock, and discovered the pass. Behind sGrolma-la lies a small lake which is supposed to be the "Swimming pool of the Dakinis". On the path downhill there are many foot-prints of Milarepa and other saints, as well as self-created figures of Simhamukha, Vajrapani, Hayagriva, Mahakala and Vajravarahi. On the small hill next to the "Secret Dakini Path" are the palaces of Tseringma and the Medicine Buddha, where many healing plants grow. In front are the palaces of Tise and Guhyasamaja, as well as eight self-created stupas and one figure of Vajravarahi. Then the pilgrim reaches the Magic Cave of Milarepa, with foot prints of the saint and a Milarepa statue which the Yogi himself has formed out of his blood and excrement.

The rGyangs grags monastery is the last station. There foot prints of the *Tise lo rgus* author himself are found there. This 'Bri gung master studied all historical texts during his journey at Kailasa and completed them with topographical accounts given by the local people. He proved that before Milarepa, Atisha (982–1055?) had already reached the region. The *Tise lo rgyus* of the 34th Hierarch 'Bri gung gdan rab is thus one of the most complete pilgrimage guides on the Kailasa.

Tise – the Soul Mountain of Bon

In the Bon tradition, the Snow Mountain Tise is, together with Pos ri nga den and the lake Ma pangs, one of the three sacred pilgrimage sites, closely connected with the hagiographies of Zhang zhung, the former kingdom. Kailasa was the centre of this kingdom and therefore also called "Soul Mountain of Zhang zhung" or "Tise – Soul Mountain of the White Snow". Tibetans believe that every region has its own deity, which may descend on a mountain which then becomes sacred. The mountains become the "soul" of the region and thus protect and secure the well being of the people around.

The region of Kailasa should be considered as the cradle of Tibetan culture. It was the centre of the Zhang zhung kingdom until its destruction in the 8th century. In this view, the close connection of Zhang zhung with the Persian realm in the east and the Iranian part of Central Asia promoted the introduction of Bon long before the introduction of Indian Buddhism into Central Asia. This tradition claims to originate with sTon pa gShen rab, who according to the Bon sources lived in sTag gzig c. 16,000 B.C.

According to a Bon tradition, the founder of the faith, sTon pa gShen rab, descended from the celestial spheres into sTag gzig, via a nine-storied mountain in the heavenly realm of Ol mo lung ring. This mountain has been identified with Kailasa in Western Tibet. But according to the text *gZer mig*,[37] the region around Kailasa is but a pale reflection of the real Ol mo lung ring, which is in the centre of the world, invisible to humans.

Other old Bon sources which relate to Kailasa are the tantric meditation cycles Ge khod sGrub skor and Me ri Sgrub skor, which in Tibet date back to the 11th century.[38] According to these texts, Tise is a palace where the 360 Ge khod deities reside. These deities are connected with the 360 days of the lunar cycle. The celestial palace has four gates, with a Chinese tiger, a tortoise, a red bird and a turquoise dragon as protectors of the four directions.[39] In the Bon po view, the universe is covered by the atmosphere like a tent, and this tent is supported by Mount Tise. The summit of the tent is open and the peak of Tise reaches out of it. This Tise peak is the centre of the higher spheres in the atmosphere. It is window and centre at the same time, and thus an *axis mundi*. Above is unlimited space. The light of space enters through the opening and illuminates sun, moon and stars. Underneath lies the earth in form of a lotus disc. Further down is the nether world, separated into nine floors.[40]

In the first phase of Bon, the mountain God Ge khod, being the local deity of Kailasa, was venerated by a special cult. Another form of Gekhod is Me ri, who later became a Buddhist protective deity. According to the text *Me ri gyad phur gyi 'phrin las* out of the *Me ri sGrub skor* it is said that:[41]

> On the Soul Mountain, the white Tise, burns a yellow fire. In the Soul Lake Dang ra Ma pangs blue turquoise smoke emerges. The Soul Rock rTa sgo emanates vibrant gold miniatures. Out of the mountain the rock and the lake emerges the three headed and six armed Ge khod. In such a way the blessing of the meditation deity manifests.

In the mythology of sTon pa gShen rab, the warrior Tise is mentioned as a local deity who resides on the mountain of the same name. "The Queen of Celestial Space", gNam phyi gung rgyal, is also located there. She belongs to the group of female sMan mo divinities, who are still worshipped by the local people today. In the first phase of Bon, the "Soul Mountain" was believed to be the sky ladder (*mthos ris them skas*) which comes down from heaven in the same way as the sky rope (*gnam thag*), which connects heaven and earth.

We already mentioned the legendary magic competition between Milarepa and the Bon Magician Naro bun chung described in chapter 22 of the *Hundred Thousand Songs*. According to this source, compiled in the 12th century by gTsang myong Heruka,[42] Milarepa was victorious over the Bonpo and chased him from Tise. Yet, it is curious that according to Lopon Tenzin Namdak, no Bon magician of that name is ever mentioned in the Bon sources. It seems rather that Buddhist saints such as Padmasambhava in the 8th and Milarepa in the 11th century used the traditional power places of the Bon po for their meditations. In the Buddhist pilgrims guides they were later referred to as "Padmasambhava caves" or "Milarepa caves".[43]

However, the importance for the Bon po of 'The Three, Glacier, Mountain and Lake' is clearly emphasised in a text of the 12/13th century called *Register text of the Three, Glacier, Mountain and Lake*.[44] In this text the author, Ye shes rgyal mthsan, describes his spiritual experiences during a pilgrimage to the holy mountain as follows:[45]

> Once, while meditating on the Meri deity in the empty stupa in front of Tise, where I have received the initiations and instructions on the Zhang zhung sNyen rgyud, it happened at

midnight, on the 11th day in the year of the ox, that I noticed a green light emerging from a secret cave of Tise. This light formed a path. Following it I reached a crystal cave where twelve Vidyadharas had assembled. They talked to me one after the other and instructed me on Tise. The first, rGyal gshen mu khir btsang po, explained that the mountain was made of four elements, and consists of slate and snow crystals. It has the shape of a crystal stupa (*shel gyi mchog rten*) of square foundation, with four doors in each direction. Consecrated as the Great Celestial Palace it holds inside four palaces.

Around the mountain lead three paths, an outer, inner and secret. According to the explanation of the second sage, dPon gshes Tha mi tsad ka, Kailasa was blessed by Samantabhadra with the white letter A and is identical as 'highest site' (*gnas mchog*) with the Body Mandala of Samantabhadra. Here gTon pa gShen rab taught the five aspects of Bon and the secret Mantras of the Zhi khro divinities, celebrated a Ganacakra and left his footprints in four directions on the rocks.

The sixth master, Zha pu ra khug, said that Buddha sTon pa gShen rab taught three times at Tise. At that time three hundred Bon practitioners descended from the sky and danced and played on musical instruments in front of sTon pa and left theirfoot prints in the rocks. They named the mountain 'White Glacier Tise' (*gangs dkar ti se*, also *rta sgo*) and the lake 'Turquoise lake of Ma spangs'.

The saint Sum pa'i Bon po dbo dkar also said that previously Vidyadharas, sages and Bodhisattvas performed religious rites at Tise and while dancing the 'lion step' (*seng stabs bro*) and 'tiger step' (*stag 'bros*) left many foot prints in the rocks. In the secret cave where Mother Tantra (*Ma rgyud thugs kyi gcer bo*) was practiced and where is the self created seed syllable of the meditation deity in the rock, they rode on their drums and flat bells and flew in the sky. Everyone connected to this sacred place will leave behind his impure body to be reborn in a pure land.

At night, the sage sPe bon thog rtse said: If one of higher capacity practices for a longer period on the Glacier Tise, he will realize the view of voidness (*stong nyid rta ba*). Prayer and ritual circumambulation of the sacred mountain will multiply the spiritual merit by ten. Recitation of Mantras cleans the impurities of speech.

In the 14th century text, *Lung stan zur dpang*, the author, bLo ldan snying po,[46] transmits prophecies which he had received from the mountain gods as oral transmission (*snyan rgyud*). There it is said:

> The snow mountain Tise is the centre of Jambudvipa. Whoever visits this mountain, will find enlightenment within three life times. Having drunk water of the holy turquoise lake, all obscurations and impurities of the past are purified.

The text *Tshe dbang gnas brgyad kyi bstod pa* is difficult to date, being a *gTer ma* text discovered in 14/15th century. According to this source, the protector of beings Tse dbang rig 'dzin resides on the peak of the Snow Mountain Tise, being the central point of Jambudvipa.

Further information we find in the fairly well known *Ti se'i dkar chag* of the 19th century. Being Buddhist-influenced, the author, dKar ru Grub chen bsTan 'dzin rin chen (born 1801), mixes early Bon sources, such the *Register text of the Three, Glacier, Mountain and Lake* (12th century) with later sources. The sacred Tise is described thus:[47]

> In the sky, directly over the centre of Jambudvipa, is the Snow Mountain Tise. At the eastern side is the Lake Ma spangs: both are in the sky. The base of the mountain is similar to ar mo li kha stone, its peak is on the level of the four trances. This mountain and this lake will not be destroyed at the moment of the destruction of the world. Directly underneath is the snow mountain Ya bag sha ra, known among humans as Tise. There is also the lake Ma dros which is known as Ma spangs. The Snow Mountain Tise is like a well proportioned stupa, the Lake Ma spangs is like an unfolded Mandala. Because they are according to their essential nature the lake and snow mountain of enlightenment, all sTon pa gshen rab of past, present and future attain enlightenment there.

Quotations and descriptions of sacred Bon pilgrimage sites in Tibet were collected by Lopon Tenzin Namdak in the 1983 text *Bod yul gnas kyi lam yig gsal ba dmig bu*.[48] Some of the sites he visited himself between 1957 and 1959, and he could therefore confirm the existence of hand- and feet prints in the rocks. In caves around the sacred lake Dang ra, where he had been hiding while recovering from a gun shot wound, he discovered rare wall paintings of the Bon tradition which he believes to be as old as the old Zhang zhung kingdom (before 8th century).

In the upper Sutlej valley, southwest of Kailasa, in the Khyung lung dngul mkha valley ("The silver palace of the Garuda valley"), near the Drikung monastery rGyangs grags, ruins are to be seen which are the remains of the old Zhang zhung capital. There a royal dynasty ruled until the late 7th century, when the last king, Lig myi rghya, was killed. At that time it was the royal residence of rJe gser gyi hya ru can, the king who asked sTon pa gShen rab for the instructions of the *mDo khri rje lung bstan* ("Sutra of the prophecies of king Khri rje").[49] In the opinion of Tenzin Namdak, the ruins left in this stony valley indicate that there must have existed in prehistoric times a once flourishing agricultural society. However, we lack archeological examinations in this region which might substantiate the sources found in written and oral tradition.

Conclusions

After examining in chronological order the written and oral sources of the Indian and Tibetan material on Mount Kailasa, we may state that:

In Indian and Tibetan Buddhist sources the identification of Kailasa with the World Mountain Meru is proposed. According to the Samkhya system the blueness of the sky is the reflection of the Southern side of Mount Meru. Tibetan Buddhist texts identify Meru with Tise (Kailasa). In Bon sources, Tise is situated in the centre of Jambudvipa. The actual visible mountain is but a symbolic reflection of an invisible, world mountain or celestial palace floating in the air.

The sacredness of Kailasa in the Hindu tradition may date to as early as 1,000 B.C., although the name Kailasa is not mentioned in the Rigveda. In the hagiographies of the Jain prophets its sacredness goes back into mythological prehistory. Buddhist texts connect Kailasa with the period of Buddha Sakyamuni, while Bon scriptures again consider the origin of the sacredness of Tise in the remote prehistoric times of sTon pa gShen rab.

The listing of meditation caves and body imprints of Buddhist saints in pilgrimage guides are chronologically much later than the Bon Register texts, which list the power places of the Bonpo. Thus the hand- and foot-prints in the rocks or the anonym wall paintings in caves around Kailasa must date to before the destruction of Zhang zhung (8th century).

Archeological excavations in that region should be of prime importance for substantiating the chronological information given in the written sources – another puzzle for the exact reconstruction of Tibetan cultural history.

Epilogue

Oh Kailasa – the holiest of all mountains,
for thousands of years the favoured goal of searching mankind,
woven with myths of world creation by the wisdom of sages
  who have gone beyond!
Where is the real source of your sacredness?
Lets keep it in accordance with the Wisdom of Tibetan tradition
– simply in the openness of 'Beginninglessness' (ye nas).

Notes

1 This contribution is mainly based on the German publication: '*Kailasa – Der heiligste Berg der Welt*', Loseries 1990.
2 On pilgrimages as a training path, see Loseries 1994.
3 See Namkhai Norbu 1984: 21ff.
4 *Tise lo rgyus*: 48b.
5 *Ibid.*
6 *Ibid*: 49a.
7 Snelling 1983: 53, 67, 70ff.
8 Gonda 1975: 23.
9 Mahabharata (MB), Sabha Parva, chap. 43, 17.
10 Gonda 1975: 15ff., and note 15.
11 Frauwallner 1953: 94.
12 Frauwallner 1953: 358ff.
13 See Mani 1975, *Puranic Encyclopaedia* entry: 'Shiva'.
14 Schleberger 1986: 150ff.
15 MB 3(33) 151, see Buitenen 1975: 510.
16 On the consecration of power places into pilgrimage sites, see Pranavananda 1949: 5.
17 Mylius 1988: 138.
18 Dowson 1891: 'Puranas'.
19 MB 3, 108, 15.
20 Schleberger 1986: 103ff
21 Frauwallner 1953: 251ff.
22 Glasenapp 1984: 247ff.
23 *Ibid*: 11.
24 Glasenapp 1984: 225ff.
25 Schleberger 1986: 173.
26 See, Mani 1975, *Puranic Encyclopaedia* entry: 'Kailasa'
27 Stevenson 1915: 254.
28 *Tise lo rgyus*: 2b. See also Rossi-Filibeck 1988.
29 *Tise lo rgyus*: 4b.

30 *Tise lo rgyus*: 15b.
31 *Tise lo rgyus*: 9b–11a.
32 *Tise lo rgyus*: 5a–9b.
33 *Mi la ras pa'i rnam mgur*: 385.
34 *Mi la ras pa'i mgur 'bum*, translated by C.C.Chang 1962 etc.; *Mi la ras pa'i rnam mgur*: 379–387.
35 *Tise le rgyus*: 23b–38b
36 *Tise lo rgyus*: 39b–49b.
37 According to Lopon Tenzin Namdak this text which describes the biography of sTon pa gShen rab was translated from Zhang zhung language into Tibetan before the 8th century.
38 Part of the *Ge khod sgrub skor* (p. 67–91), the *Ge khod mo phrom e'i dmar tshan* was translated into English by J.M.Reynolds 1989 (Bon po Translation Project); see Reynolds 1989.
39 See also Namkhai 1990, compare Namkhai 1995.
40 Nicolazzi 1995: 40ff.
41 Shortened version, translation Reynolds & Loseries, Vienna 1991 (Bon po Translation Project).
42 See Hoffmann 1950: 266f. and C.C. Chang 1962: xxiv; see also Evans-Wentz 1978; Namkhai 1995: 183ff. According to Per Kvaerne, the compilation of the 'Hundred Thousand Songs' was only completed in the 16th century, Kvaerne 1985: 8.
43 *Tise lo rgyus*: 39b–49b.
44 *Gangs ri mthso gsum gyi dkar*, 1973.
45 Shortened translation version by Reynolds & Loseries under the guidance of Tenzin Namdak, Bon po Translation Project, Vienna 1991.
46 The *Zhang zhung sNyan rgyud* is the eldest and most important transmission lineage of the *rDzogs chen* system which came from Zhang zhung into the old kingdom around Kailasa. 24 masters who had all attained the rainbow body (*mja' lus*) were historically listed before the 8th century. After that the transmission continues under the oath of secrecy till the present day, in an unbroken lineage. Its protector and meditation deity is Zhang zhung Me ri, the main god in the cycle of the 360 Ge khod: Reynolds, 1992 (Bon po Translation Project).
47 Born 1360; he is the author of the *gZi brjid*, the longest version of sTon pa gShen rab's biography (61 chapters in four volumes) which he also received as oral transmission from sTang chen dMu tsha gyer med, who lived in the 8th century; Reynolds 1992: 16
48 Free extract of a translation by Per Kvaerne, Oslo.
49 Translated by Reynolds and Loseries, Vienna 1991.

Chapter 9

Kailas-Manasarovar in "Classical" (Hindu) and Colonial Sources

Asceticism, Power, and Pilgrimage

Alex McKay

The mountain known to the Tibetans as Kang Ringpoche has become known in the West under the name Kailas, from the Sanskrit Kailasa, and much of the Western understanding of that mountain, and its attendant lake, Manasarovar, has come from Indian sources.

Modern accounts of the region, both Indian and European, by such authors as Pranavananda, Snelling, Johnson & Moran and so on, describe Kailas-Manasarovar as being one of the most sacred sites of Hinduism; one to which pilgrimages have been made since the earliest times. Yet, historically, the region does not appear to have had the structures typically associated with Hindu pilgrimage sites.

Such sites are usually institutionalised. They have *dharmasalas* or *ashrams* to house pilgrims; there are temples or at least sacred images, and there are bathing *ghats*. Resident *purohits*, or priests, advise pilgrims of the appropriate prayers to be made at the site, the most auspicious days to visit, and the type of offerings to be made there, as well as the benefits deriving from these actions. But there is no record of any such structures existing in the Kailas-Manasarovar region, at least until the 1930s, as will be seen.

This lack of structures may partly reflect the fact that the region has been outside the political boundaries of what is now India, although theoretically it is within Indian religious geography. It is also true that there are other Hindu pilgrimage sites without such structures. Another Himalayan site, Amarnath Cave, similarly has no ashrams or other symbols of a pilgrimage site but Amarnath is not a site of great antiquity, and no one claims that its sanctity is featured in Epic literature.[1] The lack of structures in the Kailas region raises the question of how many Hindu pilgrims actually visited the region.

The modern accounts previously referred to also claim that the sanctity of the region is based on an ancient Hindu understanding of Mount Kailas as the home of Shiva, and as the earthly manifestation of Mount Meru, centre of the world in traditional South Asian cosmology. But if we examine the classical texts of early Hinduism, we discover a very different understanding of the region.

In this article I want to examine the perception of Kailas-Manasarovar reflected in early Hindu literature, and contrast it with the empirical evidence concerning the region which is to be found in British imperial primary sources. We may then look again at modern understandings, and question the extent to which the Kailas region was a Hindu pilgrimage site, and whether those pilgrims have perceived it as the home of Shiva and as the cosmological Meru. We may also shed light on the lack of structures, and the sectarian identity of pilgrims there.

It should be noted that archaeological excavations at Rupar (located by the Sutlej river), which was the northernmost site of the Indus Valley civilisation which flourished during the second and third millennium's before the Christian era, do not provide any evidence of contemporary ties between the Kailas-Manasarovar region and that culture.[2] The Indus Valley culture was superseded in north India during the middle of the second millennium BC by the Indo-European culture. Aspects of the new dominant cultures' religious and cultural traditions were later recorded in the Vedic texts, the earliest of which date, very approximately, to the years 1500–1000 B.C.

Sacrificial rites were the central feature of Vedic religious practice, but the Vedas also indicate that water was seen as having sacred and ritually purifying qualities. Then, as now, sacred sites appear to have been characterised by an attendant body of water. The oldest Vedic text, the *Rg Veda*, uses the term *tirtha* to describe a river ford, or area associated with water.[3] This term later came to signify a sacred place to which pilgrims journey, hence *tirthayatra*, the Hindu term for pilgrimage, means, literally, 'a journey to a place of water'.

There are no specific references to the Kailas region in the Vedic texts. But *Rg Veda* 2.15.6 does appear to demonstrate a knowledge of the upper Indus river, for we read here that the god Indra 'made the Indus through his power flow in a northern direction'. As Frits Staal has pointed out, if the Vedic peoples had followed the Indus north to the point where it flows in a northerly direction, they could hardly have failed to continue to its nearby source, which lies around 16 kilometres from Mount Kailas.[4]

One factor apt to be forgotten, is that travellers to the Kailas region from the earliest times may well have been attracted more by the Thok Jalung gold-mines than by gods. Such gold-seekers may have had good motives for concealing their knowledge of the region's geography.

Rg Veda 10.121.4 contains the first specific reference to the Himalayas – as 'Himavant'.[5] This last book of the *Rg Veda*, considered by some to be a late addition to the text, also contains an intriguing reference to a 'long-haired' sage, apparently a religious renunciate.[6] Karl Warner, in the most comprehensive examination of the reference to date, concludes that there is no evidence that this sage is outside of Brahmanical orthodoxy.[7]

As the Indo-European peoples moved eastward into the Gangetic plains, the sacrificial rites began to give way to alternative practices such as pilgrimage. The earliest textual indications of this are in the *Aitareya Brahamana*, which praises the 'Flower-like heels of the wanderer . . . All his sins disappear, slain by the toil of his journeying.'[8]

The contemporary, or slightly later texts, the *Aranyaka*s, give further mention of renunciates, including female practitioners,[9] and in these texts we also find the first mention of a Mount Mahameru, or "Great Meru". Although the cosmological concept of a central world mountain known as Meru is widespread, this Meru has no particular status. It is simply a mountain which the eighth, celestial, son, Kashyapa, does not want to leave. Kashyapa, incidentally, was also the name of a Vedic seer, whose hymns are contained in the 9th book of the *Rg Veda*, so we may speculate that this is evidence for the early existence of renunciates within Vedic society carrying out spiritual practices in the Himalayas.[10]

The texts I have mentioned to date are all pre-Buddhist, although they may well contain material added in later periods.[11] Thus they indicate that, in the pre-Buddhist period, Indo-European culture embraced a concept of sacred water, that there were probably religious renunciates within the Brahmanical fold, and that pilgrimages were, or were becoming, an accepted religious practice. There was a knowledge of the Upper Indus and at least parts of the Himalayas, and there were indications that these mountains had spiritual associations, were coming to be regarded as the home of Vedic deities, and may have attracted gold-seekers and religious renunciates. Kailas-Manasarovar however, was, if known, not endowed with any specific sacred status, while Meru was the mountain home of a minor anthropomorphisised deity, and had no particular spiritual or cosmogonic significance.

There were a number of differences in this understanding from that which emerges from the next major series of texts within the Hindu tradition; the Epics – the *Mahabharata* and the *Ramayana*. These works may have had pre-Buddhist origins, but were recorded in a later period.[12]

We now turn to the *Mahabharata* and the *Ramayana*, the dating of which is uncertain. For our purposes it is sufficient to describe these works, very generally, as having been originally recorded in the period between the second century BC and the fourth century AD. By the time these Epics were recorded, the great age of the Brahmanical sacrificial system had passed, and many elements we now characterise as Hindu, only emerge fully in the Epics.

The Epics are concerned to, as Rommell Varma puts it, 'fix the normative values of Aryan culture',[13] and they indicate that by this period the institution of pilgrimage was an accepted religious practice within Brahmanical Hinduism. Pilgrimage may well have been one of many features originally introduced into this religious system by the renunciates, such as the 'long-haired sage' of the *Rg Veda*. But we may suspect that this acceptance had not been arrived at without opposition when we read, in the third book of the *Mahabharata*, that 'this is the highest mystery of the seers, the holy visitation of sacred fords . . . even surpasses the sacrifices'.[14]

The Epics reflect an expanded knowledge or perception – be it empirical or mythical – of the Himalayas. In addition, pilgrimage, *tirthayatra*, is now depicted as beneficial to all, in contrast to sacrifices, which are only available to the wealthy. Visits to *tirthas* are described as bestowing the same benefits as various sacrifices.[15]

In the *Ramayana*, the Kailas-Manasarovar region appears in the context of the search for Sita, abducted by the demon Ravana. The search for her encompasses the Himalayas, and there are descriptions of the route which her pursuers must follow. This takes them past various mountains, each in turn described as having fantastic characteristics. There is Mount Meru 'the king and greatest of mountains',[16] Mount Sadarsana 'a king of mountains filled with gold', and there is Kailas, rather modestly described as 'bright as a white cloud and embellished with gold'. There are others too, 'the great golden mountain . . . Somagiri . . . king of mountains, for it reaches up to heaven . . . [where] dwells Brahma', and confusingly, there is also 'the wish-fulfilling mountain Manasa'.[17]

Manasa or Manasarovar as a lake features but little in the *Ramayana*. One reference to a 'vast lotus pond' near Kailas,[18] is fairly clearly identifiable as Manasarovar, but the lake is mentioned by name only once in passing, in an account of the lake (described as being *on* Kailas), being created by the mind of Brahma at the request of renunciates who need a water source for their religious rites.[19] This incidentally, seems a comparatively colourless myth, and may be an indication of the lessening concern for Brahma, the creator God.

In the *Mahabharata*, the region is again the setting for a quest, by Arjuna, the hero who plays a central role in the *Bhagavadgita* section. As in the *Ramayana*, Meru and Kailas are clearly differentiated, and again there is a reference to a Mount Manasa.[20] Kailas does now acquire an added sanctity, however, for – 'it is there that the gods assemble'.[21]

But, in sum, Kailas has a very minor role in the *Mahabharata*. Many of its references to Kailas are simply comparative. Characters are described as, 'as tall as the Kailasa peak', or 'white-complexioned as the peak of Kailas'.[22] Kailas is not so much an actual mountain, as a metaphor of strength and purity.

Shiva features but little in the Epics, and is usually referred to under such epithets as the "Three-eyed Lord" or the "Blue-Throated God". But although a King Sagara, performing austerities at Kailas, approaches Shiva for a boon, and in another instance, a King Bhagirath travels to Kailas to placate an angry Shiva, there is no specific statement in either Epic that Shiva actually resides, or at least resides exclusively, on Mount Kailas.[23]

The section of the *Mahabharata* concerning pilgrimage sites, the "Tour of the Sacred Fords", indicates that large areas of the subcontinent were then textually assigned a particular spiritual value for visiting pilgrims. To take two examples at random; 'by passing through Vasistha all the classes become Brahmins', and again, 'after bathing at Kanakhala and staying three nights, one obtains a horse sacrifice and goes to the world of heaven'.[24] It is noticeable however, that no such benefits are ascribed to a pilgrimage to Kailas-Manasarovar.

In a recent article, Reinhold Grunendahl has discussed the geographical location of Kailas as depicted in the *Mahabharata*.[25] He demonstrates that the names Kailas and Gandhamadana are used interchangeably, and that the geographic descriptions of the region do not match the geography of the present-day Tibetan Kailas. He concludes that the Kailas described in the *Mahabharata* is a mountain located around the Badrinath region of the Garwhal Himalaya, close to the actual source of the Ganges.[26]

Grunendahl examines two versions of a particular episode in the Epic set in the Kailas region, which appear to date to different periods. He argues that the emphasis on the inaccessibility of the Gandhamadana/Kailasa region is a literary motif associated with the Narayana school, whose views are articulated in various parts of the Epic, and that that school stressed the inaccessibility of the region, which could only be overcome by ascetic practices, rather than physical endeavor.[27]

References to Kailas in the Epics do not, therefore, equate Meru and Kailas as one mountain, nor do they necessarily refer to the mountain that we know today as Kailas. Nor is Kailas associated most closely with Shiva. Rather it is identified with another deity, Kubera, originally associated with outcasts and criminals, and later to develop into a deity associated with wealth and treasures.[28]

Kailas is Kubera's mountain, it is not the cosmological centre of the world, although the reference to it as the gathering place of the gods is an indication perhaps of its growing status. But it is, at this stage, only one of a number of sacred mountains, and Meru is also referred to as the gathering place of the gods in several other sections of the *Mahabharata*, such as in a brief account of the famous creation myth of the 'churning of the oceans'.[29]

What is demonstrated in the Epic, and earlier textual references to mountains is, I believe, an example of what Max Muller, in describing the worship of various Hindu gods, each praised in turn as supreme, termed 'kanotheism'[30]; the endowing of each deity – or in this case, mountain – with supreme qualities while it is being addressed as the object of veneration. So Kailas is praised as the supreme mountain, but so are other mountains. Thus, in the "Tour of Sacred Fords" section of the *Mahabharata* , other equally sacred mountains in India are described, for example, one near the Ganges-Yamuna confluence, which is lauded as 'a mountain sacred beyond all other mountains, the holy mountain of Mahendra'.[31]

Just as Meru and Kailas are not described as the same mountain in the Epics, so it is distinctly stated that this was a sacred region, which was not within the normal range of ordinary (i.e. caste Hindu) pilgrims. The Himalayas are described as the abode of the gods and other deities of various natures – and that is not a place for men. This is made clear to Arjuna when he arrives at its boundaries. 'Here' he is told 'is the play garden of the gods, beyond the course of humans'.[32] It is emphasised that 'A mortal man cannot desport himself here',[33] and it is observed that 'No one who has failed in austerities can reach that region'.[34]

But the region *is* described as the home of those – to quote the *Mahabharata* – 'great ascetics who had regenerated their spirits and mastered their senses in quest of release . . . the equals of the sun and the fire by the power of their austerities . . . endowed with divine knowledge . . . devoted scholars of the Veda'.[35]

There are similar statements in the *Ramayana*, where these renunciates are described as beings who 'look like gods and are worshipped by the gods themselves'.[36] It is said that the power of their austerities lights up the land devoid of sun and moon.[37]

This Himalayan realm is not then, a place for ordinary pilgrims. It is the home of gods, not to be trespassed upon by ordinary men. In the 'play garden of the gods' the skills of the ordinary individual human are worthless. Arjuna, a famed warrior, is told that 'Weapons are of no use here; this is the land of the serene, of ascetic Brahmins who control their anger and joy. There is no use for bows here, nor for any fighting. Lay down your bow, you have reached the end of your journey'.[38]

Thus even Arjuna, master bowman, needs other skills there in the mountains, because he has gone beyond the worldly realm in which he is master of all necessary skills. In Indian mythology, typically, the "Hero" must be capable of great feats of asceticism.[39] The ultimate power is regarded as the power obtained by *tapas*, the power – literally 'heat' – which can only be acquired through ascetic practices. Only that power can enable an individual to cross outside of normal social boundaries into the realm of the gods.

As this land is outside of human society, and the only individuals who have the requisite ascetic power to survive there are renunciates, we may conclude that the region is in the process of being allocated to renunciates. They are the ones who may transact with the gods. The region is an anthropomorphosised landscape, to which only those who have left ordinary society may aspire. The ideal renunciate severs his ties with the world, he disappears from it, and goes beyond it; he or she (and this symbolic phrase is still used today to describe the death of a renunciate) "goes to Kailas".

Renunciates can be seen to act as pioneers, able to go beyond civilization's frontiers, negotiate with the "wilderness", and eventually bring it within the domain of ordinary citizens, whom the renunciates can protect by their power as intermediaries with the gods.

Nancy Falk has examined the issue of the "wilderness" in Indian mythology and concluded that 'In general, only ascetics took on the wilderness directly, and when they did so they broke with the common structures of the community.' As mastery of the wilderness brings worldly power over it, there existed a complex relationship between a king and the wilderness, with the king having 'to transact with it to acquire or hold kingship'.[40]

Thus, in the *Ramayana*, King Rama, the ideal Hero, is a contradictory figure. The bow-wielding Ksatriya king is fused with the Brahmin renunciate, wearing the symbols of the ascetic.[41] This dual nature enables him to confront the wilderness, and to conquer it, but also to return, whereas the ideal renunciate does not return to society. Thus the duality is essential, for the return, for the ideal "Hero", and as a literary device.

The Epics recount the journeys of "Heroes". These are sagas of archetypal mythology of the type Mercia Eliade has examined, in which the hero figure journeys to an unknown land, and returns from it with his power enhanced, or regained. Arjuna and Rama are hero figures, indeed they are gods. As possessors of ascetic powers – *tapas* – they are equipped to "transact" with the wilderness. They are no ordinary pilgrims, and there is no suggestion that their journeys are within the capabilities of the ordinary pilgrim; on the contrary, it clearly states the reverse.

Thus, to summarise the position, Kailas in the Epics is just one of many sacred mountains, one associated primarily with Kubera, and not identified with Mount Meru. This Epic Kailas may not be the Kailas we know today, and it was not a pilgrimage site considered to bestow benefits on ordinary pilgrims, but was regarded as a land of deities and of renunciates with great ascetic powers.

By the time the Epics were recorded, renunciates must have become a powerful socio-political force in northern India. Whether the renunciate movement arose within or outwith Brahmanical orthodoxy is a matter of debate,[42] but what is clear is that asceticism did raise a problem of control. Individual itinerant renunciates, living and travelling in isolated locations, devoting themselves to religious pursuits and repudiating material possessions, posed no threat to government. But renunciates tended to gather together at certain sacred places, and to gather followers, who made offerings to them. As soon as renunciates ceased to be individuals, and became a group, they turned into a secular power, and, as such, the concern of the State, which sought to control them.[43]

By the time of Kautiliya's *Arthasastra*, that most Macchiavellian of guides to Indian statecraft, which we may date to around the beginning of the Christian era, state authorities had recognised the renunciates' power and begun to try and channel it to their own advantage.[44] *Arthasastra* 1.11.4–8 recommends that kings establish monastic centres as a means of controlling renunciates. By appointing and patronising the leaders of these centres, the king could ensure that the mass of renunciates remained under a single authority, who was loyal to the king.[45]

There are doubts as to how widely known the *Arthasastra* was at that time, and we have little evidence concerning monastic Hinduism until the 8th–9th centuries, when Sankaracarya, himself a renunciate, established four religious centres in the four quarters of India and established, or at least reorganised, ten orders of Saivite renunciates. While his biography is entwined with legend, some sources have Sankaracarya dying at Kailas – the ideal renunciate's death.[46]

But it seems certain that Hindu monastic organisation did exist for some four centuries or more prior to this period. We know of the earlier existence of Saivite schools such as the Kapilikas, who must have had a basic structure, and Sankaracarya may be better seen as a renovator rather than an initiator.[47] But after Sankacarya, most Hindu sects, including Vaisnavites, developed an institutional basis.

We now come to refer to the *Puranas*, a vast corpus of texts which date at their earliest to the 2nd century of the Christian era, although most are much later. It is in these texts that the cosmological concept of Meru as the centre of the world, and the source of four great rivers, is developed.[48] It is here that we find the most colourful and exaggerated mythical descriptions of mountains. For example, the *VisnuPurana*, 11.2, describes Meru, home of Brahma, as being 84,000 leagues high, and with a summit diameter of 32,000 leagues.

What is clear, from the work of those who have attempted to understand the geography of the *Puranas*, is that there is no agreement on the location of these places. S.M. Ali, whose study of Puranic geography is probably the most comprehensive, arrives at the questionable conclusion that Mount Meru refers to the Pamir plateau, from which four major rivers also descend.[49] A more recent commentary by B.S. Syryavanshi concludes that Meru represents the Rudra Himalaya at the Ganges source (a similar conclusion to that of Grunendahl in regard to Kailas) and notes that Kedarnath, a Saivite sacred site, is traditionally regarded as Mount Sumeru/Meru.[50] Given the sacred nature of the Ganges, this conclusion has much to

173

recommend it, and we must consider the possibility that while early visitors to the Kailas region travelled to the source of the Indus, later pilgrims travelled to the source of the Ganges at Gaumukh, and identified that region as the sacred one.

But what is clear is that there is no agreement over the correspondence between the sites of the Epic and Puranic literature and the Himalayan locations known to us today, and that the identification of Meru with Kailas and even of Kailas with Shiva is almost certainly later than the time of Sankaracarya's division of Saivite sects in the 8th–9th centuries.

The Puranas present numerous problems of interpretation and dating, but it is clear that their construction of an understanding of Kailas-Manasarovar is not consistent, and that many Western authors have used these texts selectively. Thus the *Brahma Purana,* dating, as well as can be estimated, to at least the 13th century,[51] at one point lists Manasarovar but not Kailas as a pilgrimage site, while neither is included in a list of sacred places described in that text as being given by Brahma himself. This Purana thus clearly differentiates Mount Kailas from Meru.[52]

The *Sivapurana,* a text detailing rituals to be observed in the worship of Shiva, which dates to around the 9–11th centuries, has no mention of Kailas, and describes Shiva as residing at Himavat, which as we have seen, has been identified merely with the Himalayas. Nor does this text, in listing the 12 major sites of Saivite pilgrimage, include Kailas or Manasarovar.[53]

The *Skandapurana,* which dates very approximately to the 7th–11th century, is a particularly difficult text to deal with, as numerous minor texts are ascribed to it in order to strengthen their authority. Pranavananda refers to one such minor text as detailing the Kailas pilgrimage, but ascribes it to at least the 17th century. In the recent English edition in the series of Puranic texts edited by G.P. Bhatt, the *Skandapurana* differentiates between Meru and Kailas, refers at one point to Shiva as resident on the north-east peak of Meru, and does not include any suggestion that the region is a pilgrimage site. But there are references which indicate that Shiva has become more closely associated with Kailas. He dwells there, at least on occasion, for it is his favourite resort, and he rules his kingdom from there, with Kubera now described as worshipping Shiva.[54]

Suffice to say that in material over a thousand years old, there is no apparently no textual support for identifying Meru, either Meru of the Epics or Meru the Puranic world-centre, and Kailas, as the same mountain. Nor is there any textual support for regarding Kailas-Manasarovar as a pilgrimage site open to caste Hindus; it was a sacred site open only to renunciates and legendary Hero-Kings. Even the full identification of Kailas as the home of Shiva may not have been fully established by that time, and there is no conclusive evidence that the mountain in Tibet which we know today as Kailas, was then regarded as the Kailas of the Epics.

This is not to reject the possibility that Hindu renunciates did visit the Kailas we know today, but rather to suggest that it was one of many sacred mountains in a sacred land, and that the sanctity of the region had not yet come to focus on a particular mountain. In a kanotheistic system, there was no need to establish one mountain as the actual home of Shiva, or any other deity.

One indication that the identification of the Tibetan Kailas with the Kailas of the Epics was a late development, or that it was part of a wider understanding of different mountains as sacred, is the fact that several Kailas's survived, or perhaps came into existence, in northern India. Aside from such architectural Meru = Kailasa's as Ellora, or Bhorabadhur, we have a Mount Kailas 120 miles northeast of Jammu, near to Bhadrawah. This is a 4,328 metre peak which also has its lake Mansar nearby, and has a number of streams arising in the region.[55]

Himachal Pradesh has its Kailas too, Christina Noble records this Kailas as being southeast of Chamba, a 5,200 metre peak, with associated lake Manimahesh. This site attracts 1–2000 pilgrims during an annual pilgrimage.[56] Neither of these sites, however, appear to have attracted academic attention.

Yet today it is the mountain known to the Tibetans as Karingpoche Fang, which is regarded in wider circles as being the earthly manifestation of the cosmological Meru, and as the home of Shiva, and that Kailas is identified as an important Hindu pilgrimage site. But these understandings appear to have arisen within the last millennium, and there are several possible ways in which they arose.

There are some indications of sectarian developments involved here, although it is easy to overemphasise sectarianism, particularly in this period. But we have noted the apparent early eclipse of Brahma as a significant deity associated with the region, and Grunendahl's view of the Narayana influence on the *Mahabharata* account of Kailas.

Although Kubera's place in the Hindu pantheon is difficult if not impossible to classify, he is closely associated with Lakshmi, wife of Vishnu – Lakshmi is sometimes identified as Kubera's consort – and in this sense Kubera's primary association may be seen as Vaisnavite.

This eclipse of Kubera by Shiva may be seen as indicating that the Himalayas were contested ground, in which what we might today call Brahma worshippers, Saivite and Vaisnavite interests competed, with the eventual triumph of the Saivites. Certainly Kailas develops in importance as Shiva becomes an increasingly important deity.

If this is a Saivite development, we must search further into such factors as the influence of the Malla dynasty in the 12–14th century, for Tucci tells us that this dynasty, whose rule appears to have briefly encompassed the Kailas region were, while primarily Buddhist, increasingly influenced by Saivism.[57]

Alternatively, this may be a primarily Saivite Tantric development. One significant indication that this is the case is that the fully developed concept of Shiva as dwelling on Kailas, along with a highly mythologised account of Kailas as a paradise, appears in the first chapter of the *Mahanirvanatantra*, dating to around the 13th century.[58] Although the dating problems of the Puranas make it impossible to say with certainty that this is the first consistent and fully-developed account of this, it does appear likely that many of the understandings of Kailas-Manasarovar now described as 'Hindu', originate within Tantric Saivism.

There is another possibility, that different sects or groups of Hindus perceived the Kailas region in their own understanding, and that there simply was no consistent 'Hindu' understanding of Kailas-Manasarovar, until it evolved out of a response to Tibetan Buddhist understandings of the mountains by Hindu renunciates in the area, or even in response to colonial interests in western Tibet, in particular the search for the river sources of the Brahmaputra, Sutlej and so on.

Certainly, imperial interests did affect the pilgrimage in the first half of the twentieth century and it is the evidence for this latter possibility which I wish to examine in the final part of this paper, along with the question of the identity of the renunciates who travelled to Kailas – wherever that may have been.

Kailas and the West

When the British empire began to expand into the Himalayas during the 19th century, events in Tibet became the concern of the imperial power. British army officers and Indian *pandits* in imperial employ began to cross into Tibet and report on conditions there. Their accounts provide our first reliable evidence from within the Western academic tradition on the numbers of Indian pilgrims travelling to the Kailas-Manasarovar region.

Desideri and Freyre, Jesuit monks who were not unfamiliar with Hinduism, had passed through the region in 1715, and William Moorcroft, an agent of the East India Company in 1812. Both noted the sanctity of Kailas and Manasarovar, although neither mention Meru or Shiva, or refer to numbers or types of Indian pilgrims.

Lieutenant Henry Strachey, who travelled to western Tibet in 1846, records meeting two Hindu renunciates. The first, described as an 'intelligent, smart, and decent *sunyasi*' had been roughly apprehended by the Tibetan authorities on arrival, and only permitted to carry out *puja* at Lake Manasarovar under escort. He had been refused permission to make the circuit of either the lake, or of Mount Kailas. The second renunciate, whom Strachey describes as a '*yogi*' of poor appearance and as a 'half-fool' had had no such problems. Strachey attributed this to the Tibetan's not unreasonable suspicion that an intelligent renunciate could be a British Agent.

Beyond differentiating between '*sunyasi*' and '*yogi*' Strachey gives no indication of the sectarian orientation, if any, of these two men, only that the 'dirty yogi', 'propounded his own ideas about the lake and mountain, which were silly and superstitious'.[59]

But what Strachey does tell us which is significant is that these two men were the only Indian pilgrims who had been allowed into Tibet in 1846, and that none had been allowed in the year before. So 150 years ago, just two Indians, both renunciates, visited Kailas over a two year period.

We cannot assume that these figures were typical, or consistent throughout history. At that time the Tibetans were actively seeking to exclude Western influence, whereas at other times, such as during the Malla dynasty, political conditions were likely to have been much more conducive to pilgrimage to this region. But Strachey's report does suggest that what we might call the 'hard core' of pilgrims to Kailas were still renunciates, and it is consistent with the textual evidence suggesting that this was, historically, a renunciate pilgrimage.

Sven Hedin, whose perspective on the region was dominated by his determination to ascertain the river sources in the region, wrote extensively about Kailas-Manasarovar, but he is of little value to us in regard to the specifics of the Hindu presence there, although his writings added greatly to the construction of a romantic image of the region in the European mind.

Late in 1904, as a result of the Younghusband mission to Lhasa, the British established a Trade Agency at Gartok in western Tibet, and the Agent there occasionally reported on the number of pilgrims who visited Kailas-Manasarovar. These records are probably accurate. Indian visitors to Western Tibet were required to report to the Tibetan authorities, and their entry was tightly controlled. These reports make a clear distinction between pilgrims, and traders, whose entry into Tibet was strictly regulated by traditional arrangements with their Tibetan counterparts.

The establishment of Anglo-Tibetan ties transformed the modern pilgrimage to Kailas-Manasarovar. The British – or at least the 'men on the spot' – sought to bring Tibet into closer association with British India, and one means of doing this was to encourage cross-border ties. Thus Charles Sherring, an ICS officer who inspected the Gartok Agency in 1905, recommended encouraging Kailas pilgrims on the grounds that 'as elsewhere the devotee will be the pioneer of trade'.[60] In 1912, the British Trade Agent suggested that as Badrinath had thousands of pilgrims, the opening of a 'direct route' from that place to Kailas would lead to a big increase in pilgrim traffic;[61] although the Raj lacked the resources necessary for supporting such an undertaking.

Another frontier official, W.S. Cassels of the Indian Civil Service, reported in 1907 that there were around 150 pilgrims a year to Kailas, who he describes as 'fakirs', – renunciates.[62] Cassels's figures for the number of pilgrims are significantly higher than those recorded by Strachey 60 years before. One obvious reason for this was the increased ease of access, with greater security provided by the establishment of a British presence there, however tenuous, and the changing attitude of the Tibetan authorities, who no longer attempted to prevent Indian pilgrims from entering the region.

We have noted the apparent lack of structures for pilgrims to Kailas, which appears to be evidence in favour of this being seen as a renunciate pilgrimage – renunciates being less in need of such support. The early British reports do not provide any evidence which suggests any institutions housing or supporting Hindu pilgrims in the Kailas region existed in that period. Hindu renunciates apparently stayed in Tibetan Buddhist monasteries. A Tibetan Guide-book from the 1890s does recount a legend in which Buddhist monks at one monastery refused charity to seven Indian renunciates, and were turned into wolves – which presumably suggests that subsequent Hindu renunciates were more hospitably received.[63]

Professor Tucci reports that Hindu renunciates favoured Gyangtra *gompa* on the southern side of Mount Kailas, where he noted two '*saddhus*' had been living for a number of years, one of whom was a practitioner of "heat yoga". Pranavananda also refers to Hindu renunciates as staying there, and describes as unique his own residence in 'Thugolo' monastery on the southern shores of Manasarovar.[64]

The number of pilgrims to Kailas-Manasarovar began to increase dramatically in the 1930s. In 1926, according to Hugh Ruttledge ICS, around 100 Indians visited Kailas, a figure down 50 from that of twenty years before.[65] But in 1930 the Gartok Agent reported that 730 pilgrims had come from India that year, including 150 Ladakhis, whom we may presume were Buddhists. (These two reports incidentally, record that that there were 5–600 Tibetan pilgrims in 1926 and 600 in 1930, so there was no concurrent increase in the numbers of Tibetan pilgrims.)[66] Then, in 1931, the Maharajah of Mysore visited the region, along with a party reported as 700 strong;[67] a significant visit, the motives for which deserve further investigation.

One significant factor behind this increase is suggested by the Gartok Agent's report in 1928 that five 'educated' Indians had visited Kailas that year.[68] This appears to mean that they were not renunciates, and certainly from this time on there are references indicating the presence of non-renunciate Hindu pilgrims, whereas prior to this time, they are always referred to in terms denoting that they were renunciates.

The 1930s were a period in which the British and the Chinese were contesting authority in Tibet, and there was a deliberate attempt during this time by the British to emphasize the historical ties between India and Tibet, as opposed to China and Tibet. Visits to western Tibet by Professor Tucci for example, were specifically encouraged, because, in the words of Sir Basil Gould (who as Political Officer Sikkim in 1935–45 was in direct charge of Anglo-Tibetan relations), Tucci's researches 'contribute[s] in the direction of one of our main political aims, i.e. showing that Tibet has its own art etc. and that in some ways . . . Tibet is more closely allied to India than to China'.[69]

With the influx of non-renunciate pilgrims in the 1930s and '40s came a need to establish Hindu pilgrimage institutions at Kailas-Manasarovar. In 1938, it was reported that one Nityanandaji Saraswati 'promoter of the Kailas-Manasarovar Yatra Scheme at a cost of 10,000 rupees, had asked the Garpons [the local Tibetan administrators] for permission to built 21 *dharmsalas* in Tibet'. The Tibetan authorities were reported to be keen on the proposal, but nothing seems to have come of it.[70]

Swami Pranavananda, whose first visit to Kailas was in 1928, returned on a number of occasions after 1935, performing 23 *parikrama*s of Kailas and 25 of Lake Manasarovar. One recent report by an Indian journalist who met him around 1981, describes Pranavananda as having escorted 'over 5,000 pilgrims' to the region in the late 1930s and the 1940s. While this may have been an exaggeration, it does indicate an enormous increase in the numbers of pilgrims to the region, apparently mainly non-renunciates, as well as the great influence exerted on our knowledge of Kailas-Manasarovar by Pranavananda, who was a renunciate firmly within the Vedic tradition, but very much concerned to present Hindu beliefs within the light of western scientific methods.[71]

Such evidence as we have therefore, suggests that British patronage led to a dramatic increase in the numbers of Indian pilgrims to the Kailas region after the 1920s. But it appears that whereas the early pilgrims were renunciates, Kailas-Manasarovar increasingly came within the range of tours of wealthy and educated caste Hindu pilgrims, who returned to their worldly lives after their pilgrimage. What was once a land of heroes and ascetics, was now open to anyone with the necessary fitness, desire, and money.

❋ ❋ ❋

In conclusion, we return to a question raised earlier concerning the identity of those '*fakirs*' who travelled to Kailas-Manasarovar. Despite the Vaisnavite associations the region had in the Epics, with their accounts of the travels of Rama and Arjuna, Kailas is, today, described as the home of Shiva, and as such is primarily sacred to Saivites.

Of the ten branches of Saivite renunciates systemised by Sankacarya, two groups, the Giris and the Paravatas, have names indicating a particular association with ascetic practice in the mountains. The term Paravata is however, no longer used.

There is suprisingly little in the way of academic studies of renunciate movements in India, particularly those of the Saivites, and there are apparently no studies of the Giri sects activities in India. The extent to which they follow Tantric practices is thus unclear. But it is apparent that Giris do not always practice in the mountains, they may practice in other more-or-less isolated places, or remain in sectarian institutions.

Giri Saivite renunciates are, however, to be found today at the source of the Ganges, which in the present political climate is as close to Kailas-Manasarovar as they can generally aspire to. They may even be in the Kailas-Manasarovar region of the Epics – although they perceive the Kailas of Shiva as the Tibetan Kailas we know today, and that remains an *ideal* destination for them. Their numbers are not large, in 1993 and 1994 there were around half a dozen residing at Gaumukh or at Tapavan, above Gaumukh, during the months from May to October. They may spend an indefinite number of summers there, although usually retreating to Uttarkashi or Rishikesh during the winters.[72]

Pranavananda gives the names of a number of Hindu pilgrims who visited Kailas-Manasarovar which indicate they were renunciates associated with this Gangotri-Tapovan area at the source of the Ganges, although we cannot say for certain that they were members of the Giri order.[73]

Thus, while in the middle of this century, the newly emerging group of caste-Hindu pilgrims to Kailas were probably Pan-Hindu, it is this group of Giri Saivite renunciates who appear to be the spiritual successors of past travellers to Kailas-Manasarovar, and who now, as then, have the power to 'transact with the wilderness'.

Notes

1 Aziz 1982: 121–26.
2 See, *Indian Archaeology* 1954: 6–7; 1955: 9–11; Dikshit, K.N. 'Late Harappa in Northern India, in Lal, B., & Gupta, S., (eds.) *Frontiers of the Indus Civilisation*, Delhi 1984: 253–69; Joshi, J., Bala, M., & Ram, J., 'The Indus Civilisation; A Reconsideration on the Basis of Distribution Maps': 539–41 in Lal & Gupta, *loc.cit.*; Sharma, Y.D., 'Past Patterns of Living as Unfolded by Excavations at Rupar', in *Lalit Kala*, Delhi 1955–56.
3 Singh 1995: 9.
4 Staal 1990: 290.
5 Rg Veda 10.121.4, quoted in Staal 1990: 290.
6 I use the term "renunciate" as a convenient one encompassing the various terms for religious mendicants in India, *yogis, saddhus, sannyasis* etc, and in using the term "sect" I follow Dumont's definition of this term as, 'a religious grouping constituted primarily by renouncers, initiates of the same discipline of salvation, and their lay sympathizers'; Dumont 1970: 187.
7 Rg Veda 10.136; Warner 1989: 42.
8 Aitareya Brahmana 7–15, quoted in Bhardwaj 1973: 3.
9 Brhadaranyaka 111.6.1–8.1; quoted in Ghurye 1964: 28.

10 Taittiriya-Aranyaka 1.7.20, quoted in Frawley 1993: 92.
11 Gonda 1975: 20.
12 I should note that is not my intention to examine the Indian Buddhist sources. These have been the subject of a stimulating article by Frits Staal (1990), which emphasises the interaction between the Himalayan peoples, and the continuous historical interchange of ideas there, a consideration which must not be lost sight of.
13 Varma 1988-89: 13.
14 The Mahabharata [hereafter MhB] 3.80.35-40; van Buitenen edition, vol. 2: 374.
15 MhB 3.80 34-38, quoted in Eck 1981: 336. There is, however, also a consistent anti-pilgrimage thread running through Hindu texts, as indeed is the case with most other religions. The key issue here is surely one of authority.
16 Ramayana 4.41.32; Lefeber & Goldman 1994, vol. 4: 149.
17 Ramayana 4.42.16-27; Lefeber & Goldman 1994, vol. 4: 152.
18 Ramayana 4.42.21-22; Lefeber & Goldman 1994, vol. 4: 152.
19 Ramayana 1.23.7-8; Lefeber & Goldman, 1994, vol. 1: 170.
20 MhB 3.213.5-10; van Buitenen, vol. 2: 647.
21 MhB 3.140.10-15; van Buitenen, vol. 2: 490.
22 MhB 1.212.20; van Buitenen, vol. 1: 408; MhB 5.154.15; van Buitenen, vol. 3: 472.
23 MhB 3.104.5-15, van Buitenen, vol. 2: 24; MhB 3.107.20-25, van Buitenen, vol. 2: 429.
24 MhB 3.82.40-45, 3.80.25-30; van Buitenen, vol. 2: 388.
25 I am pleased to acknowledge Dr Grunendahl's assistance in translating from the German some features of this article for me.
26 Grunendahl 1993.
27 MhB 3.140.1-5; van Buitenen, vol. 2: 490.
28 Satapatha Brahmana, 13.4.3.10, quoted in Sutherland 1992: 63.
29 MhB 1.15.10; van Buitenen, vol. 1: 72; also see MhB 3.247.5-10; van Buitenen, vol. 2: 703.
30 Eck 1985: 26, quoting Muller.
31 MhB 3.85.15-20; van Buitenen, vol. 2: 400.
32 MhB 3.156.21-23; van Buitenen, vol. 2: 524.
33 MhB 3.152.5-10; van Buitenen, vol. 2: 511.
34 MhB 3.142.25-30, van Buitenen, vol. 2: 493
35 MhB 3.145.30-35; van Buitenen, vol. 2: 497.
36 Ramayana 42.25; Lefeber & Goldman, vol. 4: 152.
37 Ramayana 42.31-36.; Lefeber & Goldman, vol. 4: 153.
38 MhB 3.38. 32-34, van Buitenen, vol. 2: 297.
39 Katz 1989: 90.
40 Falk 1973: 1.
41 Lefeber & Goldman, 1994: 414 fn. 8.
42 See Olivelle 1974, Heesterman 1984, Thapar 1978, 1988, *et al.*
43 For a modern example of this process, see; Bouillier 1994: 215-18, 226.
44 Olivelle 1987: 59.
45 Olivelle 1987: 44, 50.
46 Pranavananda 1984: 218; Ghurye 1964: 5; Oberdiek 1995: 71.

47 Ghurye 1964: 42, 152.
48 Space prevents an examination of this literature in depth, as it does an analysis of the question of how the river sources relate to our identification of Mount Kailas.
49 Ali 1973: 49, 52.
50 Suryavanshi 1986: 59.
51 Rocher 1986: 155.
52 Brahma Purana 13.1–7, Batt 1986: 766–67.
53 Morinis 1984: 29.
54 Skanda Purana, 1.30.32–35, 1.37.32–33; Bhatt 1992: 256, 304.
55 Ganhar 1973: 65–68.
56 Noble 1988: 75–91.
57 Tucci 1956: 109.
58 See Avalon [ed.] 1913.
59 Strachey 1848: 1–2, 84, 87.
60 OIOC L/P&S/7/182–1656, Report of C. Sherring ICS, dated 3 September 1905.
61 OIOC L/P&S/11/54–1872, Gartok Annual Report 1912, British Trade Agent Gartok to Supt., Punjab Hill States, 30 November 1912.
62 OIOC L/P&S/7/207–1873, report of W.S. Cassels, 23 September 1907.
63 Huber & Rigzin 1995: 19–20.
64 Tucci quoted in Snelling 1990: 286; Pranavananda 1983: 238.
65 OIOC L/P&S/12/4163, report by H. Ruttledge ICS, to Commissioner, Kumaon, 30 September 1926.
66 OIOC L/P&S/12/4163, British Trade Gartok to Supt., Punjab Hill States, 1 September 1930.
67 OIOC L/P&S/12/4163–2202, British Trade Agent Gartok to Supt., Punjab Hill States, 13 September 1931
68 OIOC L/P&S/12/4163, Gartok Annual Report 1928, forwarded to Supt., Punjab Hill States, 4 December 1928.
69 OIOC L/P&S/12/4247–1022, [former Political Officer] B.J.Gould to E.P.Donaldson [India Office], c.9 February 1946.
70 OIOC L/P&S/12/4163, British Trade Agent Gartok to Political Agent, Punjab Hill States, 9 September 1938.
71 Pranavananda 1983: XIX; Bedi & Subramanian 1984: 16
72 Personal observation/discussions, Gaumukh-Gangotri, 1993–94. I am pleased to acknowledge the assistance of Siva Prasad Pujari, *pandit* of the Prasad temple, Gangnani, H.P. (India) and "Om Nagari Tapovan" and the *saddhu* community at Gaumukh and Tapovan, via Gangotri, H.P.
73 Pranavananda 1983: 225.

Chapter 10

Tibetan Pilgrimage in the Process of Social Change

The Case of Jiuzhaigou[1]

Peng Wenbin

Based on my preliminary research in the summer of 1996, I intend to discuss the social, political and economic changes in Jiuzhaigou, a Tibetan Bon-po village community in northwest Sichuan Province, PRC, and the impact of these changes on local Tibetan pilgrimage practices since the 1950s. Social transformations in Jiuzhaigou have been profound and unprecedented in history, as they have been in other parts of Tibet. Successive campaigns launched by the present Chinese regime, such as Democratic Reform, Collectivization, and the Cultural Revolution, brought about changes in all aspects of local Tibetans' traditional way of life. Religious activities, including the practice of pilgrimage, were banned from 1957 after an uprising took place here. It was not until the early 1980s – with the implementation of Deng Xiaoping's reformed religious policy – that Jiuzhaigou began to witness a revival of public religious activities. Local pilgrimage to Rdza-zhig Brag-dkar (hereafter Mt. Rdza-dkar), a sacred mountain located in Jiuzhaigou, gained momentum in the mid-1980s.

Since the 1980s, tourism has been promoted in Jiuzhaigou and its development has generated a great impact upon local pilgrimage practice. Rapid expansion of tourism in the late 1980s has increasingly drawn a large number of locals in Jiuzhaigou into the tourist industry. The consequent commoditization of ethnic culture, and its impact upon traditional values, is significant.[2] Although the impingement of the modern, secular force of tourism upon this local community is not necessarily destructive in all of its aspects, my findings at the preliminary stage of my study do indicate that the rapid development of tourism in Jiuzhaigou over the past decade constitutes one of the main factors leading to a gradual decline of pilgrimage activities during the past few years. Interviews with villagers reveal that tourism in Jiuzhaigou has engendered a preoccupation with making money and with the evaluation of many things in monetary terms. This is true particularly of the young, who see more 'tangible' benefits from their participation in the tourist business than in pilgrimage to Mt. Rdza-dkar to obtain favors from this mountain deity.

The development of tourism in regions inhabited by Tibetans is a complicated process: on the one hand, it may offer a space for Tibetans to reaffirm their cultural differences from the dominant group, thus reconstructing their ethnic identity.[3] On the other hand, it can lead to an erosion of some traditional values, introducing new strains and conflicts into local Tibetan communities. This negative consequence is real and significant, and it often cropped up in my conversation with villagers in Jiuzhaigou.

Pilgrimage to Mt. Rdza-dkar

Jiuzhaigou ('Nine Village Valley'),[4] was named after the nine Tibetan villages in a valley located in the south of Nanping County. Most of the inhabitants in the valley of Jiuzhaigou are ethnic Tibetans.[5] Local Tibetans are Bon-pos associated with Rab-dben Monastery (Chin: Zarusi), located within Jiuzhaigou valley.[6] About ten kilometers southeast of the monastery is the sacred mountain Rdza-zhig Brag-dkar ('White Clay'), a 4,400 meter-high peak that attracts pilgrims from Tibetan communities in Jiuzhaigou and its adjacent areas.

Rdza-zhig Brag-dkar appears to be a local deity whose power does not extend far beyond areas adjacent to the valley of Jiuzhaigou. Pilgrims from other Bon-po communities in the Amdo area rarely come to visit Mt. Rdza-dkar. For some locals, including the abbot of Rab-dben Monastery, Mt. Rdza-dkar is equal in rank to Bya-dur, the mountain next to Dga'-mal Dgon-pa (Chin: Gamisi); though less powerful than Shar Dung-ri in Songpan.

The local people go on pilgrimage to Mt. Rdza-dkar in summer, because for most of the year the mountain is covered with snow and the road is inaccessible.[7] To accomplish the circumambulation (*gnas-skor*) at Mt. Rdza-dkar is a two-day affair, although a few, generally young, pilgrims, are able to manage it in a single day. People usually start to climb the mountain a day earlier, stay for the night more than half-way up the mountain, then climb up to the peak on the date of the fifteenth.

On the fourteenth and fifteenth of the sixth lunar month (July 29–30, 1996, in the Western calendar), I followed a group of villagers on a pilgrimage to Mt. Rdza-dkar. Below is a list of key points on the circumambulation path:

1. Nags-steng ('above the forest'): the starting point of the pilgrimage path. A stupa is erected here. It is said that people who are unable to climb up the mountain come to this place to offer *bsangs* (incense) and throw *rlung-rta* (small prints calculated to bring good luck) to meet directly (*zhal-mjal*) the god Rdza-zhig Brag-dkar.
2. Chu-bar ('between rivers'): located on a stream, pilgrims generally take a long rest here after they start from Nags-steng. Male pilgrims replace old ritual arrows planted here.
3. Chu-phyar Gong-ma ('upper spring'): pilgrims approach a waterfall and splash water on their foreheads. It is said that the water can cure headache and eye diseases. Not far from the waterfall, clothes worn by sterile women or deceased children were discarded.
4. A simple hut: erected by people who climb the mountain to collect medicinal herbs. A prayer wheel is located on a stream not far from the hut. Pilgrims put up for the night in or near the hut. Pilgrims collect branches of junipers (*shug-pa*), and make shorter ritual arrows (*mda'-rgod*) for the second offering at the summit.
5. The summit: not far from the summit is an area of flat ground. On the fifteenth, I observed a young man light a fire for offering incense. Pilgrims purified their offerings of ritual arrows and *rlung-rta* by waving them in the smoke, then proceeded to the peak. On the way up, pilgrims, male and female, addressed the god Rdza-zhig Brag-dkar, shouting "Rlung-rta! Rlung-rta," while throwing *rlung-rta* and roasted grains. Ritual arrows were planted, mostly by men, (one old woman also carried an arrow up and planted it by herself.) Then people returned to the flat ground to picnic. Everyone shared food, beverages, and alcoholic drinks. Two old men chanted scriptures and the leftovers were offered to the deceased. After the picnic, people started on their way back.
6. Chu-bzang ('good water'): a holy spring about one third of the way down the mountain. Pilgrims wash their faces with tree leaves and filled the bottles they brought with the water. It is said the water can cure all sorts of disease. I was told by a lady that it works particularly well on women who tend to have miscarriages.

7 A prayer wheel on a stream, not far from the village of Ri-shod: the pilgrimage to Mt. Rdza-dkar concludes here. Pilgrims end their journey by circumambulating this prayer wheel three times.

The pilgrimage undertaken by locals to Mt. Rdza-dkar tends to be orientated to this-worldly concerns, such as fertility, good luck and the riddance of disease. But as is often the case among Tibetans, my interview with monks at Rab-dben Monastery offered a different perspective. They explained their pilgrimage to Mt. Rdza-dkar in term of spiritual salvation and the riddance of bad *karma*. To undertake this pilgrimage, monks have to fast. Laymen are also supposed to refrain from eating meat or vegetables that smell, such as garlic or onions. But the taboo was not observed on the day of my participation in the pilgrimage. "That's monks' business," a young villager explained to me, as he invited me to partake of the canned meat he had brought, while at the same time he consumed a piece of onion. "It's good for your appetite," he said, referring to the onion someone had just given him.

It is crucial to note the social and historical milieus both embedded in and emanating from the pilgrimage process itself, and also to register how the physical landscape of Mt. Rdza-dkar brings forth a "flash of memory" that connects pilgrims from the present to the past, and from the past to the present and to an unpredictable future. One account I collected points back to the gap between the suspension and the revival of the pilgrimage to Mt. Rdza-dkar. As we were resting in the dense woods half way between Nags-steng and Chu-bar, one informant said to me,

> I did one circumambulation of Mt. Rdza-dkar when I was about fourteen. It was prior to the Democratic Reform (around 1955). Since then, I've never been back to this place. It was not until the reformation of religious policies that I made my second trip here. It took place in 1986, about thirty years after my first trip.

The development of tourism in Jiuzhaigou also found its way into pilgrims' casual conversation. The process of pilgrimage creates a temporal space for the locals to reflect on the changes in their traditional values: to increase their awareness of the danger they are facing in a spiritual or material sense. At the place we stayed for the night, a fire was lit to combat the freezing cold. "See, we also have a 'campfire party' like those tourists," someone said jokingly, referring to the kind of festivity invented in Jiuzhaigou as a tourist attraction.

The campfire party was an imitation of the camping scene in Tibetan pastoral areas. Large colorful tents were put up in villages along the main tourist route in Jiuzhaigou. Each night in these tents, tourists were entertained with roast mutton and barley wine, as well as performances of singing and dancing by village boys and girls.

Upon hearing the joke, a lady, who was probably about thirty, seemed to be reminded of how sheep were being butchered every night in her village, and grunted her disapproval at the mass killing; "We Tibetans do circumambulations (*gnas-skor*) and believe in Ma-tri.[8] To kill and roast sheep is not something benevolent. It's the most terrible thing. But Buddha is polluted, so now we have drought and poor harvest..."

Another topic also arose when we were chatting, relating to the "resettlement plan" to be implemented within three to five years by the Jiuzhaigou Tourist Bureau. It was said that the plan was intended to resettle villagers in an area outside the valley of Jiuzhaigou, because the "primitive" and "natural" beauty of the scenery was increasingly being "polluted" by the villagers' commercial activities. The same woman said; "We're worried about this. We heard recently that the provincial governor came to address this issue. For generations we have settled in Jiuzhaigou – it's our land. It's outrageous if we're forced to move. It'll be a betrayal of our ancestors!"

Social, Political and Economic Transformations: Suspension and Revival of Pilgrimage Practices in Jiuzhaigou

The suspension of pilgrimage in Jiuzhaigou started around the time of the process of Collectivization in the late 1950s and ended in the process of implementing the Family Responsibility System and religious reform in the early 1980s.

Nanping used to be administered as a part of Songpan. The area located on the Sichuan-Gansu provincial border was not quite effectively controlled by the Songpan administrative government. In the Qing period, Nanping was a garrison station. The areas where Tibetans lived were controlled by local "chieftains" (Chin: *tusi*). Although quite a few chieftains in Nanping were deprived of their titles in the Nationalist period, the one who controlled the valley of Jiuzhaigou was not affected.

Little is known about the degree of mobility of local Tibetans during the Nationalist period. It seems that if not as high as that of the Han, their personal mobility was certainly higher in the past than it has been since the 1950s. I was told that in the past, local Tibetans in Jiuzhaigou traveled to other places for various purposes: some went to the grasslands to exchange grain for butter, some to Songpan to buy cattle, some to Wenxian in Gansu to sell home-made cloth, while others, such as monks, went on pilgrimages to Tibet to visit the sacred mountain of Kong-po Bon-ri, or the famous monastery of G.yung-drung-gling. One informant told me that in the past many people went to Tibet, Qinghai or Gansu either on pilgrimage or for commercial purposes.

In 1949, the PRC was founded. The new regime embarked on a systematic penetration into the former frontier areas largely inhabited by ethnic groups, a penetration far deeper than that of previous regimes. A series of measures were taken to enforce control of these areas, including redemarcation of administrative areas, census surveys, Democratic Reform, suppression of rebellion (if any), and Collectivization. In Nanping, all these took place within a six year period (1953–1958). As a consequence, individual mobility was greatly reduced and local pilgrimage practices were brought to a halt.

The governing principle of "divide and rule" favored by the imperial court to control ethnic minority areas certainly influenced the politics of the PRC, but in a more efficient way. Historical relationships between Tibetan communities in Songpan and Nanping were disconnected, as the latter was set up as a separate county in 1953. For instance, although Tibetans in Jiuzhaigou and in Songpan are speakers of Amdo dialects, there are regional differences between them. In the past, these differences were minimized by commercial or religious ties. In addition to purchasing cattle, villagers in Jiuzhaigou also went to Songpan, the regional center of Bon along the Min River Valley, to visit Mt. Shar Dung-ri or Mt. Bya-dur. Since the mid-1950s, the Tibetan community in Jiuzhaigou had become literally isolated from those in Songpan. This isolation had its consequences among those born after the 1950s, who found, for quite a while, that it was difficult to communicate with Tibetans from Songpan when social control was relaxed considerably in the 1980s. This problem of speech communication has been greatly reduced as contact became more frequent in the past decade, with the development of tourism and the revival of religious activities. Quite a few Tibetan merchants from Songpan are engaged in the souvenir trade in Jiuzhaigou. Meanwhile, Tibetans from Jiuzhaigou often go to Songpan to celebrate ritual festivals at Dga'-mal Dgon-pa.[9]

Census surveys played a leading role in the process of inscribing "the body politic" upon citizens in the PRC. The "knowledge" they produced facilitated the establishment of administrative units at the grass-roots level. The regular household registration system it helped to create (in 1955) became an effective means to control the flow of population. Households were registered annually, under direct control of the Bureau of Public Security. The first census survey was conducted in 1953 and the second in 1964. According to the *Nanping Gazetteer* (1994: 147–49), the first survey registered only the population figures, while the contents of the second were expanded to include professional, educational, ethnic and class status, in addition to other standard census data. In particular, the label of "class" served to differentiate "bad elements" from the general populace. In Jiuzhaigou, people of "bad class background" were former chieftains, big land owners, and monks; these were placed under tight surveillance. An old monk at Rab-dben Monastery said to me, "You asked me whether I did circumambulations in the 1960s. Certainly not! People like me were 'bad elements' associated with 'feudal superstitions.' We couldn't go anywhere. Also, others avoided contact with us as if we were lepers." Later he continued, "You asked me whether others (referring to people of 'good class background') did circumambulations. Hardly any. If someone did, he would be punished for his wrong political attitude."

The identification of class took place during the process of Democratic Reform, which lasted three years in Nanping (1955–1958). By that time, Jiuzhaigou was administered as a part of Tha-tshang Township, where the citizens were predominantly Tibetans. The Democratic Reform in Tha-tshang started in 1956. After class identification, land confiscated from landlords was distributed to peasants according to household registration data. Each household had a fixed amount of land, and each household was also fixed on their share of land. As a result, migration to other places proved to be impossible, inasmuch as the household registration system was interlocked with land distribution.

Democratic Reform triggered an uprising at the township seat of Tha-tshang and it quickly spread to Jiuzhaigou in 1957. Rab-dben Monastery was used by the rebels (land-owners and monks) as a base. After the rebellion was put down, the monks at Rab-dben were sent back to their native villages and placed under surveillance. Rab-dben Monastery was later utterly destroyed. It is said that the last annual ritual festival, Ma-tri Sgrub-chen, was held in 1956, and it was suspended ever since. In the repression of the rebellion, a process of concentration also started during which households living in remote places were forced to resettle in populous villages, for fear that they might provide shelter for rebels. The ruins of abandoned houses can still be seen at a place called Yug-gzhi-stod on the pilgrimage path to Mt. Rdza-dkar.

Collectivization in Jiuzhaigou (1958), overlapped with the first year of the Great Leap Forward Campaign (1958–1960). Tha-tshang was established as commune. Land and property were collectively owned. Villagers were organized to work and even to eat together. Until 1961 food was provided by "public dining halls" set up in each village. This period also witnessed the campaign for "anti-superstition" during which all religious activities were banned. Pilgrimage was condemned not only as "feudal remains," but as "a waste of time" which was "harmful" to production. The "work point" system introduced later in 1961 effectively regulated everyone's daily life. An informant who was once responsible for recording work points in his village recounted his experience at that time:

> At daybreak, a gong was beaten to announce the work time. When villagers were gathered, the production team leader would check attendance. If someone was absent, his or her work points for that day would be deleted. In the evening, villagers were gathered again. Evaluation of everyone's performance was held publicly. Work points were recorded every day. After the evaluation, the team leader would announce the assignment for the next day. Every two or three days, a political study session was held, newspapers or official documents in Chinese were read for public discussions. It was a bit absurd that many old people who could not understand Chinese had to be present to listen. But at that time, one's correct political attitude was a crucial thing. In the Cultural Revolution, one's political attitude was even included in the evaluation of work points. By the end of each year, the ration of one's grain was calculated on the basis of his or her work points.

Another informant made a comment on the impossibility of pilgrimage under the work point system:

> Since the 'Anti-Superstition Campaign' in 1957, there were no gods or spirits. Mao became the only god. In the Cultural Revolution, his 'Little Red Book' was read every day. People had

to report their daily behavior in front of his picture. No one dared go on circumambulation in those days. Someone would surely inform against you if you did. As a punishment, your work points would be deleted. In addition you would be taken to a 'study session' to do self-criticism. Worse, if you refused to confess, you would be sent to prison for your extreme 'anti-Party' attitude.

Severe as the punishment might be, some did manage to circumambulate Mt. Rdza-dkar despite the fact that visits to pilgrimage sites distant from the valley of Jiuzhaigou were virtually impossible. I was told that some villagers availed themselves of the opportunities to do so when they were sent to herd cattle on patches of grassland halfway up Mt. Rdza-dkar. In addition, there were times when work points were not recorded every day, such as in the busy harvest season. After work, some would sneak away in the late afternoon to Mt. Rdza-dkar, bringing their flashlights with them. Early the next morning, exhausted as they might have been, they had to return before harvest work started.

The revival of religious activities, including pilgrimage practices in Jiuzhaigou, has been a gradual process. In previous publications, the third plenary session of the Eleventh CPC Party Commission in 1978 is often cited as a reference point regarding the beginning of religious revival in China, as it publicly denounced previous "anti-religion" policy and reinstated the policy of "freedom of religious belief," suspended since the 1950s. It is true that the year 1978 marked a major about-turn in the state's attitude towards religious activities. But religious revival in specific areas varied in time. In regions inhabited by Tibetans, the restoration of religious activities proceeded slowly, under the close watch of the Chinese state. Some practices, for example monastic rituals deemed by the state as "healthy," were allowed to be restored, since monasteries, in the state's gaze, are viable places for surveillance. Moreover, "healthy" monastic ritual festivities can showcase the state's impression management project that seeks to present an image of China as a unified state with a rich diversity of ethnic cultures.[10] Popular pilgrimage practices among Tibetans, though not officially prohibited, are discouraged as they may pose a potential or real threat to the clearly demarcated administrative boundaries in Tibetan regions.

It was not until 1982 that Tibetans in Nanping began to experience a major change in their religious life. That year Document Twelve was issued by the CPC. It offered specific guidelines with regard to reestablishing the state organs in charge of religious affairs, compensating monasteries ruined since the 1950, and redressing cases of religious personnel wronged in previous political campaigns. Bon monastic activities first revived at Dar-rgyas Monastery in Tha-tshang. Dar-rgyas Monastery survived destruction after the 1958 uprising and it was reopened to Bon believers in 1982. Reconstruction of Rab-dben Monastery in Jiuzhaigou started in 1984 and was accomplished in 1988. To villagers in Jiuzhaigou, the year 1982 was also marked with a radical reform of their production system. With the introduction of the Family Responsibility System in late 1982, land in Jiuzhaigou was contracted to each household to fulfill the production quota. Villagers were given more autonomy in labor management. The 'work point' system which had served as a tough measure in supervising villagers' economic and social activities was abolished. As a result, the increase in individual mobility had a great impact on the revival of pilgrimages among the locals in Jiuzhaigou. The informant who had once been responsible for recording work points in his village described the fervor of his fellow-villagers in regard to pilgrimage to Mt. Rdza-dkar in the early 1980s:

> By that time, our Rab-dben Monastery had not yet been rebuilt. Circumambulation at Mt. Rdza-dkar was the main religious activity in this valley. The revival even occurred a bit earlier than the time when the Family Responsibility System was implemented in this valley. Experiments of the Family Responsible System started at the beginning of the 1980s in Han villages of Nanping, and its implementation did not come to Jiuzhaigou until the end of 1982. But by then everybody knew it was going to happen. The work- point system was not working very well in those days.
>
> I still remember that it was on May 15, 1982. Many went to do circumambulation at Mt. Rdza-dkar and only a few showed up in the corn fields. It happened that the deputy party secretary of our township came to inspect the production on that day. He asked me why so many were absent from work. I had to lie to him by saying that I was not sure about what happened.

The period after 1982 witnessed a rapid increase in the number of pilgrims to Mt. Rdza-dkar. Around the mid-1980s, pilgrimage to the mountain reached its climax. On auspicious days, such as the fifteenth of the summer months, more than 400 persons would make the pilgrimage. One informant told me,

> The mountain path was crowded with so many people that it was impossible to walk fast even if you wanted to. It's just strange that people in the past would try to visit that mountain even under the tight control of the work point system. Nowadays, people can come any time they wish and nobody cares if they go. Still, the number of people who come to Mt. Rdza-dkar is not as many as in 1984 or 1985. At most, only about seventy persons will show up on the fifteenth during months in the pilgrimage season.

Development of Tourism in Jiuzhaigou and its Impact on Local Pilgrimage Practices

To local Tibetans living there, Jiuzhaigou is their native place, upon which their daily lives have depended from generation to generation. The place name of Jiuzhaigou – the "Valley of Nine Villages" – confirms their ancestral ties to this place. In addition, Jiuzhaigou is a place where the sacred Mt. Rdza-dkar is located. Numerous legends concerning this deity's endeavors to protect the locals from evil spirits lurking in the valley further extend the tie of local inhabitants to a mythic past. In a sense, pilgrimage of local villagers to the holy place of Mt. Rdza-dkar is also a process of reaffirming their ties to the land protected by this deity.

To the present regime, however, the key value of Jiuzhaigou does not lie in the land that supports the daily lives of local Tibetan villagers, but in exploitable natural resources in the valley of Jiuzhaigou. In the mid-1960s, the timber industry set up in Jiuzhaigou to exploit the rich forest in the valley. It was not until the late 1970s, when the unique physical landscape of Jiuzhaigou was found to be a more profitable resource for developing tourism that the timber industry was brought to an end. Jiuzhaigou was designated a state nature reserve in 1978. In 1982, it was among the first batch of state key scenic areas. In 1992, Jiuzhaigou was admitted into the "World Heritage List" by UNESCO.[11]

Since 1984, when Jiuzhaigou was officially opened to tourists, hordes of visitors have flocked to this scenic area, noted for its beautiful lakes, waterfalls, beaches, rivers, snow-covered mountains, and forests, as well as "exotic" local Tibetan customs.[12] In my interview with administrative officials at the Jiuzhaigou Tourist Bureau, I was told that since the early 1990s, there has been a tourist industry boom in Jiuzhaigou. In 1995, the 160,000 tourists (the vast majority of whom are Han), was a number about twice that of 1987.

A tourist's experience in Jiuzhaigou can be fruitfully viewed as that of a tourist-pilgrim. The tourist-pilgrim goes on a journey in search of a place isolated in time and space. The journey to Jiuzhaigou is a journey back in time, a return to Nature. Jiuzhaigou is often promoted in the tourist brochures as a "primitive and natural fairyland." The "primitiveness" of Jiuzhaigou's physical landscape parallels that of local Tibetan customs; simply put, the "primitiveness" of local Tibetan culture is just a part of Nature, untouched by the sins of modernity. One tourist guidebook of Jiuzhaigou states, 'To this day the people of Jiuzhaigou still preserve their rich yet simple and primitive Tibetan tradition in every aspect of life, including marriage, funeral arrangements and mode of production.'[13]

According to this book, Jiuzhaigou has become "a holy land of Nature to which thousands upon thousands of tourists pay homage." This statement echoes Graburn's argument that tourism is a new form of pilgrimage or "sacred journey."[14] As modern society becomes more institutionalized, tourists often travel to remote, exotic places in search of an "authenticity" that no longer exists in their social life.

Unlike the detachment of tourists from modernity, local Tibetans' participation in the development of tourism in Jiuzhaigou serves as means in their striving to be modern. The dilemma they face is that, on the one hand, the penetration of tourism into Jiuzhaigou has reshaped their outlook and local way of life; on the other hand, however, they have to live up to the tourist imagination that their "primitive" traditions have not been "spoiled" by the forces of modernity, including tourism.

The development of tourism in Jiuzhaigou effected a bifurcation of the region into two sectors: the "front" and the "back" areas.[15] In Jiuzhaigou, the "front" area is located along the main valley of Shug-gcod (Chin: Shuzheng) and its two branches called respectively Rdzi-tsha-ba (Chin: Zechawa) and Rize.[16] This area has been turned into "tourist space" where major tourist attractions, such as waterfalls and lakes, are located. In addition, tourists are expected to interact with local villagers along this main tourist route. The "back" area is located in another branch valley called Rdza-rong. Mt. Rdza-dkar, the pilgrimage site, is situated in this valley. This area is the least frequented by tourists. Although there is a plan to develop Mt. Rdza-dkar as a mountaineering spot, only a few Westerners ventured to climb the mountain in 1995. The development of tourism in Jiuzhaigou has, in fact, redefined the place, turning Mt. Rdza-dkar into a "center out there" – on the margin of the "tourist space." In the process of reinscribing the place of Jiuzhaigou, the more than 320 meter-wide waterfall called Chu-gzigs-ngo (Chin: Nuorilang), located on the tourist route, has been transformed into the "main mark or symbol of Jiuzhaigou".[17]

Simply put, local Tibetans' participation in the tourist industry falls into two sectors: services administered by the Jiuzhaigou Tourist Bureau, and those run by the villagers themselves. At least one member of each household has been employed by the tourist bureau during the tourist season (April-October) as workers to protect the forest or clean up garbage. This kind of work is normally assigned to old people, who work from 8 a.m. to 5 p.m. every day, earning 300 yüan per month during the tourist season.

Tourist services run by local villagers themselves range from renting horses or native costumes for photography to tourists, the handicraft and souvenir trade, and folkloric entertainment, to running inns. In the valley of Jiuzhaigou, there are three administrative villages (former 'brigades' under the commune system) called Rdza-rong, 'O-zo, and Shug-gcod. Rdza-rong village is located in the "back" area, off the main tourist route. Villagers from a few households in this village do participate in tourist services, shuttling tourists from the entrance of Jiuzhaigou to the scenic areas. But the vast majority of households which cannot afford to buy pick-up trucks still concentrate on agricultural production. The villages of 'O-zo and Shug-gcod are both concentrated on the tourist route and members of each household in these villages are engaged in one or two of the touristic enterprises listed above.

Inn-keeping has been by far the most important tourism-related occupation in the villages of 'O-zo and Shug-gcod, where I conducted most of my fieldwork. Other items of tourist service are secondary in their impact upon the majority of households. For instance, the rental of horses or costumes does not contribute regular income to households involved in these kinds of business. The souvenir trade involves only a small number of households in these two villages, each having about ten stalls located on the tourist route next to the village. Folkloric entertainment, such as campfire parties, was mostly managed by only several households. Inn-keeping involves the majority of households and also contributes stable income to these households in these two villages.[18]

Most of these inns were built up in the late 1980s to meet the rapid expansion of tourism in Jiuzhaigou. Competition for tourists among households that ran hotels was tense in the late 1980s. In 1990, regulations were set up to coordinate the management of household hotels. The occupancy of each inn is limited to forty-five, and tourists' stays in these inns is operated on a rotating basis. Money gained from accommodation is distributed evenly among the households that run inns.

A social disparity exists not only between those in the same village who have regular income from running hotels and those who do not, but also between villages whose access to tourism varies. One informant in Rdza-rong complained that the annual per capita income in the villages of Shug-gcod and 'O-zo is about 3,000 yüan, while that of Rdza-rong amounts only to 700 yüan'.

Generational difference is another issue related to the development of tourism in Jiuzhaigou. One elderly informant said:

> Nowadays the young think that they can rely solely on themselves. They think they can do whatever they like with the money gained from tourism. They no longer have any respect for their elders. In the past, there used to be a village gathering at New Year to discuss affairs concerning the whole village. The discussion was presided over by the most senior person in the village. Whatever your official title was, you had to listen to him and let him speak first . . .

The development of tourism in Jiuzhaigou has also produced consequences that are not necessarily negative. Tourism has increased interactions between local villagers and tourists who come from different ethnic backgrounds. These interactions also highlight locals' self-identity vs. others. Several times during my fieldwork, I heard tourists query local villagers about their origin. Villagers always replied that they had come from Tibet. One informant, "I don't know where we came from. I was born here and so were my father and grandfather. We're just locals in this place, but the abbot of our monastery told us that we migrated from Tibet".

According to the abbot of Rab-dben Monastery, his ancestors originated from Gshen-rta-bdun about 1100 years ago. He paid a personal visit to his native place in the early 1990s when he stayed at the Bon monastery of G.yung-drung-gling. As an influential figure in

Jiuzhaigou, his personal narrative has apparently become a standardized version for locals to follow.

Village leaders in Shug-gcod are also keenly interested in constructing an "authentic" image of Tibetans. Even though they could not read Tibetan, they insisted that on any posters, such as those announcing the opening of a primary school or an ethnic folk culture village, Tibetan must be written side by side with Chinese. In addition, in the newly-opened "Ethnic Culture Village" in Shug-gcod, a dancing teacher from Khams was invited to teach local boys and girls, because Khams-pa dancing was regarded by village leaders as the most "authentic." It is fair to say that with the advent of tourism, local village identity in Jiuzhaigou now has wider implications. It is being connected to areas perceived by the locals of Jiuzhaigou to be the "core" of Tibetan history and culture.

With regard to the impact of the development of tourism upon pilgrimage activities in Jiuzhaigou, I was repeatedly told by informants that there had been a sharp decline in pilgrimage, in particular to Mt. Rdza-dkar, after the boom period in the mid-1980s. It is interesting to note the diverse views regarding the decline of pilgrimage practice, for these views reflect the interests of different groups of people. The abbot of Rab-dben Monastery, someone long engaged in promoting Tibetan culture, attributed the decline to the "backwardness" (Chin: *louhou*) of local culture as compared to that of Tibet, that is, Tibetan areas lying to the west of Jiuzhaigou, which is located on the easternmost fringes of Tibetan civilization. Local Tibetans have been much influenced by their neighboring groups, thus losing many important cultural attributes of Tibetans. He complained that the erosion of Tibetan traditional values has been accelerated in recent years by the massive influx of tourists. Locals have quickly adapted themselves to the process of commercialization and the life style of urban tourists.

To officials in the Religious Bureau of Nanping County, however, the geographical remoteness of Jiuzhaigou from other Tibetan areas does not, in any sense, indicate that local Tibetans are "backward"; rather, they are more inclined to be influenced by "advanced" Han culture. The decline of pilgrimage activities in Jiuzhaigou has been exalted as a positive sign, suggesting that locals have developed a clear sense of market economy in the development of tourism, and that they are more "open" to the outside world. In their opinion, this has proved the Marxian idea that "superstition will vanish as economy grows".

The views of local people in Jiuzhaigou on the reduction of pilgrimage activities in recent years are quite straight-forward. Lack of time is cited as the primary reason. Many attributed the decline to the overlapping of the pilgrimage season with the tourist season, which starts in April, reaches its peak in the months of July, August and September, and ends in early November. As noted previously, pilgrimages to Mt. Rdza-dkar are also undertaken by locals in the summer. Thus, the tourist season encompasses the pilgrimage season. As tourism expands in the 1990s it embraces a large and growing section of the local labor force. The souvenir trade, folkloric entertainment, horse renting, and inn-keeping in particular are often cited by informants as factors that constrain their participation in pilgrimage activities. Some replied that "people are so busy making money nowadays, they just don't have time to go," or, "people are lazy nowadays, they just don't like to walk on the difficult mountain path." Some suggest that nowadays more and more people believe in science, they see more "tangible" benefits in modern medicine, education, commodity economy, etc., than in pilgrimage. Some went on to explain pilgrimage in a more "rational" way. One village cadre said to me, "It (pilgrimage) is just a physical exercise like those in the Olympic Games, or your Han Chinese *qigong*. You see, full-length prostration is exactly the exercise of the whole body."

Many village elders expressed their concern over the decline of pilgrimage activities, and were worried that they might eventually disappear. But one informant said to me, "I'm not worried about that. It's natural that the young are fully occupied by all sorts of business and busy making money. When they grow old, they'll certainly be more concerned about their next life and also have more time in going on pilgrimage."

Concluding Remarks

Whether pilgrimages, to Mt. Rdza-dkar in particular, are declining or not is a complicated issue. If we compare the number of pilgrims to Mt. Rdza-dkar in recent years with those in the mid-1980s, when the release of control over religious activities led to a rapid boom, we can see the number of pilgrims nowadays are significantly reduced. But one informant's view is particularly valuable. He suggested that the present number of pilgrims to Mt. Rdza-dkar cannot be compared with those in the first few years of religious revival as it has now become a regular practice. Additionally, as the tourist economy grows and personal mobility increases, pilgrimage practices in Jiuzhaigou diversify, as more and more people are capable of going to pilgrimage sites in Songpan or even to Tibet. In this sense, it may have been the case that the focal role played by Mt. Rdza-dkar during the religious revival in the mid-1980s started to decrease. However, an extended period of research in Jiuzhaigou, supplemented with comparative studies of other pilgrimage sites in the Amdo area, is needed to explore this aspect further.

Notes

1 My field trip to Jiuzhaigou was made possible by a predoctoral fellowship from the Wenner-Gren Foundation for Anthropological Research. I express my gratitude for this support. I also thank Dr Toni Huber and Dr Lawrence Epstein for comment and corrections on an earlier draft of this essay.
2 Such commoditization has been noted by scholars in other parts of southwest China. See, e.g., Schein 1989; Swain 1990; Oakes 1992, 1993.
3 Klieger 1990.
4 Tib:. *Gzi-rtsa sde dgu.*
5 Out of the total population of 777, 760 are Tibetans while only seventeen are Han Chinese; Zhang 1990: 14.
6 The monastery was said to be built in the thirteenth century by a famous Bon monk called Skal-bzang Nyi-ma.
7 People in Jiuzhaigou follow the Lunar calendar of the Han Chinese. According to the abbot of Rab-dben Monastery, the fifteenth of each month from June to September of the lunar calendar is the best time for pilgrimage. "The merits you gain will be much greater if you go on the fifteenth – one circumambulation on that day will be equal to one thousand on other days" he said. No further explanations were vouchsafed on this point. "It's just a rule," he said. Only an aged man seemed to offer a plausible answer. "Well," he explained, "some say that if you are truly pious, you can see the god Rdza-zhig Brag-dkar on that day (the fifteenth)." But he soon laughed away the idea, "So far as I know, no one has ever seen him. If gods can be seen, then there will be no gods . . ."
8 The Bon-po mantra.
9 The distance between Jiuzhaigou to the county seat of Songpan is only 104 kilometers, and Tibetan settlements around Dga'-mal Dgon-pa lie at about half this distance.
10 Epstein & Peng, forthcoming.
11 Zhang 1994: 229, *et al.*
12 Statistics reveal that the number of tourists who visited Jiuzhaigou in the period of 1984–1987 totaled up to 266,020: 32,000 in 1984; 68,000 in 1985; 72,000 in 1986; 94,020 in 1987; Zhang 1990: 139.
13 Zhang *et al.* 1994: 137.
14 Graburn 1977.

15 Cohen 1979: 14.
16 Tibetan orthography uncertain.
17 Zhang *et al.* 1994: 24.
18 It was reported that in 1985, eight households in the village of Shug-gcod began to run hotels to receive tourists (Zhang 1990: 130). In this village of thirty households, until now only two have been unable to put up hotels. In the village of 'O-zo, out of sixty-six households, fifty-four own hotels, and twelve are engaged in other tourist services.

Bibliography

Aiyar, L.K.A., & Nanj-und'ayya. 1928–1936 *Mysore Tribes and Castes*, vol. 3, H.V., Mysore.
Ali, S.M. 1973 *The Geography of the Puranas*, Delhi.
Archer, M. 1972 *Company Drawings in the India Office Library*, London.
—— 1973 *Indian Paintings from the Punjab Hills*, London.
—— 1992 *Company Paintings, Indian Paintings of the British Period*, London.
Aris, M. 1975 'Report on the University of California Expedition to Kutang and Nubri in Northern Nepal', in *Contributions to Nepalese Studies*, 2.
—— 1979 *Bhutan. The early history of a Himalayan kingdom*, Warminster: Aris and Phillips.
—— (ed.), 1979a 'Introduction' to *Autobiographies of Three Spiritual Masters of Kutang*, Thimpu.
—— 1988 *Hidden treasures and secret lives. A study of Pemalinga (1450–1521) and the Sixth Dalai Lama (1683–1706)*, Delhi: Motilal Banarsidass / Shimla: Institute of Advanced Study.
—— 1995 *'Jigs-med-gling-pa's "Discourse on India" of 1789: A critical edition and annotated translation of the lHo-phyogs rgya-gar-yi gtam brtag-pa brgyad-kyi me-long*, (Studia Philologica Buddhica Occasional Paper Series IX), Tokyo: The International Institute for Buddhist Studies.
Aufschnaiter, P. 1976 'Lands and places of Milarepa', in *East and West*, vol. 26.
Avalon, A. 1913 *Mahanirvanatantra: The Tantra of Great Liberation*, London.
Awasty, I. 1978 *Between Sikkim and Bhutan. The Lepchas and Bhutias of Pedong*, Delhi: B. R. Pub. Corp.
Aziz, B.N. 1982 'A Pilgrimage to Amarnath: The Hindus' Search for Immortality' in *Kailash*, 9.2–3.
—— 1978 *Tibetan Frontier Families: Reflections of Three Generations from D'ing-ri*, New Delhi: Vikas Publ. House.
Baber, E.C. 1882 *Travels and researches in Western China*, Royal Geographical Society, Supplementary Papers, vol. I, part 1. London: John Murray.

Bacot, J. 1908 'Le pèlerinage du Dokerla (Tibet oriental)', in *La Géographie*, vol. XVII, I.
—— 1909 *Dans les marches tibétaines. Autour du Dokerla, novembre 1906 – janvier 1908*, Paris: Plon-Nourrit et Cie.
Bailey, F.M. 1957 *No passport to Tibet*, London: Rupert Hart-Davis.
Balfour, E., (ed.), 1871 *Encyclopedia of India, Eastern and Southern Asia*, vol. 2, Madras.
Ball, V. 1977 *Travels in India by Jean Baptiste Tavernier*, 2 vols., New Delhi.
Bayley, C.A. 1988 *Rulers, Townsmen & Bazaars, North Indian Society in the Age of British Expansion, 1770–1870*, Cambridge: C.U.P.
Bedi, R., & Swamy, S. 1984 *Kailas & Manasarovar. After 22 Years in Shiva's Domain*, New Delhi: Allied Publishers.
Bell, C.A. (Sir) 1924 *Tibet, Past and Present*, Oxford: OUP.
—— 1924a 'A year in Lhasa', in *The Geographical Journal*, vol. LXIII.2.
Benett W.C. 1877 *Gazetteer of the Province of Oudh*, vol. 1, Lucknow.
Berg, E. 1994 'Journeys to the Holy Center. The Study of Pilgrimage in Recent Himalayan research', in the *European Bulletin of Himalayan Research*, No. 6.
Berglie, P.-A. 1981 'Mount Targo and Lake Dangra: a contribution to the religious geography of Tibet', in Aris, M., and Aung San Suu Kyi (eds.), *Tibetan studies in honour of Hugh Richardson*: Warminster: Aris and Phillips.
Beveridge, H. 1857 *A Comprehensive History of India*, vol. 2, London.
—— (ed.), 1914 *The Tuzuk-i-Jahangiri*, London, (& Rogers, A., trans.).
Bharati, S.A. 1963 'Pilgrimage in the Indian Tradition', in *History of Religions* 3.1.
Bhardwaj, S.M. 1973 *Hindu places of pilgrimage. A study in cultural geography*, Berkeley: University of California Press.
—— 1965 *The Tantric Tradition*, London.
Bhatt, G.P. (ed.), 1986 *The Brahma Purana*, New Delhi.
—— (ed.), 1992–94 *The Skandapurana*, New Delhi.
Blondeau, A.M. 1960 'Les pèlerinages tibétains' in *Sources Orientales, vol. III – Les pèlerinages*, Paris: Editions du Seuil.
—— 1985 'mKhyen-brce'i dban-po: La biographie de Padmasambhava selon la tradition du bsGrags-pa Bon, et ses sources', in Gnoli, G., & Lanciotti, L., (eds.), *Orientalia Iosephi Tucci Memoriae dicata*, Serie Orientale Roma LVI, 1, Rome: IsMEO.
Blondeau, A.M., & Steinkellner, E., (eds.), 1996 *Reflections of the Mountain: Essays on the History and Social Meaning of the Mountain Cult in Tibet and the Himalaya*, Wien: Österreichische Akademie der Wissenschaften.
Boeck, K. 1903 *Durch Indien ins verschlossene Land Nepal. Ethnograpische und photographische Studienblätter*, Leipzig: Verlag von Ferdinand Hirt und Sohn.
Bouillier, V. 1985 'The Ambiguous Position of Renunciants in Nepal: Interrelation of Asceticism and the Social Order', in *Journal of the Nepal Research Center*, V11.
Bourreau, A. 1983 'Narration cléricale et narration populaire. La Légende de Placide-Eustache', in *Les Saints et les Stars. Le texte hagiographique dans la culture populaire*, Etudes réunies par J. C. Schmitt, Paris: Beauschene.

Bower, H. 1894 *Diary of a journey across Tibet*, London: Rivington, Percival, (Reprinted: Kathmandu: Ratna Pustak Bhandar, 1976).
Brauen, M. (ed.), 1983 *Peter Aufschnaiter: sein Leben in Tibet*, Innsbruck: Steiger Verlag.
—— 1994 'Why not "Translate" into Pictures', in *Tibetan Studies*, Kvaerne, P., (ed). *op. cit.*
Buffetrille, K. 1994a *The Halase-Maratika caves (Eastern Nepal). A sacred place claimed by both Hindus and Buddhists*, Pondy Papers in Social Sciences, No. 16, Pondicherry: French Institute.
—— 1994b 'Revitalisation d'un lieu-saint bouddhique: les grottes de Halase-Maratika, Népal oriental (district de Khotang)', in, *Tibetan Studies*, Kvaerne, P., (ed.), *op. cit.*
—— 1994c 'A Bon po Pilgrimage Guide to Amnye Machen mountain', in *Lungta*, 8.
—— 1996a *Montagnes sacrées, lacs et grottes, lieux de pèlerinage dans le monde tibétain. Traditions écrites et réalités vivantes*, unpublished Ph.D. dissertation, Université de Paris X, Nanterre.
—— 1996b 'One Day the Mountains Will Go Away . . .: Preliminary Remarks on the Flying Mountains of Tibet', in Blondeau & Steinkellner, (eds.), *op. cit.*
—— 1997 'The Great Pilgrimage of A myes rMa chen: Written Tradition, Living Realities', in Macdonald, A.W., (ed.), *op. cit.*
—— (forthcoming). 'Inceste et pèlerinage: le cas de mChod rten nyi ma' in *Tibetan Studies*: Proceedings of the 7th Seminar of the International Association for Tibetan Studies, Graz, June 1995.
Buitenen, J.A.B. van, (ed./ trans.), 1973 *The Mahabharata*, (3 vols.) Chicago.
Burrard, S.G. 1915 *Records of the Survey of India*, vol. VIII (in two parts), Dehra Dun: Office of the Trigonometrical Survey.
Bynum, C., Harrell, S., & Richman, P., (eds.), 1986 *Gender and Religion: On the Complexity of Symbols*, Boston: Beacon Press.
Bysack, G.D. 1890 'Notes on a Buddhist monastery at Bhot Bhagan in Howrah', in *Journal of the Royal Asiatic Society of Bengal*, 59.
Calhoun, A.B. 1929 'Burma – an important source of precious and semi-precious stones', in *Engineering and Mining Journal*, vol. 127.18.
Cammann, S. 1951 *Trade Through the Himalayas*, Princeton.
Cantwell, C. 1989 *An Ethnographic Account of the Religious Practice in a Tibetan Buddhist Refugee Monastery in Northern India*, Unpublished Ph.D. thesis, Univ. of Kent at Canterbury.
—— 1994 'Buddhist Ritual and Tibetan identity', in *Tibetan Studies*, Kvaerne, P., (ed.), *op. cit.*
—— 1995 'Rewalsar: Tibetan Refugees in a Buddhist Sacred Place', in *The Tibet Journal*, 20.1.
Carrasco, P. 1959 *Land and polity in Tibet*, Seattle: University of Washington Press.
Chan, V. 1994 *Tibet handbook. A pilgrimage guide*, Chico (Cal.): Moon.
Chang, C.C. 1962 *The Hundred Thousand Songs of Milarepa*, New Hyde Park.
Clarke, J. 1995 *A Regional Survey and Stylistic Analysis of Tibetan Non-Sculptural metalworking c.1850–1959*, Unpublished Phd thesis, School of Oriental and African Studies, London University.

Cohen, E. 1979 'The Impact of Tourism on the Hill Tribes of Northern Thailand', in *Internationales Asienforum*, 10.1–2.
Cohn, B.S. 1963–64 'The Role of the Gosains in the Economy of 18th and 19th century Upper India', in *Indian Economic and Social History Review*, vol. 1.
Cooper, T.T. 1871 *Travels of a pioneer of commerce in pigtail and petticoats: Or, an overland journey from China towards India*, London: John Murray.
Cutting, C.S. 1940 *The fire ox and other years*, New York: Charles Scribner's Sons.
Dargyay, E. 1977 *The Rise of Esoteric Buddhism in Tibet*, Delhi: Motilal Banarsidass.
Das, S.C. 1902 *Journey to Lhasa and Central Tibet*, London, (reprinted, 1970, New Delhi: Majushri).
David-Néel, A. 1953 'Les marchands tibétains', in *France-Asie*, vol. IX, no. 83, avril: I, vol. IX, no. 84, mai: II.
Deasy, H.H.P. 1901 *In Tibet and Chinese Turkestan. Being the record of three years' exploration*, London: T. Fisher Unwin.
Dixey, R. (ed.), 1993 *Heart Drops of Dharmakaya. Dzogchen Practice of the Bön Tradition. Lopon Tenzin Namdak on the Kun Tu Bzang po'i Snying Tig of Shardza Tashi Gyaltsen*, Ithaca, New York: Snow Lion Publications.
Douglas, N., & White, M. 1976 *Karmapa:The Black Hat Lama of Tibet*, London: Luzac & Co.
Dowman, K. 1988 *The power-places of Central Tibet: the pilgrim's guide*, London: Routledge and Kegan Paul.
Dowson, J. 1891 *A classical Dictionary of Hindu Mythology and Religion, Geography, History & Literature*, London.
Dubey, D.P. (ed.), 1995 *Pilgrimage Studies: Sacred Places Sacred Traditions*, Allahabad: The Society of Pilgrimage Studies.
Dudjom Rinpoche, & Jikdrel Yeshe Dorje. 1991 *The Nyingma School of Tibetan Buddhism: Its Fundamentals and History*, 2 vols, Gyurme Dorje & Kapstein, M., (transl./ed.), Boston: Wisdom Publications.
Dumont, L. 1970 *Homo hierarchicus: The caste system and its implications*, London, (Paris, *Homo Hierarchicus: essai sur le systeme des castes*, 1970).
Dunbar, G.D.S. 1915 'Abors and Galongs: notes on certain hill tribes of the Indo-Tibetan border', in *Memoirs of the Asiatic Society of Bengal*, vol. V, (Extra Number), Calcutta: The Asiatic Soc.
Duncan, J. 1801 'An Account of Two Fakeers with their Portraits', in *Oriental Memoirs*, London.
Duncan, M.H. 1929 *The mountain of silver snow*, Cincinnati: Powell and White.
—— 1952 *The Yangtze and the yak. Adventurous trails in and out of Tibet*, Alexandria, Virginia/Ann Arbor, Michigan: Edwards Brothers.
Eck, D.L. 1981 'India's Tirthas: "Crossings" in Sacred Geography', in *History of Religions*, 20.4.
—— 1985 *Darsan: Seeing the Divine Image in India*, Chambersburg PA: Anima Publications (First published, 1981)
—— 1983 *Benares: City of Light*, London.

Ehrhard, F-K. 1990 *Flügelschläge des Garuda* Literar-und ideengeschichtliche Bemerkungen zu einer Liedersammlung des rDzogschen, Tibetan and Indo-Tibetan Studies 3, Stuttgart:Franz Steiner Verlag.
Ekvall, R.B. 1939 *Cultural relations on the Kansu-Tibetan border*, Chicago: University of Chicago Press.
—— 1964 *Religious Observances in Tibet*, Chicago: University of Chicago Press.
Eliot, J. 1880 *Indian Industries*, London.
Entwistle, A.W. 1981–82 *Vaisnava Tilakas*, London.
Epstein, L. 1982 'On the History and Psychology of the "Das log"', in *The Tibet Journal*, 7.4.
Epstein, L. & Peng Wenbin. 1994 'Ganja and Murdo: the social construction of space at two pilgrimage sites in Eastern Tibet', in *The Tibet Journal*, vol. 19.3.
—— (forthcoming), Ritual, Ethnicity and Generational Identity.
Evans-Wentz, W.Y. 1978 *Milarepa, Tibets groáer Yogi*, Munchen (first published 1928, as *The Life of Milarepa, Tibet's Great Yogi*, London: John Murrray).
Everding, K-H. 1993 *Tibet: Lamaistische Klosterkulturen, nomadische Lebensformen und bäuerlicher Alltag auf dem Dach der Welt*, Köln: DuMont.
Falk, N.E. 1973 'Wilderness and Kingship in Ancient South Asia', in *History of Religions*, 13.1.
Ferrari, A. 1958 *Mk'yen Brtse's guide to the holy places of Central Tibet*, Series Orientale Roma, vol. XVI, Roma: IsMEO.
Filchner, W. 1906 *Das Kloster Kumbum in Tibet. Ein Beitrag zu seiner Geschichte*, Berlin: Ernst Siegfried Mittler und Sohn.
—— 1933 *Kumbum Dschamba Ling. Das Kloster der hunderttausend Bilder Maitreyas*, Leipzig: F.A. Brockhaus.
Filibeck, E. De R. 1988 *Two Tibetan Guide Books to Ti se and La phyi*, Monumenta Tibetica Historica Abt.1, Band 4, Bonn:VGH Wisseschaft.
—— 1990 'A guide-book to Tsari', in Epstein, L. & R.F. Sherburne (eds.), *Reflections on Tibetan culture*, Lewiston: The Edwin Mellen Press.
Fletcher, H.R. 1975 *A quest of flowers. The plant hunting explorations of Frank Ludlow and George Sherriff told from their diaries and other occasional writings*, Edinburgh: Edinburgh University Press.
Forbes, J. 1813 *Oriental Memoirs*, vol. 2, London.
Foreman, H. 1936. *Through Forbidden Tibet*, London: Anchor Press.
Francke, A.H. 1914 *Antiquities of Indian Tibet, Part 1, Personal Narrative*, Calcutta: Superintendent Government Printing.
—— 1972 *Antiquities of Indian Tibet, Part 2, The Chronicles of Ladakh and Minor Chronicles*, New Delhi: S.Chand, (first published, 1926).
Frauwallner, E. 1953 *Geschichte der indischen Philosophie*, Salzburg:Bd.I.
Frawley, D. 1993 *Vedic Secrets of Ancient Civilization*, New Delhi.
French, R. 1995 *The Golden Yoke. The Legal Cosmology of Buddhist Tibet*, Ithaca, N.Y.
Fuller, C.J. 1992 *The Camphor Flame, Popular Hinduism & Society in India*, Princeton: University Press.
Futterer, K. 1900 'Land und Leute in Nordost-Tibet', in *Zeitschrift der Gesellschaft für Erdkunde, Berlin*, vol. 35, part 5.

Ganhar, J.N. 1973 *Jammu Shrines and Pilgrimages,* New Delhi.
Gendun Chomphel (dGe-'dun chos-'phel), 1939 *rGya-gar-gyi gnas-chen khag-la 'grod-pa'i lam-yig. Guide to Buddhist Sacred Places in India,* Calcutta (Maha Bodhi Society).
Gerard, A. 1841 *An Account of Koonawur in the Himalayas,* London.
Ghosh, J.M. 1930 *Sannyasi & Fakir Raiders in Bengal,* Calcutta.
Ghurye, G.S. 1964 *Indian Saddhus,* Bombay: Popular Press, (1953).
Gill, W. 1880 *The river of golden sand. The narrative of a journey through China and Eastern Tibet to Burmah,* (2 vols). London: John Murray.
Glasenapp, H. 1984 *Der Jainismus. Eine indische Erl sungslehre,* Hildesheim.
Gokhale, B.G. 1930 *Surat in the 17th century,* London and Malmo.
Gonda, J, 1975 *Vedic Literature,* (Gonda, J., (ed.), *A History of Indian Literature, vol. 1.*), Weisbaden.
Govinda, A. 1962 *Der Weg der weissen Wolken. Erlebnisse eines buddhistischen Pilgers in Tibet,* Zürich/Stuttgart (Rascher Verlag), (first English translation, 1966, as *The Way of the White Clouds,* London: Rider & Co.)
Graburn, N. 1977 'Tourism: the Sacred Journey', in V. Smith (ed.), *Hosts and Guests,* Philadelphia: University of Pennsylvania Press.
Grapard, A.G. 1982 'Flying Mountains and Walkers of Emptiness: Toward a Definition of Sacred Space in Japanese Religions', in *History of Religions,* 21.3.
Gregory, J.W. & Gregory, C.J. 1923 *To the Alps of Chinese Tibet,* London: Seeley Service and Co.
Grunendahl, R. 1993 'Zu den beiden Gandhamadana-Episoden des Aranyakaparvan', in *Studien Zur Indologie und Iranistik,* 18., Reinbeck.
Grünwedel, A. 1919 *Die Tempel von Lhasa. Gedicht des ersten Dalailama, für Pilger bestimmt,* Sitzungsberichte der Heidelberger Akademie der Wissenschaften, Heidelberg: Carl Winter's Universitätsbuchhandlung.
Hackmann, H. 1907 *Vom Omi bis Bhamo. Wanderungen an den Grenzen von China, Tibet und Birma,* Berlin: Karl Curtius.
Hamilton, F.B. 1819 *An account of the kingdom of Nepal and the territories annexed to this dominion by the house of Gorkha,* Edinburgh: Archibald Constable and Co, (Reprinted New Delhi: Manjusri Publishing House, 1971).
Hamsa, B.S. 1934 *The holy mountain, being the story of a pilgrimage to Lake Manas and of initiation on Mount Kailas in Tibet,* London: Faber and Faber.
Handel-Mazzetti, H. 1927 *Naturbilder aus Südwest-China. Erlebnisse und Eindrücke eines österreichischen Forschers während des Weltkrieges,* Wien/Leipzig: Oesterreichischer Bundesverlag.
Hanna, S. 1994 'Vast as the Sky: The Terma Tradition in Modern Tibet', in Samuel, G., Gregor, H. & Stuchbury, E., (eds.) *op. cit.,* Delhi: Aditya Prakashan.
Harrer, H. 1952 *Sieben Jahre in Tibet,* Wien: Ullstein. (First published in English 1954 as *Seven Years in Tibet,* New York: E.P. Dutton.).
Havnevik, H. 1990 *Tibetan Buddhist Nuns: History, Cultural Norms and Social Reality,* Oslo: Norwegian Univ. Press.

—— (forthcoming) The Autobiography of Jetsun Lochen Rinpoche (1865–1951). 'A Preliminary Study', in Proceedings of the 7th Seminar of the International Association for Tibetan Studies, Graz 1995.

—— (ongoing) *The Religious Ideal for Women in Tibetan Biographical Literature*, Ph.D. thesis, University of Oslo.

Hedin, S. 1910–1913 *Trans-Himalaya. Discoveries and adventures in Tibet*, (3 vols), London: Macmillan and Co.

—— 1917–1922 *Southern Tibet. Discoveries in former times compared with my own researches in 1906–08*, (Band I-IX), Stockholm: Lithographic Institute of the General Staff of the Swedish Army.

—— 1922–1923 *Tsangpo Lamas Wallfahrt*, (2. vols.), Leipzig: F.A. Brockhaus.

—— 1909 *Transhimalaja. Entdeckungen und Abenteuer in Tibet*, Leipzig.

Heesterman, J. 1984 '"Orthodox" and "Heterodox" Law: Some Remarks on Customary Law and State', in Eisenstadt, S.N., Kahane, R., & Shulman, D. (eds.), *Orthodoxy, Heterodoxy and Dissent in India, Religion and Society* (23), N.Y./Amsterdam.

—— 1988 'Householder and Wanderer', in Madan, T.N., (ed.), *Way of life: King, Householder, Renouncer, Studies in Honour of Louis Dumont*, (New Delhi: Vikas, 1981).

Heim, A. 1933 *Minya Gongkar. Forschungsreise ins Hochgebirge von Chinesisch Tibet*, Bern-Berlin: Verlag Hans Huber.

Heron, A.M. 1930 'The gem-stones of the Himalaya', in *The Himalayan Journal*, vol. II, April.

Hocart, A.M. 1936 *Rois et courtisans*, Le Seuil, Paris: Le caire.

Hoffmann, H. 1950 *Quellen zur Geschichte der Bon-Religion*, Wiesbaden.

Hooker, J.D. 1854 *Himalayan Journals. Notes of a naturalist in Bengal, the Sikkim and Nepal Himalayas, the Khasia mountains, etc.*, London: Murray. (Reprinted New Delhi: Today and Tomorrows Printers and Publishers, 1980).

Hornbein, T.F. 1965 *Everest: the West Ridge*, San Francisco: Sierra Club.

Hosie, A. 1905 *Report on a journey to the eastern frontier of Tibet*, London: His Majesty's Stationery Office.

Hsieh, Shih-chung. 1993 *Dai Lue: Xishuangbanna de Zuqun Xiangxiang (Dai Lue: Ethnicity in Sipsongpanna)*, Taipei: Zili Wanbao Press.

Huber, T. 1989 *A pilgrimage to La-phyi: A Study of Sacred and Historical Geography in South-Western Tibet*. Unpublished M.A. dissertation, University of Canterbury, New Zealand.

—— 1990 'Where exactly are Cāritra, Devikoṭa and Himavat? A sacred geography controversy and the development of tantric Buddhist pilgrimage sites in Tibet', in *Kailash. A Journal of Himalayan Studies*, vol. XVI, nos. 3–4.

—— 1991 'Traditional Environmental Protectionism in Tibet Reconsidered', in *The Tibet Journal*, 16.3.

—— 1993 *What is a Mountain? An Ethnohistory of Representation and Ritual at PureCrystal Mountain in Tibet*. Unpublished Ph.D. thesis, University of Canterbury, N.Z.

—— 1994a 'When what you see is not what you get. Remarks on the traditional Tibetan presentation of sacred geography', in Samuel, G., Gregor, H., & Stutchbury E., (eds.), *op. cit*.

—— 1994b 'Why can't women climb Pure Crystal Mountain? Remarks on gender, ritual and space at Tsari', in Kvaerne, P., (ed.), *Tibetan Studies, op. cit.*

—— 1994c 'Putting the Gnas Back into Gnas-Skor: Rethinking Tibetan Buddhist Pilgrimage Practice', in *The Tibet Journal*, vol. X1XX.2.

—— 1997 'A Guide to the La-Phyi Mandala', in Macdonald, A.W., (ed.), *op. cit.*

—— 1998a *The Cult of Pure Crystal Mountain. Popular Pilgrimage and Visionary Landscape in Southeast Tibet*, N.Y.: Oxford University Press, (forthcoming).

—— (ed.), 1998b *Powerful Places and Spaces in Tibetan Religious Culture*, Dharamsala: LWTA., (forthcoming).

Huber, T. & Rigzin, T. 1995 'A Tibetan guide for pilgrimage to Ti-se (Mount Kailas) and mTsho Ma-pham', in *The Tibet Journal*, vol. 20.1.

Huc, E.-R. & Gabet, J. 1987 *Travels in Tartary, Thibet and China, 1844–1846*. London: George Routledge and Sons, (Translated from the original French edition of 1850, Reprinted: New York: Dover Publications).

Ihara Shoren & Yamaguchi Zuiho (eds.), 1992 *Tibetan Studies. Proceedings of the 5th Seminar of the International Association for Tibetan Studies, 2 vols., Narita 1989*, Narita: Naritasan Shinshoji.

Imhof, M. 1974 *Die großen kalten Berge von Szetschuan. Erlebnisse, Forschungen und Kartierungen in Minya-Konka-Gebirge*, Zürich: Orell Fussli Verlag.

Jackson, D. 1984 *The Mollas of Mustang: Historical, Religious and Oratorical Traditions of the Nepalese-Tibetan Borderland*, Dharamsala: LTWA.

Jest, C. 1987 'Valeurs d'échange en Himalaya et au Tibet: l'ambre et le musc', in *De la voûte céleste au terroir, du jardin au foyer*, Paris: Editions de l'Ecole des Hautes Etudes en Sciences Sociales.

Jha, M. 1995a *The sacred complex of Kathmandu, Nepal. Religion of the Himalayan kingdom*, New Delhi: Gyan Publishing House.

—— 1995b 'Buddhist pilgrimage centres of Kathmandu, Nepal: a study in anthropo-historical approach and methodological perspective', in Jha, M., (ed.), *Pilgrimage. Concepts, themes, issues and methodology*, New Delhi: Inter-India Publications.

Johnson, R. & Moran, K. 1989 *Kailas. On pilgrimage to the sacred mountain of Tibet*, London: Thames and Hudson.

Johnston, R.F. 1908 *From Peking to Mandalay. A journey from North China to Burma through Tibetan Ssuch'uan and Yunnan*, London: John Murray.

Kapstein, M. 1992 'Remarks on the Mani bKa'-'bum and the Cult of Avalokitesvera in Tibet', in Goodman, S.D. & Davidson, R.M., *Tibetan Buddhism: Reason and Revelation* Albany: SUNY.

Karmay, S.G. 1972 *The Treasury of Good Sayings: A Tibetan History of Bon*, London Oriental Series, vol. 26, London: OUP.

—— 1977 *A Catalogue of Bonpo Publications*, Tokyo: The Toyo Bunko.

—— 1988 *The Great Perfection. A Philosophical and Meditative Teaching of Tibetan Buddhism*, Leiden: E.J. Brill.

—— 1991 'L'homme et le boeuf: le rituel du glud (rancon)', in *Journal Asiatique*, CCLXXIX.3-4.

—— 1992 'A pilgrimage to Kongpo Bon-ri', in Ihara Shoren & Yamaguchi Zuiho (eds.), *op. cit.*

—— 1994 'Mountain Cults and National Identity in Tibet', in Barnett, R. & Akiner, S., *Resistance and Reform in Tibet,* London: Hurst and Co.

Karmay, S. & Sagant, P., (eds.) 1997 *Les habitants du Toit du Monde: Homage à Alexander W. Macdonald,* Nanterre, Société d'ethnologie.

Katz, R.C. 1989 *Arjuna in the Mahabharata: Where Krishna Is, There is Victory,* Columbia: Uni., of South Carolina Press.

Kawaguchi, E. 1909 *Three years in Tibet,* Madras: The Theosophist Office, (Reprinted: Kathmandu: Ratna Pustak Bhandar, 1979).

Kingdon Ward, F. 1913 *The land of the blue poppy. Travels of a naturalist in Eastern Tibet,* Cambridge: Cambridge University Press. (Reprinted: London: Cadogan Books, 1986).

—— 1924 'The snow mountains of Yunnan', in *The Geographical Journal,* vol. LXIV.3.

—— 1926 'Explorations in South-Eastern Tibet', in *The Geographical Journal,* vol. LXVII.2.

—— 1936 'Botanical and geographical exploration in Tibet, 1935', in *The Geographical Journal,* vol. LXXXVIII.5.

Kirkland, J.R. 1982 'The spirit of the mountain: myth and state in pre-Buddhist Tibet', in *History of Religions,* vol. XXI.3.

Klieger, P.C. 1990 'Close Encounters: "Intimate" Tourism in Tibet', in *Cultural Survival Quarterly* 14.2.

—— 1992 *Tibetan Nationalism (The Role of Patronage in the Accomplishment of a National Identity),* Berkeley: Folklore Institute.

Kolff, D.H.A. 1971 'Sannyasi Trader-Soldiers', in *Indian Economic and Social History Review,* vol. 8.

Kollmar-Paulenz, K. 1993 *'Der Schmuck der Befreiung.' Die Geschichte der Zi byed-und gCod-Schule des tibetischen Buddhismus,* Wiesbaden: Harrassowitz.

Korom, F.J. 1992 'Of Navels and Mountains: A Further Inquiry into the History of an Idea', in *Asian Folklore Studies,* 51.

Kulke, H. 1993 *Kings and Cults. State Formation and Legitimation in India and Southeast Asia,* New Delhi: Manohar.

Kvaerne, P. 1970 'Remarques sur l'administration d'un monastère bon po', in *Journal Asiatique,* 258.

—— 1976 'Who Are the Bonpos?', in *Tibetan Review* II, 9.

—— 1985 *Tibet – Bon Religion. A Death Ritual of the Tibetan Bonpos,* Leiden: Brill.

—— (ed.), 1994 *Tibetan Studies: Proceedings of the 6th International Seminar of Tibetan Studies,* 2 vols., Fagernes 1992. The Institute for Comparative Research in Human Culture. Oslo.

—— 1995 'The Bon Religion of Tibet: A Survey of Research', in Skorupski, T., & Pagel, U, (eds.), *The Buddhist Forum, Papers in honour and appreciation of Professor D.S. Ruegg's contribution to Indological, Buddhist and Tibetan Studies,* vol. 3, 1991–1993, New Delhi: Heritage.

—— 1995a *The Bon Religion of Tibet. The Iconography of a Living Tradition,* London: Serindia Publications.

Lamb, A. 1960 *Britain and Chinese Central Asia, The Road to Lhasa 1767–1905*, London.
Le Beck, H.J. 1801 'An Account of the Pearl Fishery in the Gulph of Manar in March & April 1797', in *Asiatick Researches*, vol. 5.
Lefeber, R., & Goldman, R.P., (eds./trans), 1994 *The Ramayana of Valmiki*, Princeto: University Press.
Lemaire, T. 1970 *Filosofie van het landschap*, Baarn: Ambo.
Lesdain, Count de. 1908 *From Pekin to Sikkim. Through the Ordos, the Gobi desert, and Tibet*, London: John Murray (original French edition: Paris, 1908).
Lévi, S. 1905–1908 *Le Népal. Etude historique d'un royaume hindou*, Paris: Ernest Leroux. [Annales du Muséé Guimet, tomes 17, 18, 19]. (Reprinted Paris: Toit du Monde – Raj de Condappa – Editions Errance, 1985).
Lha-mo, Rin-chen [Mrs. Louis King]. 1926. *We Tibetans. An intimate picture, by a woman of Tibet, of an interesting and distinctive people. . .*, London: Seeley Service and Co.
Li An-che. 1948 'Our pilgrimage to a Tibetan sacred mountain', in *Asian Horizon*, vol. 2, summer.
—— 1982 *Labrang. A study in the field,* (Chie Nakane, ed.), Tokyo: Institute of Oriental Culture, University of Tokyo.
Lo Bue, E. 1994 'A case of mistaken identiy: Ma-gcig Labs-sgron and Ma-gcig Zha ma.', in Kvaerne, P., (ed.), *op. cit.*
Longman Dictionary. 1988 *Longman dictionary of the English language*, London: Longman.
Loseries, A. 1990 'Kailasa – Der Heiligste Berg der Welt', in Gratzl, K., (ed.), *Die heiligsten Berge der Welt*, Graz.
—— 1994. 'Sacred Geography and Individual in Central Tibet: Terdrum Sanctuary, a Training Path within the Drikung Mandala', in *The Tibet Journal*, vol. 19.4.
Ludlow, F. 1938 'The sources of the Subansiri and Siyom', in *The Himalayan Journal*, vol. X.1.
MacDonald, A.W. 1967 *Matériaux pour l'étude de la littérature populaire tibétaine* Paris: Presses Universitaires de France.
—— (ed.), 1982 *Les royaumes de l'Himâlaya. Histoire et civilisation*, Paris: Imprimerie nationale.
—— 1985 'Points of view on Halase, a holy place in East Nepal', in *The Tibet Journal*, vol. 10.3: (translated with additions in: *La Nouvelle Revue Tibétaine*, vol. 13, 1986).
—— 1990 'Hindu-isation, Buddha-isation, then Lama-isation or: what happened at La-phyi?', in Skorupski, T. (ed.), *Indo-Tibetan studies,* Buddhica Britannica Series Continua 11, Tring: Institute of Buddhist Studies.
—— (ed.), 1997 *Mandala and Landscape,* New Delhi: D.K. Printworld.
Ma Lihua. 1993 'Shamanic Belief among Nomads in Northern Tibet', in *Anthropology of Tibet and the Himalaya*, Ramble, C., & Brauen, M., *op. cit.*
Mabbett, I.W. 1983 'The Symbolism of Mount Meru', in *History of Religions*, vol. 23.1.

Mani, V. 1975 *Puranic Encyclopaedia. A comprehensive Dictionary with special reference to the Epic and Puranic Literature*, Delhi.
Markham, C.R. 1876 *Narratives of the mission of George Bogle to Tibet and of the journey of Thomas Manning to Lhasa*, London: Trübner and Co (Reprinted: New Delhi: Manjusri Publishing House).
Massonaud, C. 1982 'Le Sikkim', in *Les Royaumes De l'Himalaya*, Paris: Collectien orientale de l'Imprerie nationale.
Meyer, F. 1987 'Des dieux, des montagnes et des hommes. La lecture tibétaine du paysage', in *Etudes Rurales*, nos. 107–108.
Migot, A. 1961[?] *Caravane vers Bouddha. Un français à travers la Haute-Asie mystique*, Paris: CAL, Edition revue par l'auteur.
Monier-Williams, M. 1974 *A Sanskrit-English Dictionary*, Oxford: OUP, (first published 1899).
Montaigne, H. 1991 *Histoire et géographie sacrée du grand pèlerinage*, La Place Royale, Recouvrance.
Morinis, E. 1984 *Pilgrimage in the Hindu Tradition*, Delhi.
Mylius, K. 1988 *Geschichte der altindischen Literatur*, Bern, Munchen, Wien.
Namkhai Norbu. 1984 *The necklace of gZi. A cultural history of Tibet*, Dharamsala: LWTA.
—— 1990 *sGrung lde'u bon: Tradizioni magico-religiose dell'antico Tibet*, Arcidosso.
—— 1995 *Drung, Deu and Bon. Narrations, Symbolic languages and the Bon tradition in ancient Tibet*, Dharamsala: LTWA.
Namkhai Norbu & Prats, R. (eds.), 1989 *Gangs ti-se'i dkar c'ag. A Bon-po story of the sacred mountain Ti-se and the blue lake Ma-pang*, Serie Orientale Roma, LXI, Roma: IsMEO.
Nanpingxian Difangzhi Biancuanweiyuanhui. 1994 (Editorial Board of Nanping Gazetteer), *Nanping Xianzhi (Nanping Gazetteer)*, Beijing: Minzu Chubanshe (Nationality Press).
Nebesky-Wojkowitz, R. von. 1956 *Oracles and demons of Tibet. The cult and iconography of the Tibetan protective deities*, The Hague: Mouton.
Nicolazzi, M. A. 1995 *Monche, Geister und Schamanen. Die Bon Religion Tibets*, Dusseldorf.
Noble, C. 1988 *Over the High Passes: A Year in the Himalayas with the Migratory Gaddi Shepherds*, London: Fontana, (1987: William Collins).
Oakes, T.S. 1992 'Cultural Geography and Chinese Ethnic Tourism', in *Journal of Cultural Geography*, 12.2.
Oberdiek, U. 1995 'Functions of Hindu Pilgrimage: Secular traits in Tirthayatra', in Dubey, D., *op. cit.*
Oldfield, H.A. 1880 *Sketches from Nipal*, (2 vols.). London: W.H. Allen. (Reprinted Delhi: Cosmo Publications).
Olivelle, P. 1974 'The Notion of Asrama in the Dharmasastras', in *Wiener Zeitschrift fur die Kunde Sudasiens*, 18.
—— 1987 'King and Ascetic: State Control of Asceticism in the arthasastra', in *Festschrift Ludo Rocher, Adyar Library Bulletin*, 50, Madras.
Ossendowski, F. 1923 *Beasts, men and gods*, London: Edward Arnold.
Petech, L. 1973 *Aristocracy and Government in Tibet 1728–1959*, Rome: Is.M.E.O.

—— 1988 'The 'Bri gung pa Sect in Western Tibet and Ladakh', in *Selected Papers on Asian History*, Rome: Is.M.E.O.
Pommaret, F. 1989 *Les revenants de l'au-delà dans le monde tibétain*, Paris: C.N.R.S.
Pranavananda, S. 1950 *Exploration in Tibet*, University of Calcutta.
—— 1984 *Kailas-Manasarovar*, Delhi: Pranavananda (first published 1949).
Prejevalsky, N.M. 1876 *Mongolia, the Tangut country and the solitudes of Northern Tibet*, (2 vols.), London: S.Low, Marston, Searle and Rivington. (Reprinted New Delhi: Asian Educational Services, 1991).
Prindle, P.H. 1983 *Tinglatar. Socio-economic relationships of a Brahmin village in East Nepal*, Kathmandu: Ratna Pustak Bhandar.
Ramble, C. 1984 *The Lamas of Lubra: Tibetan Bonpo Householder Priests in Western Nepal*, Unpublished Ph.D. thesis, University of Oxford.
—— 1995 'Gaining Ground: Representations of Territory in Bon and Tibetan Popular Tradition', in *The Tibet Journal*, 20.1.
Ramble, C., & Brauen, M., (eds.), 1993 *Anthropology of Tibet and the Himalaya*, Zurich: Volkerkundemuseum der Universitat.
Rangachar, N. 1931 *Diary of a pilgrimage to Lake Manasarowar and Mount Kailas with H.H. the Maharaja of Mysore in 1931*, Mysore: Government Branch Press.
Regmi, D.R. 1961 *Modern Nepal*, Calcutta.
Rey, A. (ed.), 1992 *Dictionnaire Historique de la langue française*, Paris: Dictionnaires le Robert.
Reynolds, J.M. 1989 *The Cult and Practice of Zhang-zhung Meri: Translation of the Sadhana Practice for Meri from the Meri sGrub skor, together with the original myth of the Walchen Gekhod*, (Bon po Translation project), Berkeley.
—— 1992 *Bon po Dzogchen: Teachings according to Lopon Tenzin Namdak*, (transcribed and edited by Vajranatha), Freehold and Amsterdam.
Ricard, M. et al. 1994 *The life of Shabkar. The autobiography of a Tibetan yogin*. Albany: State University of New York Press, SUNY.
Richardson, H. 1962 *Tibet and Its History*, London: OUP.
Richardus, P. 1989 *The Dutch orientalist Johan van Manen: his life and work*, Leiden: Kern Institute.
Rijnhart, S.C. 1901 *With the Tibetans in tent and temple. Narrative of four years' residence on the Tibetan border, and of a journey into the far interior*, Edinburgh and London: Oliphant, Anderson and Ferrier.
Risley, H.H. 1892 *Tribes and Castes of Bengal*, Calcutta.
Rocher, L. 1986 *The Puranas*, (A History of Indian Literature, Gonda. J., (ed.), vol. 2.), Wiesbaden.
Rock, J.F. 1930a 'Seeking the mountains of mystery. An expedition on the China-Tibet frontier to the unexplored Amnyi Machen Range', in *The National Geographic Magazine*, vol. LVII.2.
—— 1930b 'The glories of Minya Konka', in *The National Geographic Magazine*, vol. LVIII.4.
—— 1931 'Konka Risumgongba, holy mountain of the outlaws', in *The National Geographic Magazine*, vol. LX.1.

—— 1947 *The ancient Na-khi kingdom of Southwest China*. [Harvard-Yenching Institute, Monograph Series, vols. VIII and IX], Cambridge, Mass.: Harvard University Press.
—— 1953 'Excerpts from a History of Sikkim', in *Anthropos*, vol. 48.
—— 1956 *The Amnye Ma-Chen range and adjacent regions. A monographic study*, Serie Orientale Roma, XII, Rome: IsMEO.
Roerich, G. N. de 1931 *Trails to inmost Asia. Five years of exploration with the Roerich Central Asian Expedition*, New Haven, Yale University Press, (Reprinted: Moscow: Izdatel' stvo, Nauka, 1967).
—— 1967 *Izbrannye Trudy*, ("Selected Articles"), Moscow: Editions Nauka.
—— 1976 *The Blue Annals*, Delhi: Motilal Banarsidass, (Calcutta, 1949).
Rose, H.A. 1911 *Glossary of the Tribes & Castes of the Punjab & the North West Frontier Provinces*, vol. 2, Lahore.
Russell, R.V. 1916 *Tribes & Castes of the Central Provinces*, vol. 3, London.
Ryall, E.C. 1879 'Explorations in Western Tibet, by the trans-Himalayan parties of the Indian Trigonometrical Survey', in *Proceedings of the Royal Geographical Society*, vol. I.
Sadananda Giri. 1976 *Society and Sannyasin, A History of the Dasnami S.S. Sannyasins*, Rishikesh.
Samkrtyayan, R. 1990 *Kinnar des me*, (3rd ed.), New Delhi: Kitab Mahal Agencies Pvt. Ltd, (first published, 1948).
Samuel, G. 1993 *Civilized Shamans: Buddhism in Tibetan Societies*, Washington: Smithsonian Institution Press.
Samuel, G., Gregor, H., & Stuchbury, E., (eds.), 1994 *Tantra and Popular Religion in Tibet*, Delhi: Aditya Prakashan.
Sarcar, J.N., (Sir). 1955 *A History of the Dasnami Naga Sanyasis*, Allahabad.
Sarcar, S.C. 1940 'Some Notes on the Intercourse of Bengal with the Northern Countries in the 2nd half of the 18th century', in *Bengal, Past and Present*, vol. 41.
—— 1942 'A note on Puran Gir Gosain', in *Bengal, Past and Present*, vol. 43.
Schein, L. 1989 'The Dynamics of Cultural Revival Among the Miao in Guizhou', in Tapp, N., & Chao, C., (eds.), *Ethnicity and Ethnic Groups in China*, Hong Kong: The Chinese University of Hong Kong Press.
Schleberger, E. 1986 *Die indische Gotterwelt. Gestalt, Ausdruck und Sinnbild. Ein Handbuch der hinduistischen Ikonographie*, Darmstadt.
Schoff, W.H. (Trans.) 1912 *The Periplus of the Erythraean Sea*, New York.
Seeland, K. 1993 'Sanskritisation and Environmental Perception among Tibeto-Burman Speaking Groups', in Ramble & Brauen, *op. cit*.
Senft, W. 1983 *Tibets Götter leben. Unvergängliches und Unbekanntes vom Dach der Welt nach der Kulturrevolution*, Graz-Stuttgart: Leopold Stocker Verlag.
—— 1984 *Chinas Bergwelt*, Graz-Stuttgart: Leopold Stocker Verlag.
Sherring, C.A. 1906 *Western Tibet and the Indian borderland*, London: Edward Arnold, (reprinted, Delhi: Cosmo Publications, 1974).
Singh, S.P. 1995 'Origin and Growth of the Institution of Pilgrimage' in Dubey, D.P., *op. cit*.
Sleen, W.G. van der, 1927 *Vier maanden kamperen in den Himalaya*, Rotterdam: Nijgh & Van Ditmar.

Smith, E.G. 1970 'Introduction' to *Kongtrul's Encyclopaedia of Indo-Tibetan Culture,* Lokesh Chandra, (ed.), New Delhi: International Academy of Indian Culture.
Snellgrove, D. 1979 'A Description of Muktinath, The Place of Promenade, Ku-Tsab-Ter-Nga, Mount Mu-li, The Guru's Hidden cave and the sNa ri Lord', in *Kailash,* VII.2.
—— 1987 *Indo-Tibetan Buddhism: Indian Buddhists and Their Tibetan Successors,* London: Serindia Publications.
—— 1989 *Himalayan Pilgrimage,* Boston: Shambala, (first published London, 1981).
Snellgrove, D., & H. Richardson, H. 1980 *A cultural history of Tibet,* Boulder: Prajna Press, (original edition, London: Weidenfeld & Nicolson).
Snellgrove, D., & Skorupski, T. 1979 *The Cultural Heritage of Ladakh,* 2. vols, Warminster: Aris & Phillips (1977).
Snelling, J. 1983 *The sacred mountain. Travellers and pilgrims at Mount Kailas in Western Tibet, and the great universal symbol of the sacred mountain,* London and The Hague: East West Publications, (2nd, revised edition, 1990).
Sørensen, P.K. 1994 *The Mirror Illuminating the Royal Genealogies,* Wiesbaden: Harrasowitz.
Sørensen, P.K., & Vinding, M., (forthcoming), *Himalayan Myths of Origin; The rabs of the Tamang Thakalis,* (in *Nepalica*).
Spengen, W. van, 1992 *Tibetan Border Worlds. A geo-historical analysis of trade and trader,* Unpublished Ph.D. dissertation, University of Amsterdam.
—— 1995 'The Geo-History of Long-Distance Trade in Tibet 1850–1950, in *The Tibet Journal,* vol. XX.2
Sperling, E. 1994 'Rtsa-Mi Lo-tsa-Ba Sangs-Rgyas Grags-Pa and the Tangut Background to Early Mongol-Tibetan Relations', in Kvaerne, P., (ed.), *op. cit.*
Staal, F. 1990 'The Lake of the Yaksa Chief', in *Indo-Tibetan Studies,* Skorupski, T., (ed.), Buddhica Britannica Series Continua 11, Tring: Insititute of Buddhist Studies.
Stein, R.A. 1959 *Recherches sur l'épopée et le barde au Tibet,* Paris: Presses Universitaires de France.
—— 1980 *La civilisation tibétaine,* Le Sycomore, L'Asiathèque, (first published, 1962, Dunod, Paris), (first published in english as *Tibetan Civilization,* Stanford Ca.: Stanford Univ. Press, 1962).
Steinmann, B. 1996 'Mountain deities, the invisible body of the society: a comparative study of the representations of the mountains by the Tamangs and the Thamis of Nepal, the Lepchas and the Bhotias of Sikkim' in Blondeau, A. M., & Steinkellner, E. (eds.), *op. cit.*
Stevenson, S. 1915 *The Heart of Jainism,* London.
Stoddard, H. 1985 *Le mendiant de l'Amdo,* Paris: Société d'ethnographie.
Stoll, E. 1966 'Ti-se, der heilige Berg in Tibet', in *Geographica Helvetica,* vol. 21.
Strachey, H. 1848 *Narrative of a Journey to the Lakes Cho Lagan or Rakas Tal, and Cho Mapan, or Manasarowar . . .,* Calcutta: Baptist Mission Press.
Sukthankar, V.S. 1969–1970 *The Mahabharata,* Critical Edition. Poona.

Suryavanshi, B.S. 1986 *The Geography of the Mahabharata*, Delhi.
Sutherland, G.H. 1992 *Yaksha in Hinduism and Buddhism: The Disguises of the Demon*, New Delhi (First published 1991, as *The Disguises of the Demon: The development of the Yaksa in Hinduism and Buddhism*, State Uni. of N.Y. Press).
Swain, M.B. 1990 'Commoditizing Ethnicity in Southwest China', in *Cultural Survival Quarterly*, 14.1.
Sweet, M.J. 1996 'Mental Purification (Blo sbyong): A Native Tibetan Genre of Religious Literature', in *Tibetan Literature; Studies in Genre*, Cabezon, J.I., & Jackson, R.R., Ithaca, NY.: Snow Lion.
Tafel, A. 1914 *Meine Tibetreise: Eine Studienfahrt durch das nordwest-liche China und durch die innere Mongolei in das östliche Tibet*, (2 vols.), Stuttgart/Berlin/Leipzig: Union Deutsche, Verlagsgesellschaft.
Teichman, E. 1922 *Travels of a consular officer in Eastern Tibet; together with a history of the relations between China, Tibet and India*, Cambridge: Cambridge University Press.
Thapar, R. 1978 'Renunciation: The Making of a Counter-Culture?', in Thapar, R., (ed.), *Ancient Indian Social History: Some Interpretations*, New Delhi.
—— 1988 'The householder and the renouncer in the Brahmanical and Buddhist traditions', in Madan, T.N. (ed.), *Way of Life: King, Householder, Renouncer, Studies in Honour of Louis Dumont*, (1981, New Delhi: Vikas).
Tichy, H. 1937 *Zum heiligsten Berg der Welt. Auf Landstrassen und Pilgerfahrten in Afghanistan, Indien und Tibet*, Wien: Verlag von L.W. Seidel und Sohn.
Tsybikoff, G. 1904 'Journey to Lhasa', in *The Geographical Journal*, vol. 23.
—— 1992 *Un pèlerin bouddhiste dans les sanctuaires du Tibet. D'après lesjournaux de voyage tenus entre 1899 et 1902*. Paris: Editions Peuples du Monde, (Translated by Bernard Kreise from the original Russian edition of 1919).
Tucci, G. 1940 *Travels of Tibetan Pilgrims in the Swat Valley*, The Greater India Society, Calcutta.
—— 1956 *To Lhasa and beyond. Diary of the expedition to Tibet in the year MCMXLVIII*, Roma: Libreria della Stato.
—— 1956a *Preliminary Report on two Scientific Expeditions in Nepal*, Rome (ISMEO).
—— 1973 *Les religions du Tibet et de la Mongolie*, Paris: Payot, (first published as Die Religionen Tibets, 1970, in *Die Religionen Tibets und der Mongolei*, Tucci, G. & Heissig, W., Stuttgart/Berlin etc.: W.Kohlhamman Gmbtt.).
—— 1989 *Sadhus et brigands du Kailash. Mon voyage au Tibet occidental*, Paris: Editions Raymond Chabaud – Peuples du Monde (original edition: Milan: Casa Editrice Ulrico Hoepli, 1937).
Tucci, G, & Ghersi, E. 1935 *Secrets of Tibet. Being the Chronicle of the Tucci Scientific Expedition to Western Tibet (1933)*, London/Glasgow: Blackie and Son Limited.
Tulku Thondup. 1996 *Masters of Meditation and Miracles. The Longchen Nyingthig Lineage of Tibetan Buddhism*, Boston: Shambhala.

Turner, S. 1800 *An Account of an Embassy to the Court of the Teshoo Lama in Tibet*, London.
Turner, V. 1969 *The Ritual Process*, London.
—— 1973 'The Center Out There: Pilgrims Goal, in *History of Religion*, vol. 12.
Varma, R. 1988–89 'Meru and Kailasa; Reflections on a Tangible "Sacred Space", Unpublished M.A. thesis, S.O.A.S., London University.
Vaurie, C. 1972 *Tibet and its birds*, London: H.F. and G. Witherby Ltd.
Vinding, M. 1996 *The Thakalis: A Himalayan Ethnography*. Unpublished Ph.D. thesis, University of Aarhus.
Vitali, R. 1996 *The Kingdoms of Gu.ge Pu.hrang. Tho. ling gtsug. lag. khang. lo. gcig .stong 'khor.ba'i rjes.dran. mdzad sgo'i go.sgrig tshogs. chung*, Dharamsala: LTWA.
Walker, B. 1968 *The Hindu World*, vol. 1, London.
Warikoo, K. 1988 'Central Asia & Kashmir: A Study in Political, Commercial & Cultural Contacts During the 19th and Early 20th Centuries', in *Central Asian Survey*, vol. 7.1.
Welch, S.C. 1978 *Room for Wonder, Indian Painting during the British Period 1760–1880*, New York.
Waddell, L.A. 1899 *Among the Himalayas*, London: Constable, (Reprinted Kathmandu: Ratna Pustak Bhandar, 1978).
Walker-Watson, M. 1983 'Turquoise – the gemstone of Tibet', in *Tibetan Review*, vol. XVIII.6–7.
Walsh, E.H. 1906 'An Old Form of Elective Government in the Chumbi Valley', in *Journal of the Asiatic Society of Bengal*, July.
Wangdu, Pasang & Diemberger, H. 1996 *Ngag dbang skal ldan rgya mtsho, Sheldkar Chos 'byung / History of the "White Crystal:" Religion and Politics of Southern La stod*, Wien: Verlag der Osterreichischen Akademie der Wissenschaften.
Warner, K. 1989 'The Longhaired Sage of RV 10.136: A Shaman, A Mystic or a Yogi?', in Warner, K.(ed.), *The Yogi and the Mystic: Studies in Indian and Comparative Mysticism*, London.
Wilson, A. 1979 *The abode of snow. Observations on a tour from Chinese Tibet to the Indian Caucasus, through the upper valleys of the Himalaya*. Kathmandu: Ratna Pustak Bhandar, (Original edition, London, 1875).
Wollaston, A.F.R. 1922 'The natural history of South-Western Tibet', in *The Geographical Journal*, vol. LX.1.
Wright, D. 1877 *History of Nepal*, Cambridge: Cambridge University Press.
Wylie, T.V. 1962 *The Geography of Tibet According to the 'Dzam gling rgyas bshad*, Rome: Is.M.E.O.
Yogev, G. 1978 *Diamonds and Corals, Anglo-Dutch Jews and 18th Century Trade*, Leicester.
Yule, H. (Sir), 1903 *The Book of Ser Marco Polo*, vol. 2, London,
Yule H. & Burnell A.C. 1996 *Hobson-Jobson, The Anglo-Indian Dictionary*, Ware.
Yuthok D.Y. 1990 *House of the Turquoise Roof*, Ithaca: Snow Lion Publications.
Zhang, Shanyun. 1990 *Jiuzhaigouzhi (Records of Jiuzhaigou)*, Chengdu: Sichuan Minzu Chubanshe, ("Sichuan Nationality Press").

Zhang, Shanyun, Ze Renzhu & Zhang Xiaoping. 1994 *Jiuzhaigou Ziran Jiaoxiangqu* (*The Natural Symphony of Jiuzhaigou*), Beijing: Kexue Puji Chubanshe, ("Science Propagation Press").

Tibetan Texts

Bod yul gnas kyi lam yig gsal ba dmig bu: Lopon Tenzin Namdak, Dolanji 1983.

Gangs ri mthso gsum gyi dkar: in Two rare Bon po dkar chag to the sacred Kailash and Manasarovar, written by Yeshes rgyal mthsan and dKar ru Grub dbang bStan 'dzin rinchen. Reproduced from rare mansucripts preserved at bSam ling Monastery in Dolpo (NW Nepal) by Tashi Dorji. Tibetan Bonpo Monastic Centre, New Thobgyal, P.O. Ochghat (via Solan), H.P.1973.

Gangs shug ma ni lo chen rig 'dzin chos nyid bzang mo'i rnam par thar pa rnam mkhyen bde ster. Autobiography of the Shug gseb rje btsun rig 'dzin chos nyid bzang mo. The Autobiographical Reminiscences of the Famed Religious Master and Reinbodiment of Klong chen pa Shug gseb rje btsun Rig 'dzin chos nyid bzang mo. The Ngagyur Nyingmay Sungrab series, vol. 22, Gangtok, 1975. (271 folios).

Kah thog Si tu Chos kyi rgya mtsho, Gangs ljongs dbus gtsang gnas bskor lam yig nor bu zla shel gyise mo do / An Account of a pilgrimage to Central Tibet during the years 1918 to 1920. Tashijong, Palampur, 1972. [KaSi].

Khetsun Sangpo Rinpoche, *rGya gar pan chen rnams kyi rnam thar ngo mtshar padmo'i 'dzum zhal gsar pa* / Biographical Dictionary of Tibet and Tibetan Buddhism. Dharamsala:LTWA, 1973- [BDTT]

Khyab-bdag 'khor-lo'i mgon-po mkhas-grub 'Jigs-med nam-mkha'i rnam-thar dad-brgya'i rma-bya rnam-par rtse-ba. The Biography of Khyun-sprul 'Jigs-med-nam-mkha'i-rdo-rje . . . together with the Zalgdams and Nams mgur of Khyun sprul, dPal-ldan tshul-khrims, Reproduced by sonam Dakpa from a lithographic print published in Delhi in 1957, 2 vols, Ochghat (Tibetan Bonpo Monastic Centre), 1972.

Mi la ras pa'i rnam mgur: rNal 'byor gyi dbang chen po Mi la ras pa'i rnam mgur. Compiled by Rus pa'i rgyan canmTsho sngon mi rigs dpe skrung khang. Ti se'i dkar chag: by dKar ru Grub chen bsTan 'dzin rin chen. Tibetan block print.

Ti se lo rgyus: Gangs rin po che Ti se dang mtsho Ma dros pa bcas kyi mngon byung gi lo rgyus mdor bsdus su brjod pa'i rab byed shel dkar melong, by the 34th 'Bri gung gdan rab bTsan 'dzin chos kyi blo gros, 1896, 'Bri gung thil.

Tshig mdzod Bod rgya tshig mdzod chen mo, (3 vols), Beijing: Nationalities Publ. House, 1985.

Contributors

Katia Buffetrille did her Ph.D. dissertation at the University of Paris X, Nanterre, on the subject of pilgrimages around sacred mountains, lakes and caves in Tibet and in the Sherpa area of Nepal. She lived for several years in Nepal and is currently working in Paris at the *Centre d'études des religions tibétaines*. Her main current projects are bringing out her Ph.D. in book form and publishing editions of the pilgrimage guides she used in her Ph.D., along with their translations. More recent projects include work on *Kha ba dkar po*'s pilgrimage (Yunnan) and a study of the cult of the *yul lha* in Reb kong (Qinghai).

Winand Callewaert has a B.A.(hons.) in Hindi and Sanskrit from Ranchi Shastri Sanskrit University of Benares, a B.A. in Philosophy from Pune, a Ph.D. and a D.Litt. from the Catholic University of Leuven, where he is a Professor teaching Sanskrit. He is the author of a number of books, mostly in the field of Bhakti Hindu literature.

John Clarke has recently (1995) completed a doctorate on the regional non-sculptural metalworking industries in traditional Tibet, a degree awarded by The School of Oriental and African Studies in London. He is currently Assistant Curator in the Indian and South East Asian Department at the Victoria and Albert Museum, London, where he curates the collection of Tibetan art. He is at present working on a catalogue of this collection.

Hanna Havnevik has a B.A. (1991) in anthropology, history and history of religions from the University of Oslo. She took a *magistergrad* in the History of Religion (1996) at the University of

Oslo, with her thesis *Tibetan Buddhist Nuns: History, Cultural Norms and Social Reality*, which was published by the Norwegian University Press, Oslo 1990 (translated into French and published by *Editions Dharma* 1995). She has been employed by the Norwegian State as advisor for refugees/immigrants 1987-1990 and was a Research Fellow at the University of Oslo from 1991-1996, in the Department of Cultural Studies, History of Religions section, where she is now employed as an Associate Professor. Her ongoing research, *The Religious Ideal for Women in Tibetan Biographical Literature*, based on the autobiography of Jetsun Lochen Rinpoche (1865-1951), is expected to be completed in 1997 and will be submitted for the doctoral degree at the University of Oslo.

Per Kværne has a Ph.D. from the University of Oslo, where he is currently Professor in the History of Religions. A Member of the Norwegian Academy of Science and Letters, and Convenor of the 6th Conference of the International association for Tibetan Studies in Fagernes in 1992, he is particularly well known for his work on the Bon-po, and his most recent major publication is *The Bon Religion of Tibet: The Iconography of a Living Tradition*.

Andrea Loseries-Leick studied Tibetology and Ethnology in Paris, India and Vienna. She is living as a free-lance scholar in Graz. Her research focuses on cultural history particularly in regard to the Tibetan Tantric traditions, their rituals and arts, including Bon. Her methodological approach combines textual studies with oral transmission and intensive field-work in Tibet and India. Her publications range from thesis and analysis of the use of skulls and bones in Tibetan rituals, to charnel ground practices and sacred geography and the individual. Recently she has concentrated on aspects of the Mother cult in gCod-tradition of the gYung drung Bon in comparison with the Buddhist versions of gCod-rituals. She is also working on the subject of the Mothercult in the Bengali context of the wild goddess Kali.

Alex McKay has been a fellow at the International Institute for Asian Studies, Leiden, The Netherlands. He has a B.A.(hons.) in Religious Studies and History and a Ph.D. in South Asian History from the London University School of Oriental and African Studies. He is the author of *Tibet and the British Raj: The Frontier Cadre 1904-1947*, (Curzon Press, London 1997) and has published a number of articles on Tibetan history and culture. He is currently working on a history of the pilgrimage to Mount Kailas.

Wim van Spengen is lecturer in the Department of Human Geography at the University of Amsterdam, where he was awarded a Ph.D. in 1992 for his thesis on the socio-economic history of Tibetan trade. His research interests include the historical geography of Inner Asia and Asian travel literature.

Brigitte Steinmann is 'Maître de conférences' in Ethnology, at the University Paul Valéry of Montpellier, France, and the author of 'Les Tamang du Népal, usages et religion, religion de l'usage' (1987) and 'Les Marches tibétaines du Népal' (1988). She has done extensive field research among the Eastern Tamangs of Kathmandu Valley and has gone back every year to Nepal for more than fifteen years. For the past five years she has also worked on Sikkim. She stresses the necessity to add historical enquiry to anthropological research, in order to compare the specific forms that Buddhism has taken among the Tibeto-Burman speaking groups throughout the Himalayas. She has published several articles on Sikkimese society.

Peng Wenbin is a Ph.D. candidate in the Department of Anthropology at the University of Washington, Seattle. He has conducted research on the Qiang nationality and, with Dr. Lawrence Epstein, on pilgrimage in Eastern Tibet (1989–1991). He has co-authored with Dr. Epstein the articles "Labtse and the Reinscription of Sacralized Social Space." *China Tibetology* (Special Issue), 1992, and "Ganja and Murdo: The Social Construction of Space at Two Pilgrimages Sites in Eastern Tibet." *The Tibet Journal* 19(3), 1994. His fields of interest cover pilgrimage, ethnic tourism and ethnic identity in southwest China.

Index

Afghanistan 42, 66
Agni 109
Ali, S.M. 173
Allahabad 55, 58, 78, 81
Almora 56
Amarnath cave 165
Amdo 21, 32 n12, 39, 43, 72, 86, 90–1, 185, 189, 200
Amritsar 9, 72, 78, 80
Amyes rMa chen (Amye Machen) 19, 21, 24, 27–8, 39, 45
Anagorika Govinda, Lama 11, 81–3, 115
Andrade, Padre A. 115
Arhat 26, 119, 121, 130, 140, 154, 156–7
Aris, Michael 46, 91, 142 n3
Arjuna 169–72, 180
Aryan (also see Indo-European) 145, 147, 168
Ashoka 81
Atisha 157
Avalokiteśvara 29, 87–90, 103 n33, 122–4, 130

'Bri gung pa 20, 32 n7, 152 155–7
Bailey, Lt-Col. F.M. 48
Belgium 108, 116
Bell, Charles. 17 n23
Benares 58–9, 61–3, 70 n68, 72, 75, 77–8, 81, 109
Bengal 52–6, 58–9, 61, 65, 148–9

Bernard, Theos. 17 n23
Bharati, Swami A. 4, 67
Bhardwaj, Surinder 4
Bhatt, G.P. 174
Bhotia/Bhutia 12, 120–1, 125–6, 128, 134, 136, 139
Bhutan 38, 54, 63, 65, 73–4, 120, 125–6, 135, 138–40
Blondeau, A.M. 4, 32 n1, 37
Bodh Gaya 9, 28, 38, 43, 72, 75, 77, 81
Bodleian library 9, 52–3
Bodnath 42–3
Boeck, Kurt. 42
Bogle, George. 54, 56, 63–6
Bon(po) 7, 9–10, 12–4, 25–6, 33 n18, 71–5, 78, 80, 82–3, 155, 158–162, 184–5, 189, 193, 197
Bower, General H. 44–5
Brahma 109, 115, 168–9, 173, 176
Brahmaputra 55, 59, 110–1, 143, 176
Brahmin 60–1, 172
British (empire etc.) 13–4, 43, 64, 66–7, 121, 141, 166, 176–9
British Library 61
Buddha (Sakyamuni) 8, 12, 26–7, 41, 93, 149, 152–7, 162
Buddhacisation 6–8, 11, 17 n16, 21–30, 33 n18, 37
Buddhism 6, 10–13, 18–20, 22, 25, 27–30, 37–8, 57, 65, 71–2, 74,

223

76–7, 80, 82–3, 85, 90, 100, 115–6, 119, 121, 123, 130, 140, 143–4, 152, 159, 161, 167–8, 176, 178–9, 182 n12
Buffetrille, K. 6–7, 11, 220
Buriats 39

Cakrasamvara 21, 25, 27, 152–4, 156–7
Cakravartin 134, 150–1
Calcutta 43, 64–5, 67
Callewaert, W. 11, 13, 220
Cambridge 39
Cassels, W.S. 178
Central Place System 41
Chamdo 14–5
Chan, Victor. 36–8, 46
Chang-tang 44, 143
Chenrezig – see Avalokitśvara
China 1, 5, 14, 18, 20, 28, 30, 41–3, 55, 67, 79, 85, 108, 111–2, 114, 135, 144–5, 179, 184, 188–91, 198–9
China, Emperor of. 66, 124
Chogyal – see Maharaja of Sikkim
Chorten (mchod rten) – see Stupa
Chronicle of the Rulers of Sikkim 117, 120–1, 125, 130, 135, 138–9, 141,
Chumbi Valley 22, 75, 120–2, 125–6
Circumambulation 6–7, 19, 21, 25–6, 37, 66, 102 n1, 108–9, 116, 120, 143–4, 149, 152, 157, 160, 180, 185, 188, 190, 192
Clarke, J. 9, 220
Cohn, Bernard. 59, 67
Cornwallis, Lord 66
Cultural revolution 184, 191

Dakini 26, 74, 100, 124, 157
Dalai Lama(s) 33 n25, 38, 43, 64, 93, 95, 136
Darchen 69 n36, 108, 111
Darshan/darsana 63, 120
David-Neel, A. 47
Delhi 72, 76, 78, 81, 83, 116
Desideri, Ippoliti. 17 n23, 144, 177
Dowman, K. 36, 38

Drepung 93, 96
Dunhuang 20

East India Company 9, 54, 65, 67, 177
Eastern Nepal 18–9, 29
Eastern Tibet 12, 14, 19, 42, 43, 99, 121
Ekai Kawaguchi – see Kawaguchi, Ekai
Ekvall, R. 4, 47
Elephanta 147
Eliade, Mircia. 172
Ellora 147, 175
Epics (also see *Mahabharata* & *Ramayana*) 148, 165, 167, 169–70, 172, 174–5, 180–1

Fakirs (also see *Gosain, Sannyasi*) 40, 53, 55–6, 60, 63, 178, 180
Falk, Nancy. 172
Forbes, James. 54
French 'school' (of pilgrimage studies) 4
Freyre, Manuel. 144, 177

Ganden 93, 95–6, 101
Ganesh 115
Ganges (Ganga) 55, 58, 61–3, 65, 70 n68, 77, 80, 147–8, 151, 153, 170, 173–4, 181
Gartok 56–7, 178–9
Garwal/Gharwal 55, 80, 88, 170
Gedun chospel (dGe 'dun chos 'phel) 71, 83 n1
Gelugpa/Gelukpa (dGe lugs pa) 33 n24, 37–9, 74, 79, 95–6
Gerze 108, 110, 112
Ghersi, Captain E. 79
Gill, William. 42
Giri 65, 180–81
Gnas ri 7, 20–4, 27–8, 31, 32 n10
Gnas skor (also see circumambulation) 16, 17 n13, 19, 185, 188
Gosains 9, 52–69
Gould, Sir Basil. 179
Graburn, N. 195
Grappard, A.G. 26

INDEX

"Great Leap Forward" 191
Grunendahl, Reinhold 169–70, 173, 175
Gurkhas/Ghurkhas 56, 120, 125
Gurla Mandhata 155
Guru Nanak 78
Guru Rinpoche – see Padmasambhava
Gyanima (rGya ni ma) 56–7, 69 n36, 92, 105 n82
Gyantse 79, 93, 96, 101

Halase-Maratika 19, 29, 39
Hamsa, Sri. 56
Hardwar 55, 69 n49, 72, 77, 80
Hastings, Warren. 54–5, 58, 63, 65–7, 70 n86
Havnevik, H. 10–11, 220–1
Hedin, Sven. 17 n23, 144, 177
Hidden Lands 12
Himachal 36
Himachal Pradesh 71–2, 78, 175
Himalaya(s) 4, 38, 42–3, 54, 57, 85–6, 143, 146, 152, 167–8, 170–1, 173–4, 176
Himavat (also see Himalayas) 147, 150, 167, 174
Hindu(s) 5, 9, 13–14, 29, 55, 57, 59, 61, 63, 66–7, 79, 108–9, 112, 114, 116, 143, 147, 149, 152, 156, 162, 165–6, 168, 170, 175–81
History of Sikkim, see *Chronicle of the Rulers of Sikkim*
Hocart, A. 23
Huber, T. 4–5, 37
Hundred Thousand Songs of Milarepa 159

India 5, 7–10, 13, 16, 19–20, 28, 30, 37–8, 42–3, 52–60, 65, 67, 71–3, 75–7, 79–83, 87, 109, 121–2, 136, 141, 143, 145–6, 149, 151, 158, 162, 165, 171–3, 175–80
Indo-Europeans (also see Aryans) 167
Indra 109, 123, 130, 146, 166
Indus 112, 143, 145, 166–7, 174
Islam 4, 149

International Institute for Asian Studies 4, 32 n1

Jahangir, Emperor. 52
Jain(s) 13, 143, 149–52, 162
Jambudvipa 146, 150, 152–5, 161–62
Japan(ese) 26, 144
Jesuits 115, 144, 177
Jetsun Lochen, Lama. 10, 85–107
Jiuzhaigou 14, 184–201
Jo nang pa 25, 33 n25
Jokhang 96

bKa' brgyud 20, 28, 32 n6 & 7, 153, 155
Kachenjunga 119, 121–3, 141 n2
Kailas(h)/Kailasa 5–6, 10, 12–3, 17 n24, 19–21, 24–8, 38–41, 45–6, 63, 66–7, 72–3, 77, 81, 87, 91–2, 96, 105 n76, 108–16, 143–83
Kailas-Manasarovar Yatra Scheme 179
Kali 149, 154
Kalidasa 147
Kalimpong 43, 71, 75
Kalka-Howrah Mail 76
Kalmuks 39
Kang Rinpoche – see Kailas
Kapilikas 173
Karmapa 80, 84 n21, 91
Karmay, S.G. 83
Karnali 143
Kashmir 19, 56, 69 n34, 77, 115, 144, 148
Kathmandu 42–3, 75, 81, 88, 92, 96, 110
Kawaguchi Ekai 17 n23, 144
Kazakh 80
Kedernath 173
Kham 39, 48, 74, 79, 86, 119, 198
Khumb mela 41, 55, 67, 69 n49
Khyung-lung 72–3, 77, 79–81, 162
Khyung Sprul, 9–10, 71–84
Kinnaur 9, 71–2, 76–9, 81
Kirkpatrik, Capt. 59
Kongpo Bon-ri 39, 73, 84 n5, 189
Krishna 53, 114
Kuber(a) 109, 146, 170, 72, 174–6

225

Kumaon 56
Kumbum 39–40, 45, 96
Kværne, P. 9, 221

La phyi 20, 38–9, 43, 93, 96, 155–6
Ladakh 38, 56, 77, 80, 88–90, 156, 179
Lah(a)ul 87–8, 90
Lakshmi 175
Leh 56
Leiden 4
Lemaire, Ton. 36, 48
Lepcha 12, 119–22, 125–6, 128–30, 132–40, 142 n7
Lhasa 20, 38–40, 45–6, 56–7, 64, 66–7, 85, 92–5, 97–8, 101, 102 n1, 108, 111– 2, 144, 178
Limbu 12, 119–20, 136, 138
Lingam 63, 116, 147–9, 154, 156
Lopa/Loba 48
Lopez, Donald. 11
Losar (New Year) 38
Loseries-Leick, A. 13, 221

Ma Pangs – see Manasarovar (lake)
Macdonald, A.W. 4–5
Mahabharata 13, 145–6, 151, 168–9, 171, 175
Mahameru – see Meru (Mount)
Mahant 58–9
Maharaja of Mysore. 179
Maharaja of Sikkim 12, 117, 119, 121, 125, 129, 134–8, 140
Mallas 42, 56, 176–7
Manasarovar (lake) 26, 48, 63, 66–7, 69 n36, 72–3, 92, 105 n80, 109–112, 116, 143, 153, 158, 160–1, 165, 168–9, 174–81
Mandala 21, 25, 90, 115, 124, 130, 154, 157, 161
Mandala state 13, 120, 139
*Mandala*isation 6, 12, 26
Mani wall 98, 100, 105 n94
Mani(pas) 10, 88–90, 95–7, 100, 103 n35, 104 ns 48 & 49
Mantra 27, 81, 89–90, 114, 144, 155, 160
Mao, Chairman. 191

Marco Polo 54
Math 58–9, 61, 67
McKay, A. 13, 221
Meru (Mount) 109, 145–8, 150, 152–3, 162, 166–70, 172–5, 177
Messnier, Rheinhold. 145
Milarepa 10, 12, 37, 39, 91–2, 94, 96, 110–11, 152, 155, 157, 159
Mongolia 8, 39, 41, 43
Moorcroft, William. 177
Muktinath 87–8, 92
Muller, Max. 170
Muslim(s) 63, 82
Mustang 56, 91–2, 96

Nepal 19–20, 30, 38, 42–3, 52, 54–6, 58, 63, 66–7, 73, 75, 81, 86–7, 111, 126, 138
Noble, Christine. 175
Nuns (Buddhist) 95, 99, 101
Nyingma (rNying ma) 9–10, 25, 30, 37, 79, 91, 94–6, 99–101

Olympic Games 199
'Ol-mo-lung-ring 17 n17, 158
Omei Shan 8, 43
Oudh 9, 55, 68 n2
Ousley, Sir Gore. 52–6, 58–9, 61–2, 67 n2
Oxford 52

Padmasambhava 10, 37, 74, 87, 91, 93–6, 98, 101, 107 n138, 122, 124–6, 136, 138, 157, 159
Panchen Lama 9, 38, 60, 63–7, 70 n78
Parvati 146–7, 154, 156
Peking 9, 66
Pilgrimage – *passim*
Potala (Mount) 29
Potala (Palace) 96
Pradaksina – see circumambulation
Pranavananda, Swami. 17 n23, 165, 174, 180–1
Puranas 146–8, 173–4, 176
Purangir 9, 60, 65–6, 70 n86

Rad-dben 185, 187, 190, 193, 200 n7

Rama 63, 172, 180
Ramayana 168–9, 171–2
Ramesvaram 55, 63
Ravana 63, 146–7, 168
Rdza-dkar (Mount) 14, 184–87, 191–200
Rewalsar (mTsho Padma/Tsopema) 72, 76, 78, 80, 87–8
Rijnhart, Susie. 40
Ris med (movement) 10, 85, 91
Rishis 147
River of Golden Sand 42
Rudra – see Shiva
Russia 66
Ruttledge, Hugh. 179

Saddhu(s) – see *Sanyasi*(s)
Sagara, King. 146, 169
Sakya (Sa Skya) Pandita 31, 124
Sakya(pas) 38, 93, 96, 117, 119, 122, 125
Samkhya 146, 150, 162
Samye 98, 130
Sangskar – see Zangskar
Sankaracharya 65, 173–4, 180
Sanskrit 5, 52, 114, 130, 165
Sanskritisation 7, 17 n16
Sanyasi 46, 52–3, 59–61, 63, 66–7, 177
Saparam 110, 115
Sarnath 9, 72, 75
Sera 96
Shabkar 10, 91–7, 99
Shaivites 53, 60–1, 173–4, 176, 180–1
Shang-shung – see Zhang zhung
Shen rab (gShen rab) 17 n17, 158–60, 162, 164 ns 37 & 47
Sherpa 18, 29–30, 126
Sherring, Charles. 56, 67, 178
Shigatse 38
Shiva 63, 108–9, 111, 114, 116, 146–9, 156, 166, 169–70, 174–7, 180–1
Siddha(s) 10, 75, 95, 99, 101, 132
Sikhs 9, 114
Sikkim 12, 29, 38, 43, 56, 101, 117–42
Simla (Shimla) 56, 77

Sino-Tibetan Agreement 5
Sita 55, 168
Sleen, W.G.N. van der. 78
Snellgrove, D. 11
Songsten Gampo 37
Spengen, W. van. 8, 11, 222
Spiti 89–90
Sri Lanka 46, 55
Staal, Frits. 166, 182 n12
Steinman, B. 12, 222
Strachey, Lt. H. 177–78
Stupa 22, 25, 27, 77, 81, 83, 92–3, 109–10, 112, 115, 122–3, 134, 159–61
Sutlej 56, 71, 73, 110, 143, 162, 166, 176
Sutras 152–54
Swami Pranavananda – see Pranavananda Swami
Swat 19, 77
Swayanbunath 42, 75
Szechuan 8, 43, 184, 188

Tachienlu 43
Taklakot (Pu rang) 56, 69 n36, 88, 92
Tantra/Tantrik(s) 13, 22, 37, 143, 148–9, 152–4, 158, 160, 176, 180
Tapas/tapasya 66, 116, 146, 149, 171–2
Tashilumpo 45, 54, 56, 63, 66–7, 93, 96, 101
Teichman, Eric. 46
Terma (gTer ma) 12, 95, 117, 161
The Life of Shabkar 46
Tholing (mTho ling) 73, 76, 110, 114–5
Ti se – see Kailas
Tibet "Zone of Peace" 8
Tibet – *passim*
Tibet and its Birds 44
Tibet Journal 4
Tibetan army 80
Tibetan identity. 5, 14, 30, 185, 197–8
Tirtha 146, 151, 166, 168
Tirthankara(s) 149–51
Tsa ri 20, 38–9, 45, 48, 91, 98, 155–6

Tsangpo 98, 100
Tucci, Giuseppi. 4, 11, 79, 115, 176, 179
Tulsidas 109
Turner, Captain. 54, 66–7
Turner, Victor. 4
Twain, Mark. 11

Ujain 55, 58
UNESCO 194
Upanishads 148
Urga 8, 43

Vairocana 25, 33 n27, 103 n26
Vaishnavites 53, 60–2, 69 n43, 173, 175–6, 180
Varanasi – see Benares
Varma, Rommell. 168
Vedas (Rg Veda etc.,) 109, 145, 148, 162, 166–8, 171, 180
Victoria and Albert Museum 60, 62, 68 n1, 70 n68
Vinaya 95, 99, 144

Visnu/Vishnu 109, 175
Vyasa 145, 147

"Workers of the Great Pilgrimage" (*skor chen las pa*) 28
"World Mountain" 143, 153–4, 162
Walsh, E.H. 22–3
Warner, Karl. 167
Way of the White Clouds 11, 81, 115
Wenbin, Peng. 7, 14, 222
Western Tibet 10, 19, 63, 72, 77, 89, 105 n82, 158, 176–9
Wollaston, A.F. 39
World Heritage List 194

Yarlung 97–8
Younghusband Mission 98, 178
Yul lha 6–7, 9, 14, 17 n15, 20–5, 27–8, 30–1, 78–9

Zangskar 45, 88, 112
Zhang zhung 17 n17, 73, 76–7, 83, 158, 161–2, 164 nns37 & 46

For Product Safety Concerns and Information please contact our EU
representative GPSR@taylorandfrancis.com
Taylor & Francis Verlag GmbH, Kaufingerstraße 24, 80331 München, Germany

www.ingramcontent.com/pod-product-compliance
Lightning Source LLC
Chambersburg PA
CBHW062214300426
44115CB00012BA/2059